To Ann
From Lee-Ann
October 1993

To Ann
From Lee-Ann
October 1993

SEEDS
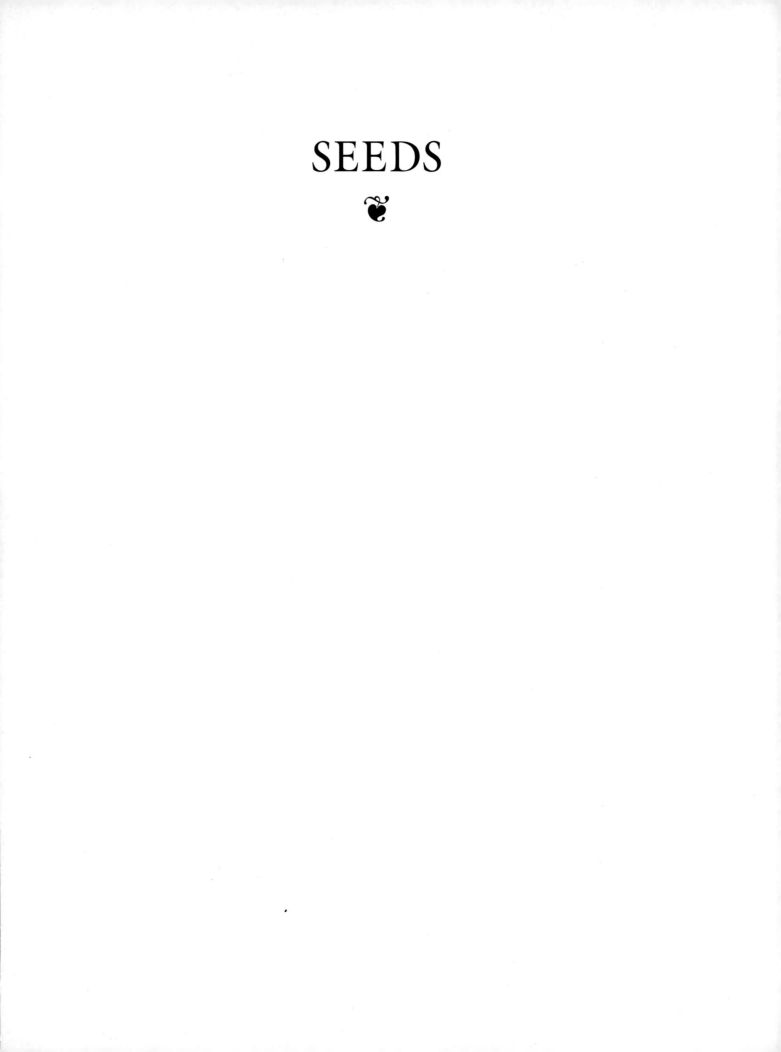

SEEDS

The Ultimate Guide to Growing

Vegetables, Herbs & Flowers

SAM BITTMAN

BANTAM BOOKS

TORONTO · NEW YORK · LONDON · SYDNEY · AUCKLAND

SEEDS
A Bantam Book/April 1989

Project Editor: Sharon Squibb
Designer: Beth Tondreau Design
Illustrations: Mona Mark
Illustrations (pages 20, 34, 109, 116): Sharon Squibb

LIBRARY OF CONGRESS CATALOGING-IN-PUBLICATION DATA
Bittman, Sam, 1943–
Seeds : the ultimate guide to growing vegetables, herbs & flowers.
Includes index.
1. Vegetables—Seeds.   2. Herbs—Seeds.   3. Flowers—
Seeds.   4. Vegetable gardening.   5. Herb gardening.
6. Flower gardening.   I. Title.
SB324.B57   1989   635'.0421   88-47933
ISBN 0-533-05366-3

Published simultaneously in the United States and Canada

PRINTED IN THE UNITED STATES OF AMERICA

0 9 8 7 6 5 4 3 2 1

DEDICATION

As always, for Maggie and my sons:
Jondavid, Peter and Simeon.

ACKNOWLEDGMENTS

I would like to thank Cia Elkin, whose continuing
input helped bring this work to fruition. Thanks also to
Ed Soldo, a great gardener, for his wisecracks and intuitions.

For their invaluable help in putting together this book, grateful thanks to the following people:

Angela Miller and all the staff of IMG Publishing for their unrelenting dedication and perseverance; Elvin McDonald for his heartfelt generosity, expertise and love for growing things; Coleen O'Shea of Bantam Books; Beth Tondreau and Jane Treuhaft for their commitment and talent; Joe Marc Freedman of The Sarabande Press; K. Russell Glover for his photographs.

For inviting us into their gardens, thanks also go to: Berezny's Farm Stand, Riverhead, NY; Kathy Jahrsdorfer; Bob and Mary Van Nostrand of Old Orchard Farm Store, Orient, NY; Fred Terry's Farm Stand, Orient Point, NY; Shelter Island Nursery, Shelter Island, NY; Mrs. Bartilucci of Shelter Island, NY; Lorraine Dusky; The Green Thumb, Watermill, NY; Wesnofske's North Fork Farm, Peconic, NY.

CONTENTS

❧

INTRODUCTION

*"He who sees things grow from the beginning
will have the best view of them."*

—ARISTOTLE

To the practical minded, growing from seeds is a way of saving money. And, while the seeds for a given plant may have to be purchased initially, the bottom-line gardener strives to grow only nonhybrid seeds, particularly those of edible plants, to be more self-reliant.

To the realist, growing from seeds means never having to settle for only the popular commercial cultivars (cultivated varieties) available that season from local garden centers and nurseries in transplant form. True, it takes time to grow from seeds, but not the precious hours that can be lost shopping for transplants when one would much prefer to be out planting in the garden.

To the colorist, the gardener as artist, growing from seeds means having more colors and shades in the palette.

To the gourmet, the person who savors life through reverence and appreciation of food, growing from seeds means achieving ever new heights of taste and joyful combinations of ingredients.

Quite simply, growing plants from seeds lets each of us, at all ages and stages of life, participate in the procreative process. It is a desirable and beneficial habit that can regenerate and enrich all aspects of ourselves—physical, emotional, and spiritual.

All my life, from as far back as I can remember, I have been involved in the world of seeds. My parents are dry-land farmers in western Oklahoma. I grew up knowing that our livelihood depended on their ability to produce the food we ate and the grains we fed to animals or sold. Throughout my long career as a professional journalist who specialized in gardening, growing a plant from seed has never failed to be a wonderful experience for me.

In addition to all the essentials for success with seeds, which Sam Bittman so generously and plainly sets forth in this book, I would like to offer one more thought. There are, in my view, only three mistakes one can make with seeds: The first is not to plant any seeds at all. The second is to plant too many seeds at once. And the third is not to immediately try again when a batch of seeds fails to meet one's expectations. Growing plants from seed is a way of life. People who adopt it are a special breed who speak the universal language of optimism. Growing a plant from seed is a miraculous experience that everyone deserves to witness. Whether the seed is quick or slow to sprout, the miracle always occurs—something wonderful to see again and again.

ELVIN McDONALD
Director of Special Projects,
Brooklyn Botanic Garden

PART 1

❦

Preliminaries

ABOUT SEEDS ❦ PLANNING THE
VEGETABLE AND FLOWER GARDEN
❦ STARTING SEEDS INDOORS ❦
PLANTING SEEDS AND SEEDLINGS
OUTDOORS

A rock pathway winds through the garden to the hideaway gazebo.

❦ 1 ❦
ABOUT SEEDS

While there is much to be said for the arrival of seed catalogues in January's mail to drive off those dead-of-winter blues, nothing, for sheer pleasure, surpasses the day a few weeks later when those boxes tightly packed with the future contents of this year's garden arrive at your front door.

Gardening from seed—or onion set or asparagus root crown or whatever else you've ordered—is one of life's most magical pleasures. Although to some the process might seem intimidating, cultivating seeds is in fact relatively easy to do and can provide an endless source of wonder and fun as well as accomplishment. Put a seed into a growing medium, give it a little warmth and moisture, and most of the time, it will start growing. If you have doubts, plant two instead for insurance and one will surely germinate. Then you have only to watch the fun begin.

Seeds themselves are fascinating. The largest in the world are coconuts, of which the very largest is a gigantic nut called *coco de mer* (coconut of the sea) which grows on Praslin Island in the Indian Ocean and weighs between 40 and 50 pounds. At the other end of the scale are some American Figworts with seeds so small it takes more than eight million to make a single ounce.

Some plants, like the garden pea, produce relatively few seeds—several dozen at best. But consider *amaranthus graeicizans,* a common Tumbleweed, which produces as many as six million seeds per plant. There are also wide variations in gestation. Some plants, like the Pine Tree or Sea Palm, take years to produce a crop of mature seeds, while others, including certain garden weeds, take only weeks.

Plants can—and will—produce seed under almost impossible conditions. The lowly Chickweed, for instance, has a survival urge so determined that you can uproot one which has barely flowered, toss it clear out of the garden, and it will still mature its seeds lying out there in the open field.

The drive in plants to produce seed is as powerful as it is because seed is the vehicle through which almost all plant life reproduces itself. The earth—including the earth in most backyard gardens—accommodates the process by allowing itself to become packed thick with seeds of all kinds, each waiting to come alive. One botanist actually counted thirty thousand viable weed seeds in a patch of ground one yard square and ten inches deep.

DORMANCY INSURES SURVIVAL

All seeds—not just weeds, but the seeds you buy for your garden—should be looked upon as dormant plants awaiting the moment when they, too, will spring to life, grow to maturity, and produce yet more seeds for future generations. Because dormancy is not an accident; it's part of nature's overall scheme. To understand how it works, imagine that it is August. A ripe tomato falls to the ground and bursts, its seeds scattering onto fertile ground. They are soon pressed into the soil by you or your dog or children. Yet even though the weather is warm, the seed will not germinate. Why? Because if it did, the young plant would be destroyed by cold weather long before it could produce new seeds of its own—and the seed knows this!

I DREAMT OF A WEED-FREE GARDEN

When I started my first garden, I resolved to have no weeds. I used only seedless oat straw or salt hay for mulch; I searched out and destroyed any weed that poked its head above ground. Yet it seemed that the more weeds I pulled, the more I had to pull. So I tried black plastic, and newspapers, and wood chips, and cocoa hulls, and every other smothering mulch I could get my hands on. I gave up deep cultivation during the growing season to avoid bringing those tiny weed seeds I knew were lurking below up to the surface where they might germinate from the sun's warmth. At season's end, I let no weeds mature; the garden was bare as winter came on.

But next spring, the weeds reappeared and I despaired. I came to think of myself as incompetent, a gardener who didn't have the knack. Then I learned the truth from a magazine article a sympathetic friend gave me. It said, among other things: that there are trillions of weed seeds in every garden, and that weed seeds can remain dormant in the ground for a long time—up to several decades even, in the case of evening primrose and mullein.

Furthermore, the weed seed that germinates in today's garden could easily have been produced not only years ago but miles away and been transported unceremoniously to the spot by a bird flying overhead. Assuming spring came and the garden got tilled, the seed on the surface could have been turned under to a depth where it remained viable but unable to germinate. Twenty years later you come along and turn it up with your tilling, whereupon it springs to life as a weed among your lettuce. And as if birds weren't enough as weed seed carriers, there were also water, wind, and other animals at work.

Both relieved and dismayed, I soon realized weeds had their uses. Since you can't eliminate them, you should put them to work. If gathered before they flower and produce those persistent seeds, you can lay them along garden walkways as mulch where they will rot and add valuable organic matter to your soil. You can even eat some weeds; lamb's quarters and purslane, for instance, are quite edible when picked young.

Miraculously, nature protects against such destruction by programming into seeds a growing cycle that is sensitive to the rhythm of the seasons. This time-delay mechanism insures that the seeds will remain dormant until the start of another full growing season. Both the length and the actual mechanics of dormancy vary widely among species and varieties. Dormancy in seeds with water-resistant or "hard" seedcoats, for example, may last for years, or until enough water soaks into the seed through small nicks and scratches (called scarifications) in the seedcoat to allow germination. Other seeds must be exposed to extended periods of cold and damp—apparently simulating winter soil conditions—before they can be aroused to grow. Still others may remain dormant until exposed to light, while certain parasitic plants will only come to life when an appropriate host plant germinates nearby.

THE ANATOMY OF A SEED

In a sense, seeds truly are programmed to accomplish their task, and once set in motion they contain all the instructions required to transform themselves into thriving plants. They also contain ingredients to support themselves the first few weeks of life. So when you plant a seed, you're placing into the soil a tiny plant-to-be, equipped with its own agenda and time clock, all wrapped in a perfect package. You, the gardener, are merely providing the conditions—growing medium, light, nutrients, moisture and air—it needs to burst into life. This can be illustrated by a look at a simple bean seed to see the tiny but inactive plan waiting within.

Under the seedcoat of most seeds you'll find shapes called cotyledons (pronounced cottyleedns) fitted neatly into the space and attached to the plant's rudimentary stem. Most vegetable and flower seeds have two cotyledons pressed together, as you see here in the bean seed, and are called *dicots*. Others, such as corn, rye, oats and other cereal crops contain a single cotyledon and are called *monocots*. Unleaflike as they appear, the cotyledons actually become the young plant's first visible leaves. The emergent dicots send up two "wings" as they sprout, while the monocots send up a single "spike." If you separate the two halves of a dicot as shown in the illustration, you'll see, lying flat on the inner wall of each, the first tuft of the "true" leaves that will appear some days after the cotyledon wings first emerge from the soil. At the other end of the seed is the root tip, which will elongate and form the first root, or radicle, once germination has taken place.

The cotyledons of most plants are loaded with enough stored carbohydrates, fats and protein to supply the young plant during the first weeks of its life after germination. In some seeds, such as corn, buckwheat and rye, this sustenance is to be found instead in the endosperm, the layer which surrounds the seed.

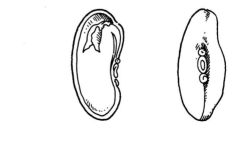

Bean seed

HOW SEEDS ARE PRODUCED

A plant's flowers carry its reproductive organs and are the cradle where its seeds are born. In order to produce seeds, a plant must first produce a flower—and they all do. Flowers can be almost microscopic in relation to the plant, or huge, like the 12-inch-across Sunflower, but for the process to unfold, the flower must be there. Light, temperature, moisture and the presence in the soil of certain nutrients all affect the plant's ability to create its flowers.

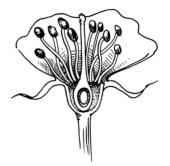

The male organs, called stamens as you can see in the illustration, consist of a group of stalks called filaments with knobby tops called anthers. They produce the fertilizing agent pollen, a word taken from the Greek word for "dust." The female parts, called pistils, consist of a single stalk called a style with a sticky area on top, called the stigma, which receives the pollen, and the ovaries, or body cavities holding the ovules, or unfertilized seeds-to-be at its bottom. (Some plant botanists take exception to the use of the terms ovary and ovules since the plant parts they name bear little similarity to their counterparts in female animals.) All these reproductive parts are surrounded by petals, in the aggregate known as the perianth, and below that is the vestige of the original bud covering that burst open when the flower emerged, called the sepals.

PLANTS SEE TO THEIR FERTILIZATION IN A NUMBER OF WAYS: *Many have a complete flower with both male and female organs and can self-pollinate. The tomato's an example. Others also bear a complete flower but require pollen from another variety in order to achieve fertilization; so the wind, birds, bees and other insects must do the work. Still others, like the melons, have male and female flowers on the same plant. And recently hybrids have appeared with only female flowers (which are the fruit-producers). Both of these also enlist the animals and elements for pollination.*

THE SEED INDUSTRY

According to a recent Gallup poll, more than 40 million American families have at least one garden, and the number is rising every year. In 1978, six million households purchased garden products by mail. By the mid-1980s the number had jumped to 13 million, and 63 percent of the purchases were seeds.

Commercial seed growers have been quick to respond to this tremendous market. In recent years, they have developed the greatest variety of flowers and vegetables ever, and new strains are appearing all the time. You can now get seed for a white Marigold, a yellow tomato, a green Carnation, a white eggplant, or a purple cauliflower. Even more startling are a bean that grows a yard long, a pumpkin that weighs a hundred pounds, or a melon that fits into the palm of your hand.

Although it takes plant breeders about eight seasons to bring a new cultivar (meaning bred or cultivated by a grower, not found in nature) to market, the possibilities for specialized breeding are endless. What this means for start-from-seed home gardeners is infinite opportunity for horticultural adventure. Though the local nursery can never offer more than a limited number of cultivars as seedlings, you can order a spectacular choice of seeds from the catalogs listed in the back of this book and raise some of the most esoteric, gorgeous and impressive cultivars to be found anywhere.

❦ 2 ❦
PLANNING THE VEGETABLE AND FLOWER GARDENS

Tempting as it is to jump immediately into ordering seeds from all those delightful catalogues, a little planning beforehand is in order. In fact, the best and most successful gardens are often created not in the springtime, but over those long winter nights when the gardener mulls over how much to plant, what crops and varieties to use (not just carrots, but which *kinds* of carrots), where to place the crops in the garden for best yield, and other such considerations. For many, planning a garden, like planning a vacation, is a pleasurable necessity filled with happy anticipation.

PLANNING THE VEGETABLE GARDEN

First, if you don't have a vegetable, herb or flower garden, or are considering creating a new one, you must decide where to put it. We'll start with vegetables, and then do flowers. Herb gardens are discussed in chapter 6.

Siting the Vegetable Garden

You should first have an idea of how much space you need. Techniques for estimating this are on page 9, but for a general idea, a garden 20 by 40 feet will feed a family of four. Once you know how much space you need, the major considerations for locating a vegetable garden—or flower bed or herb border for that matter—are sun, soil and slope.

S U N . Without 6 to 8 hours of direct sunlight every day, most flowers and vegetables will not thrive. Look for a south-facing site with no shade-producing obstructions such as tall or bushy trees, buildings, or walls of any kind. If you cannot avoid a certain amount of shade, try to make sure it doesn't occur at midday, when sunlight is at its brightest, and when your plants can least tolerate its absence. In tomatoes, peppers, melons and corn, blossom and fruit set may be negatively affected. If you can't avoid midday shade, try to make sure it falls only over a certain section of the garden, where you can plant leaf and root crops which don't mind a brief shadow. Save the bright areas with all-day sun for fruiting crops such as peppers, melons, squash and tomatoes.

S O I L . Situate the garden where the soil is richest. If you've never grown anything on your property, look for a particularly lush section of lawn. If you don't want to carve a piece out of the grass, look for a sunny area with a thick stand of growth among the weeds. A soil that can grow stout weeds will probably be suitable for flowers and vegetables. If it's fall and you have a choice of possible spots, you might investigate having your soil tested for the optimal place. See details in chapter 4.

Drainage is another important consideration. Plants cannot find sufficient oxygen in waterlogged soil, so avoid bogs or any areas that are always wet. Even if they're rich with vegetation, the soil may not grow the plants you want to see there. If you have no choice, you'll need to drain off the water by digging a ditch completely around your plot and laying in gravel and a drainage pipe. If undertaking that doesn't appeal to you, you can try raised planting beds (see page 38).

SLOPE. The tilt of the land can also affect the success of the garden. A slight pitch of a few degrees to the south, for example, will dry out and warm up your soil earlier in the spring, allowing for earlier planting. Too much slope, however, means problems. More than a 10-degree pitch is not only difficult to work on, it can mean your topsoil will wash away with every heavy rain. If a sloped surface like this is your only option, you may have to consider building terraces—not an easy job.

Handiness to the house is important to some gardeners: they like to run out the door into the salad or flower bed and be back in the kitchen with their bounty in five minutes or less. If the other conditions are right, there's no reason you can't have the garden as close to the house as you can get it.

FENCING A VEGETABLE GARDEN

Whether or not to fence a vegetable garden is an often-asked question, and the answer depends on two more: Do you *want* a fence? and Do you *need* a fence? If you do or don't want a fence for looks, it's just a yes or no. But you may *need* a fence, to support vine-growing crops or to fend off hungry rabbits, raccoons, deer, and other animal pests that can undo weeks of hard labor in a single nocturnal feeding.

The simplest fence can be made from inexpensive four- or five-foot-wide chicken wire stapled to a frame of two-by-four posts and rails. Sink the wire a foot or so into the soil to keep burrowing animals out, and you might add a strand or two of electric fencing along the top for climbers, such as raccoons in zealous pursuit of your sweet corn. Electric fencing involves additional expense, but if you value that sweet corn, it's worth it. Deer will jump over almost anything to get to food, but can be dissuaded from entering the neighborhood altogether if there's a dog tied out nearby.

Choosing Your Crops and Determining the Size of Your Garden

The size of your garden depends on how much food you want to grow and your ability to handle the necessary upkeep. Do you just want a few ingredients for summer salads, or are you set on a season-long supply of many different vegetables? Perhaps you want even more—all you can eat and a surplus to put up for the winter.

The choice is yours. Just remember as you make your lists of crops that the larger the garden, the more work there is. Will you have help? Or will your shoulders alone bear the responsibility? Think this over. All is calm when the seeds are underground or just emerging. But when the real growing begins, everything—weeds included—seems to burst forth at once and keep bursting. And there is nothing more agonizing for a new gardener than the sense of things rapidly getting out of hand.

THE FEET OF ROW FORMULA. Once you've established how much labor is available for all the watering, weeding, fertilizing and harvesting ahead, you can start thinking about your garden's size in terms of the quantity of food you want to grow. A traditional measure for most crops is "five feet of row" to supply one person from spring through frost. If you want carrots for a family of four, for example, you'll want 20 feet of carrots in single file, whether it's two 10-foot rows, four 5-foot rows, or what-have-you. This will give you a quick idea of how many feet of row you need to have in your garden, but you should know that planting in single file is by no means the only way to grow vegetables.

MULTIPLE-ROW PLANTING FOR HIGHER YIELD. If you were to rely exclusively on seed packets for planting instructions, you'd soon believe that almost all garden plants must grow in single-file rows with two- or three-foot walkways in between. It doesn't take long to figure out that when arranged in this traditional manner, the garden is given over more to walkways than to food. Garden paths are a delight, especially if you have lots of land, but if space is at a premium, as it is in many gardens, you may want to devote more of it to growing crops. This can be easily done just by creating rows more than one plant wide.

If a carrot plant can thrive, according to the seed packet, with other carrot plants three inches in front and back of it, it should do equally well with plants three inches to either side, and it does. Planting three rows side by side this way is known as triple-row planting. You can see that a triple row of carrots would only have to be about seven feet long to get the same 20 feet of row you need to feed the family of four—not the 20-foot-length taken up by single-row planting. You can plant double rows too, or rows as wide as you can comfortably lean over and cultivate from either side.

OTHER PLANTING FORMATS. Besides double- and triple- (or more) row planting, there are wide-row and block planting, other tried and true planting formats that suit certain crops and ease the work of sowing and cultivation while maximizing yield.

In wide-row planting, a band of soil perhaps two feet wide or more is sown broadcast—uniformly all over instead of in rows. Sometimes more than one crop is mixed into a wide-row planting.

Block planting seems to suit crops that like to be surrounded by each other rather than lined up in rows next to other crops. It gives the same solid-mass effect as wide rows once the plants mature, but is seeded differently, usually in a diamond or crisscross pattern. Both are effective use of rectangular space, allowing you to tailor the width to your own cultivating and reaching range. Techniques for setting them up are given in chapter 4.

What this means is that, as a garden planner, you have considerably more flexibility than the seed-packets suggest. Further, you have the right to try anything. If a particular experiment doesn't work, then you can always try a different approach later in the season or next year.

Managing the Crops in the Garden: Succession, Companions, Flowers, Double Patches

There are interesting and useful ways you can manage the crops in your garden, where advance planning can pay off in success. We'll start with succession planting, a technique I've used very successfully for years.

SUCCESSION PLANTINGS. Many vegetables take only a portion of the growing season to come to maturity. To harvest the plants and leave the ground they occupied unused is a waste of good space. For example, the spinach I like best matures in about 45 days, just about the time I'm ready to plant beans. I pull up the spent spinach, re-dig the bed, and plant my snap beans. Similarly, when my peas are done, I can use the bed for a late planting of carrots or scallions. Other cool weather crops which start and finish early are radishes, beets, onion sets for scallions, cabbage, kohlrabi, mustard and cauliflower. They can be replaced with beans, fall lettuce, spinach and other cool weather crops that will mature before the first killing frost in autumn.

So, in truth, you actually have two plans for this year's garden: the first for the crops you start out with, and the second for the crops which follow.

If you use succession plantings, you don't necessarily need two sheets of paper; just put the names of the succession crops in parentheses on the main chart. Remember to consider early varieties for these succession plantings so you can harvest before frost.

COMPANION PLANTING. Experienced gardeners know that certain crops are more productive when planted together or near one another than when planted alone or beside crops they "dislike." For instance, pole beans like to be planted near corn, but dislike onions, beets and Sunflowers. Sunflowers like cucumbers, but dislike being near potatoes.

Much controversy has grown up around this practice of companion planting or intercropping as it is also known. The "show-me" gardeners consider it all balderdash and want scientific proof. I find the entire notion of likes and dislikes

quite entertaining, and have practiced certain standard groupings for many years. Potatoes grown near bush beans, for instance, seem to keep away the Mexican bean beetle; aromatic herbs and flowers tend to deter the cabbage moth from laying her eggs on cabbage, broccoli, cauliflower and the rest of the crucifers, or cabbage-family crops.

There are other companion-planting approaches that have a visibly practical base. Taller plants such as corn and tomatoes are generally planted in the north or east ends of the garden to avoid shading shorter plants. But for some crops, shade is a welcome commodity. For that reason I plant out second-wave lettuce seedlings among my corn to give them much needed shade during the heat of midsummer.

Other companions make for simultaneous succession plantings. Onion plants set out among early cabbage or cauliflower, for example, will continue to mature long after their bed-mates have been removed to the table. And pumpkins, melons and winter squash planted among the early corn will not only create an obstacle for thieving raccoons (who detest stepping across prickly foliage), but will continue to grow and provide color well after the corn has been harvested.

If space allows, I urge you to try several different combinations and keep production records for comparison.

FLOWERS IN THE VEGETABLE GARDEN. Flowers can appear regularly in the vegetable garden, both for aesthetic and practical reasons. A ring of dwarf French Marigolds around a double row of bush beans, for instance, is not only a charming sight but serves as a deterrent to the Mexican bean beetle. As you contemplate different layouts, consider adding a mini-bed of flowers in corners or other spots where you might have a bit of space, for a light-hearted antidote to the serious vegetable business at hand.

TWO PATCHES OF THE SAME VEGETABLE. Creating a varied environment in the garden by setting out two or three separate patches of the same crop is another idea, one which can also help reduce pest damage. Don't put all the corn, or cabbage, or tomatoes in one location. Put a few cabbage plants here, near the beans, and then a few way over next to the onions. So if the pests hit the patch here, perhaps those near the onions will be spared.

Drawing Up Your Plan

Armed with all your horticultural knowledge, you're now ready to set down your ideas on paper. If there's any of the frustrated artist in you, this may be the time to express it; some gardeners use orange pencils to draw in the carrot rows, red for the radishes, green for the lettuce, and so on. Others just write in the names of the crops along the lines or in the patches where they go.

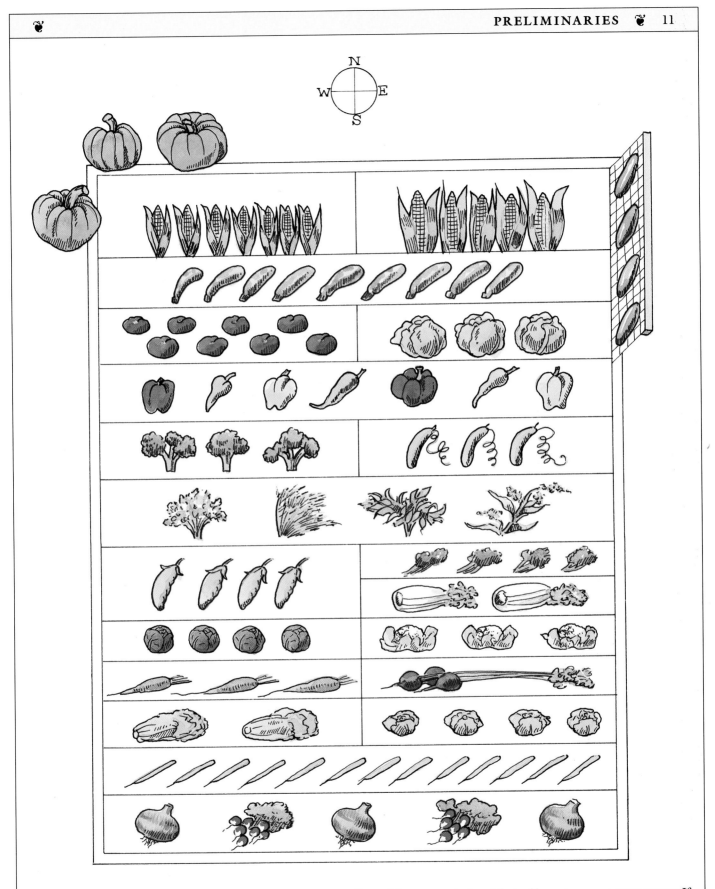

I worked out this garden plan some years ago. Use it just as it appears if you wish, or as a springboard for working out your own arrangement. If you're using succession plantings, you don't need to start from scratch on another sheet of paper. Just put the names of your succession crops in parentheses alongside those on the chart now. Remember to consider early varieties for the succession plantings so you can harvest before a killing frost occurs.

EXPLORE VARIOUS OPTIONS. Though most gardeners plant in straight lines because vegetables require a good deal of care and straight lines are the easiest to tend, you may choose circles, or triangles, or whatever you wish. For years I have maintained a circular flower bed in the middle of a rectangular vegetable garden, and I have experimented with circles of broccoli, circles of beets, and wagon wheels of Marigolds—just for the fun of it, and, of course, to entertain my children. That's part of the fun and creativity of gardening. We've included a few examples of such gardens, but you should let your own imagination guide you.

A BASIC 20-BY-40-FOOT GARDEN. If you haven't computed your feet of row to the last carrot, you can always work with the 20-by-40-foot garden for the family of four. These 800 square feet should supply food from spring through frost with a little left over for putting by. The example provided here is one that's proven its merit and illustrates many of the suggestions we have discussed: at one corner, pumpkins have space to sprawl among the corn, thus deterring animals who dislike its prickly surface. At another, cucumbers are trained on a trellis just to keep them off the ground and spare the space for other crops. The corn is at the far end to avoid shading lower plants down front. (However, the beans are a little too close to the onions to be officially correct.)

Ordering Your Vegetable Seeds

Fresh seeds from proven seed houses (only slightly more expensive than the bargain brands, and in some cases even cheaper) are the greatest insurance for a successful home garden. They'll provide you with strong, healthy young plants. But start with weak, spindly plants from some no-name, fly-by-night operation, and no fancy tiller, tool or watering gadget is going to save you from a season of doom. Experimentation with new and interesting varieties from untried sources, or well-stored seeds from earlier growing seasons is worth the effort, but it is a good idea to back your garden up with proven sources. Seeds can be selected from a catalogue or at the garden store. I prefer ordering most of my seeds from catalogues—for two reasons. Most garden shops carry only two or three brands of seeds, and often limit their inventory to what they feel are the interests of the "average" buyer. This reduces your possibilities. Catalogues, however, not only offer greater choice to home gardeners, but almost invariably present more information about individual cultivars than the backs of seed-packets. If you're going to experiment with new varieties, you should know as much about them as you can.

A WORD ABOUT HYBRIDS

Hybrid plants, often designated as "F1" in catalogues, are bred to improve yield, flavor, and disease resistance, as well as for other features which make them attractive to both home and commercial growers. For instance, while flavor is of paramount importance to the home gardener ("Extra sweet and delicious!" the catalogues rave about their hybrid tomatoes), durability ("firm-fleshed" or "good keeper") is of much greater concern to commercial growers. Hybrid seeds offer a wonderful opportunity to experiment, but don't plan to save seeds from your hybrid crops—they will never bear true in future seasons.

Selecting Your Varieties

Although there is usually a lot of hype associated with catalogue sales in general, I have found the claims made by major seed houses for their outstanding varieties to be reliable. If a catalogue says a tomato cultivar will produce delicious, disease-free, abundant crops of fruit on compact vines in 55 days from transplanting, I tend to believe it's so.

When ordering seeds for the home garden, look carefully at the following five considerations: maturity date, yield, flavor, disease resistance and garden space required.

MATURITY DATE. This is of special importance because it helps you plan for succession plantings, and also assists in prolonging the harvest of certain crops. For example, because I know my favorite lettuce matures in 45 days and will be out of its growing bed in about 60 days, I can make definite plans to follow with fall peas. As for prolonging the harvest, knowing the maturity dates of different sweet corn varieties allows me to make simultaneous plantings of several varieties (early, mid-season and late) that will start producing ears in 63 days (Early Sunglow), and continue through day 90 (Silver Queen), with a nice bi-color (Sugar and Cream) maturing in between at 78 days.

YIELD. Catalogues often use phrases like "bears a tremendous crop," or "heavy yields," or "abundant producer over long periods." Since these descriptions are not applied to every cultivar, you can assume that when they are, it is for good reason. If abundant yields are important to you, select accordingly.

FLAVOR. While many of gardening's delights are in the growing, the taste of the food you've so ably brought to table is of more than passing pleasure. Look for terms such as "excellent taste," "delicious flavor," "superb sweetness," "luscious and juicy," "tender and rich-flavored," and the like.

DISEASE RESISTANCE. The ability of certain strains to resist common diseases which have proven capable of major destruction is equal to all other considerations. Many varieties of beans and tomatoes, for example, are advertised as disease-resistant. While you may not want to limit yourself to such crops (certain old-fashioned varieties lack the protection), you'd be wise not to ignore them entirely—or you might find yourself with a blighted crop of your favorite vegetable.

GARDEN SPACE REQUIRED. There was a time when gardeners with smallish plots despaired of ever being able to grow cucumbers, melons, squash and pumpkins, the vine-grown plants that sprawl everywhere. But the seed industry rose to the challenge and created a number of excellent, compact-growing versions for small home gardens. Dwarf peas and beans, and determinate tomato plants (that grow to a certain size and no further) have also been developed. And truly midget-type cultivars have been developed specifically for container or tub growing.

Additional Options

Beyond these considerations, two other choices are available to the seed buyer: treated seed and seed tapes.

TREATED OR UNTREATED SEED. Young seedlings are occasionally threatened by certain fungus diseases known commonly as "damping off" and "seed rot," whose organisms lurk in the cool, wet ground of early spring. This, of course, is no problem for indoor starters if you use a sterile planting medium (of which more in chapter 3). To combat the problem for direct-seeded cultivars, whose seeds are planted directly into the ground instead of into seed pots, seed houses routinely used to treat seeds with fungicides. But then many gardeners, concerned over the use of toxic chemicals on food-growing seeds, began buying from houses that did not add the fungicides.

Today, much seed available through retail catalogues is untreated, with the likely exception of corn, beans and peas. Burpee, for example, treats none of its seeds, but does sell Captan, a fungicide for gardeners who wish to treat their own. Other houses offer options and request that customers specify "UT"—untreated—(as is the case with Stokes), or a similar designation when ordering. Be guided by your own preferences.

SEED TAPES. Seed tapes are a great resource for gardeners who are uncomfortable handling tiny seeds, or making straight rows or who hate to thin out young seedlings. Fifteen-foot strips of paper tape are impregnated with seeds spaced just so. Scratch out a shallow furrow in the soil or planting medium, lay in the tape (cut to any length), and cover with soil. The paper soon dissolves, leaving behind perfectly spaced rows of flowers or vegetables. Unfortunately, you get fewer seeds for more money than the price of seeds in packets, but for some, the rewards are well worth the price. Seed tapes are not available in all catalogues, and come only in the most popular varieties.

Storing Seed

Just as metabolism in a hibernating animal slows to ensure the creature's survival over the winter, so must sleeping seeds remain dormant if they are to retain their vigor for spring awakening in your seed flats and garden. Because dormant seeds get their loudest wake-up calls from heat and moisture, it is essential that they be kept both cool and dry while in winter storage. This applies equally to seeds you have purchased and wish to save from one season to the next and seeds you produce in your garden for future use.

Store seed packets in rodent-proof and insect-proof containers, such as metal cans with tight-fitting metal lids or glass jars and bottles with metal screw-top lids. Avoid wooden or plastic containers. Keep seed containers in an unheated room, or, if space allows, in the refrigerator. To absorb any moisture that develops, you can follow Nancy Bubel's suggestion in her *Seedstarter's Handbook:* Roll up powdered milk in a paper towel and place it in the container. It should be replenished in midwinter.

PLANNING THE FLOWER GARDEN

This is, if anything, even more fun than mulling over your vegetable choices because its only function is pleasure—for you in growing the flowers you like, and for the eyes of others in your handiwork.

Siting the Flower Beds

The most important considerations for determining the location, type, size and shape of your flower gardens are aesthetic: that is, where and how will flowers create the most beauty? As in siting a vegetable garden you must be mindful of existing conditions: sun, shade, lay of the land, and soil and the needs of the flowers you'll be raising. Still, all things being equal, your best spots for flowers will be where you can see them.

Walk around your property. How do people approach or pass it? Where do they enter the house? Are there pathways which can be enhanced by flowers? Or a bare fence or wall

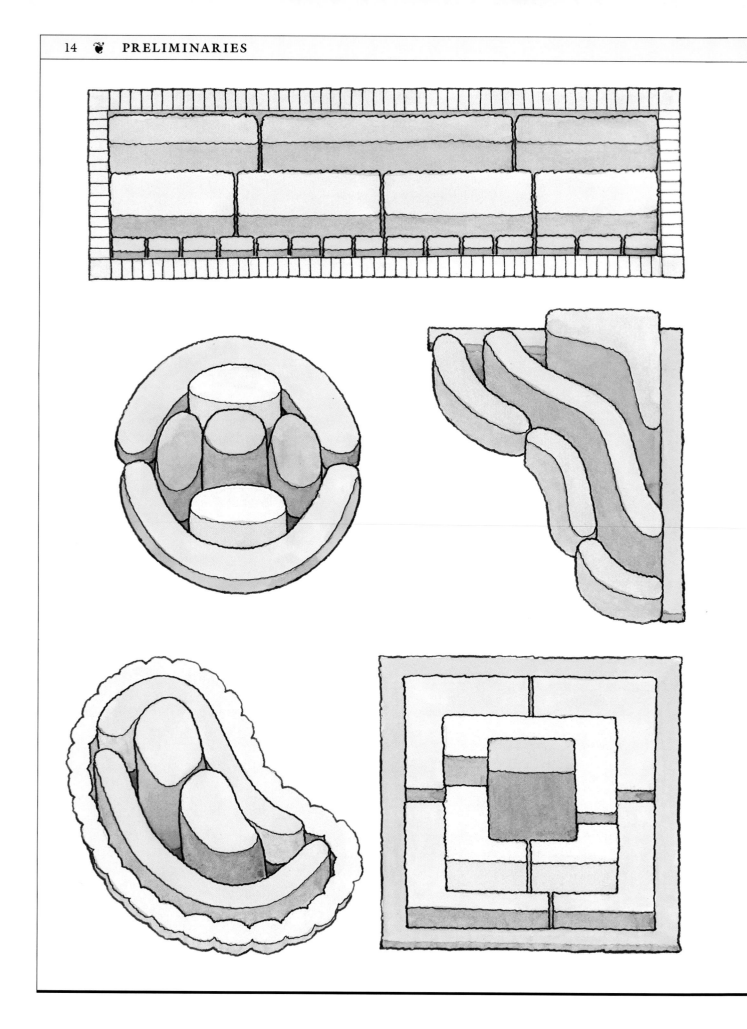

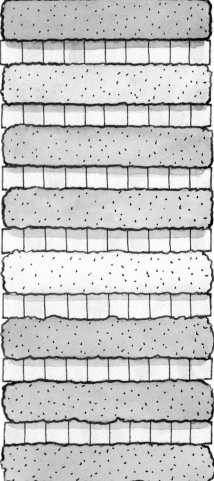

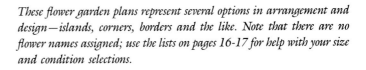

These flower garden plans represent several options in arrangement and design—islands, corners, borders and the like. Note that there are no flower names assigned; use the lists on pages 16-17 for help with your size and condition selections.

CUTTING FLOWERS

African Daisy
Ageratum
Amaranthus
Aster
Baby's Breath
Bachelor Button
Bells of Ireland
Blanket Flower
Butterfly Flower
California Poppy
Canterbury Bells
Carnation
Celosia
Chrysanthemum
Clarkia
China Pink
Columbine
Cosmos
Dahlia
Delphinium
Foxglove
Gloriosa Daisy
Golden Coreopsis
Larkspur
Lupine
Love in a Mist

Marigolds
Mexican Sunflower
Mignonette
Nasturtium
Painted Tongue
Pansy
Petunia
Phlox
Pincushion Flower
Poppy
Pot Marigold
Shasta Daisy
Snapdragon
Spider Flower
Stocks
Sunflower
Sweet Peas
Transvaal Daisy
Tree Mallow
Verbena
Yarrow
Zinnia

TALL FLOWERS
(Over 24" High)

Amaranthus Tricolor
Celosia

Canterbury Bells
Cosmos
Dahlia
Delphinium
Flowering Tobacco
Foxglove
Hibiscus
Hollyhock
Larkspur
Marigold
Mexican Sunflower
Morning Glory
Painted Tongue
Pincushion Flower
Snapdragon
Spider Flower
Statice
Sunflower
Zinnia

MID-HEIGHT FLOWERS
(12"-24" High)

Ageratum
Amaranthus Tricolor
Aster
Bachelor Button

Balsam
Blue Lace Flower
Blue Sage
California Poppy
Chinese Forget-Me-Not
Chrysanthemum
Clarkia
Cosmos
Dahlia
Geranium
Globe Amaranth
Golden Coreopsis
Love in a Mist
Marigold
Mignonette
Nasturtium
Painted Tongue
Petunia
Pincushion Flower
Poppy
Pot Marigold
Snapdragon
Snow-on-the-Mountain
Spider Flower
Strawflower
Summer Forget-Me-Not
Swan River Daisy
Vinca
Wallflower

Zinnia

EDGING OR LOW-GROWING FLOWERS
(Under 12" High)

Ageratum
Alyssum
Aster
Baby Blue Eyes
Basket of Gold
Begonia
Candytuft
China Pink
Cupflower
Dahlberg Daisy
Dusty Miller
Dwarf Morning Glory
Firecracker Plant
Flowering Kale
Impatiens
Livingstone Daisy
Lobelia
Pansy
Petunia
Phlox
Portulaca

A cutting flower garden can be designed for garden site, flower height, fragrance, or color.

Sapphire Flower
Toadflax
Treasure Flower
Vinca
Viola
Wishbone
Yarrow
Zinnia

FLOWERS FOR SHADE OR PARTIAL SHADE

Ageratum
Baby Blue Eyes
Begonia
Black-Eyed Susan
Canterbury Bells
Columbine
Garden Balsam
Impatiens
Flowering Tobacco
Foxglove
Gloriosa Daisy
Larkspur
Lobelia
Lupine
Monkey Flower
Nasturtium

Pansy
Petunia
Primrose
Sapphire Flower
Scarlet Sage
Shasta Daisy
Summer Forget-Me-Not
Vinca
Viola
Wishbone

FLOWERS FOR DRY SOILS

African Daisy
Alyssum
Baby's Breath
Bachelor Button
Basket of Gold
Black-Eyed Susan
Blanket Flower
California Poppy
Candytuft
Celosia
Golden Coreopsis
Cosmos
Creeping Zinnia
Dianthus

Four O'Clock
Gloriosa Daisy
Globe Amaranth
Hawk's Beard
Ice Plant
Marigold
Mexican Sunflower
Morning Glory
Nasturtium
Petunia
Phlox
Poppy
Portulaca
Snow on the Mountain
Spider Flower
Treasure Flower
Vinca
Yarrow

FLOWERS FOR MOIST CONDITIONS

Flowering Tobacco
Forget-Me-Not
Garden Balsam
Hibiscus
Impatiens
Lobelia

Monkey Flower
Nasturtium
Pansy
Primrose
Snow on the Mountain
Spider Flower
Stock
Transvaal Daisy
Vinca
Viola
Violet
Wishbone

FLOWERS THAT LIKE COOL SUMMERS

Butterfly Flower
Clarkia
Columbine
Delphinium
Godetia
Iceland Poppy
Larkspur
Lupine
Monkey Flower
Nasturtium
Painted Tongue
Pansy

Primrose
Stocks
Swan River Daisy
Sweet Pea
Toadflax
Wallflower

FLOWERS FOR FRAGRANCE

Alyssum
Carnation
Dianthus
Flowering Tobacco
Four O'Clock
Heliotrope
Marigolds
Mignonette
Nasturtium
Petunias
Primrose
Snapdragons
Stocks
Swan River Daisy
Sweet Pea
Sweet William
Wallflower
Yarrow

that needs softening? Is there a place where people congregate outside for meals and conversation that would benefit from the presence of an island bed, or maybe just a swatch of color or texture? Remember, above all, to consider areas that are visible from your most looked-out-of windows—on rainy days, or whenever you are indoors, there is nothing as spirit-lifting as glancing out at a symphony of color. (For the same reason you will want to consider the many flowers found in the listings here and in seed catalogues that attract bees, moths, bats, and birds—all of which, especially humming-birds, are exciting to watch from inside.)

Designing the Flower Beds

Once you've accepted the limitations, if any, of the site—shade, slopes, and soil conditions—the design of your flower gardens are really a matter of personal preference. Design ideas are rarely right or wrong; they either please you or they don't. You can choose among formal, highly structured and traditional designs, or informal flower beds and borders. Select what delights you most. We've given a few illustrations as examples.

Given all the choices of color, height, length of blooming season, and specific functions of some flowers, it will be both time- and agony-saving to work out some ideas on paper before you order seeds, just as you did with vegetables.

One other note before selecting varieties. You may want to grow some flowers for cutting or dried arrangements in block plantings—perhaps in the vegetable garden. This way you'll have a continuing source of table decoration without having to steal from, and thereby diminish the intensity of, your showier beds and borders.

Ordering Flower Seeds and Selecting Your Varieties

Going through a seed catalogue for the purpose of selecting flowers can be a maddening business. Everything is so beautiful that, before you know it, you've selected sixty varieties you'd love to grow, but don't have the space for. The following list of considerations, plus the lists of flowers for various sites and uses, will make the selection process a bit more organized—though no less agonizing—when you are forced to make the final cut.

COLOR. You have several pattern choices here: you can choose a monochromatic scheme, in which flowers are all in the same color range (e.g., reds, or red-oranges, or pinks); or

you can have an analogous scheme which includes colors that are near each other on the color wheel (e.g., reds, oranges, and yellows; or violets, blue-violets, and blues); or you may have a complementary scheme of colors opposite one another on the color wheel, such as violets and yellows, or reds and greens. The human eye responds to color in certain calculable ways that may help you to make your choices. Warm colors, like reds, oranges, yellows tend to pop out at the viewer, while the cooler greens and blues tend to recede. Having said all that, any color combination is in fact worth trying. Trial and error is the best way to discover what works best for you.

PLANT HEIGHT. All flower offerings in seed catalogues clearly state the approximate height of the mature plants. The heights of different plants in a flower bed have an effect on the beholding eye. Low, spreading mounds of flowers make the eye move laterally, while tall upright spikes of flowers move the eye vertically. Variety in height clearly creates visual interest, but you should not be dissuaded by this from planting occasional beds of low-growing or tall-growing flowers. The colors, textures and shapes of plants can create variety enough. When making your sketches, remember that in mixed borders the tallest plants should be placed in the rear so they do not shade shorter ones; and in island beds, the tallest plants should be in the middle for the same reason.

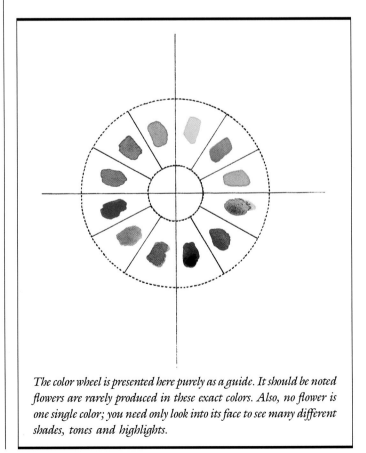

The color wheel is presented here purely as a guide. It should be noted flowers are rarely produced in these exact colors. Also, no flower is one single color; you need only look into its face to see many different shades, tones and highlights.

BLOOMING SEASON. Since flowers are grown for the color they provide, what could be finer than to have constant waves of color throughout the growing season? But the fact is that some flowers bloom only in early spring, and others continue further into summer. Still others refuse to flower in very hot weather, but experience a resurgence of blooming as the cool weather of fall approaches. So, if you want color the season through, you'll have to order seeds accordingly. Seed catalogues are not consistent with their information in this area, but I've included it with every flower in the listings.

OTHER CONSIDERATIONS. Finally, you may want to think about flowers of bewitching fragrance planted near the entrance to the house, or beside a much-used sitting spot. Or, for purposes of visual interest and diversity, you might make your selections according to bloom-size.

TOOLS, WATERING, AND POWER EQUIPMENT

Getting a gardening job done right—whatever the job—depends on having the right tools. If you're just starting your gardening career, an investment in a set of high-quality gardening tools, watering gear and equipment is well worth the money. Whenever possible, select tools and implements for their comfort and ease of use. If you're a tall person, for example, long-handled tools are a must. If you're not particularly brawny, try lighter-weight tools.

Basic Set of Garden Tools: Tilling and Planting

If I were forced to limit my tilling collection to just four, I'd choose the D-handled garden spade, a spading fork, a common hoe, and a steel garden rake.

SPADE. This is indispensable for digging or shoveling. Kept sharp, it makes a wonderful sod-slicer when starting new plots. And when it comes to prying up surprisingly large stones, this is your tool of choice.

SPADING FORK. This is the most constantly used tool in my garden. It has four heavy-gauged metal tines that make it perfect for breaking new ground, aerating the soil, digging root crops, turning the compost pile, and even spreading hay mulch (though a pitchfork, with five slender tines, is generally used for moving hay and leaves).

COMMON HOE. When you start looking at garden hoes, you'll soon realize there are many to choose from, some quite specialized. The narrowest are excellent for cultivating between plants, the widest for weeding and cultivating between rows. The heaviest-duty hoes, with stout handles, can be used to open deep furrows or even irrigation ditches.

STEEL GARDEN RAKE. Seedbed preparation is impossible without a good steel rake. It snags up rocks and roots, clumps and clods and smooths out the soil surface. It's ideal for mixing lime and other additives into the top several inches of soil.

TROWELS. For my planting collection, I'd throw in a good set of smaller tools, such as a trigger-handled hand fork and strong, single-piece construction hand trowel.

Care of Hand Tools

While all garden tools are designed to be used outdoors, they must not be allowed to remain outdoors, or they will go the way of all things left to the mercy of the elements. Metal parts will rust; wooden handles will become pitted and brittle.

A tool shed is ideal, but not necessary, so long as you discipline yourself to bring your tools in when you're through with them. Because few of us do, a little preventive maintenance can add years to our garden implements. One popular practice is to paint the handles bright orange or yellow. This protects the wood and makes the tool visible—and is a reminder to bring it under cover. Another common practice is to sand the handles at the beginning and end of each season and apply a soaking coat of linseed oil.

When storing tools for winter, clean all the metal parts thoroughly, sand away any rust, sharpen the edges with a file and coat them with a thin layer of machine or motor oil.

Watering Equipment

No gardener should begin a horticultural enterprise without the assistance of good-quality watering equipment. First, you need a hose long enough to reach comfortably from the nearest outdoor spigot to the garden. Garden stores carry many types of nozzles, and there is a universe of sprinklers to choose from.

Soaker, or drip irrigation hose is an excellent and efficient means of bringing moisture to the roots of your crops. Recommendations for its use are in chapter 4. But a good water-

BASIC GARDEN TOOLS

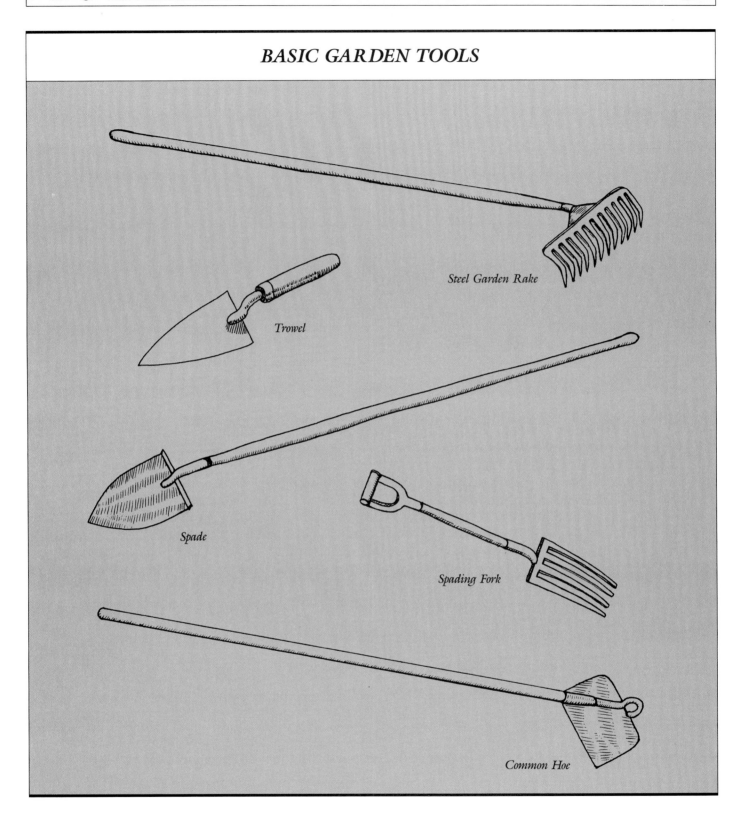

Steel Garden Rake

Trowel

Spade

Spading Fork

Common Hoe

ing can does a good job too, so long as you're willing to make the number of necessary refills. Special wands that attach to hoses are perfect for watering individual plants without knocking them off their feet in the deluge.

Power Equipment

For nearly 10 years, I have gardened with the aid of a rear-tined rototiller. It is a magnificent and versatile machine, and has made it easier for me to turn in the tons of organic material I've added to my soil. But because I garden intensively, and mulch my walkways with hay, I find that my tiller-use is confined to both ends of the gardening season, with no activity in between—hardly a justification for spending a thousand dollars or more.

But many, many gardeners make excellent use of their tillers all season long. It turns the soil in spring, cultivates during the growing season, turns new beds when space becomes available, and turns under crop residues and cover crops in the fall. The most popular are the Troy-bilt, available in several sizes and prices, and the Ariens and the Mantis.

Power chippers and shredders, which make fast work of leaves and brush, are excellent for preparing fibrous material for the compost pile.

❦ 3 ❦
STARTING SEEDS INDOORS

The minute you begin handling packets of seed and getting your hands into planting medium, it starts feeling like spring. Even if it's snowing outside and temperatures will plunge below zero several times before the earliest crocus blooms, if you're planting seeds, it's spring.

BENEFITS

Starting seeds indoors can give you more than just a psychological edge on winter. In practical terms, it gives you a jump on the growing season—regardless of when it actually arrives. The lettuce you started indoors in February and set out in the garden as seedlings at the beginning of April can be on your table just a few weeks later, when the lettuce you direct-seeded outdoors the same April day will still be only a couple of inches tall. The trick is doing both—that way you get new lettuce plants coming to maturity all season long. The same is true for cool-season flowers. Start them indoors early, and you'll get early blooms. Seed some outdoors at the "right" time, and you'll get more. (Planting outdoors is covered in detail in the next chapter.)

And, of course, the vast choices available: not one commercial nursery in ten thousand will have the variety to play with you have, as a seed-starter. Their seedling work must be limited to the few most popular—and salable—varieties.

Even if the local nursery carried seedlings in every variety you ever dreamed of, you could never be certain about the environment under which they were grown. For example, were the seeds treated or untreated? Were they started too early? Were they fed properly? And so on. Obviously most nurseries do a pretty good job or they wouldn't be in business, and you can count on them if some of your seedlings don't turn out well—particularly temperamental starters like small-seeded flower varieties and long-time germinators such as celery and certain herbs.

By creating your own indoor nursery, you can practically guarantee quality control—once you know what you're doing. You can use the seed you want, the soil mixes you've decided are best, the fertilizers you deem ideal. You can thin and transplant according to your own methods. And, of course, you are free to experiment.

SETTING UP YOUR INDOOR PLANTING STATION

The ideal place to establish an indoor planting station, as we'll call your mini-nursery, is in a spare room, away from traffic. Or you can share a room already in use, picking a corner and shifting a few pieces of furniture to establish a protected area that will be your three-month center of operations. Avoid setting up your area near a source of direct heat, like a radiator or wood stove. This could dry out your seedlings and lower the humidity too far.

Constructing the Unit

The area does not need water or even windows. The essential ingredients for this hub of horticultural activity will just be shelves or tables with lights suspended above them. You can

In this five-shelf unit, the middle shelf functions as a worktable and storage space, while shelves above and below hold trays of young plants. The unit shown is four feet wide, but you can make yours wider or narrower. Fluorescent fixtures come in seven lengths ranging from 12 to 96 inches to accommodate almost any shelf width.

make your own or buy fully-assembled systems at garden stores, but these often only have room for a limited number of plant trays. And small as they are, these setups can run into hundreds of dollars. If you can afford the money, by all means go for it, particularly the larger versions. But for a fraction of the cost, you can build a station not only with much greater capacity, but that takes up only 32 square feet of wall space. You can make your unit narrower or wider, but a five-shelf unit measuring 4 feet wide by 2 feet deep by 8 feet tall will hold almost 20 trays of plants and provide workspace as well.

To put this station together, you'll need:

10   two-tube fluorescent fixtures, sometimes called shop lights (see below), 48″ long each, plus hooks and chains to suspend them
6   two-by-fours, 8 feet in length
5   one-by-twelve boards, 8 feet in length
2   one-by-twos, 10 feet in length

If you can find the lights on sale, which they frequently are, you should be able to build the unit for under $200, including nails and an inexpensive electrical timer to connect to the lights and provide a set amount of light each day. If you're handy, you can put this together in about an hour. Add another hour if, like me, you have two left hands.

Fluorescent Lighting

Strange as it may seem, fluorescent lighting more closely duplicates the spectrum of rays available in natural sunlight than any other artificial light source. It also consumes less power and gives brighter light than do incandescent lamps.

The interior walls of fluorescent tubes are coated with different powders to achieve various effects: cool white, natural white, daylight and warm white. Research shows that plants do best when exposed to a combination of these effects, such as one cool white tube plus either a daylight or warm white one. These are both effective combinations in a two-tube fixture. Specialty single-tube grow-lights are also available, under such names as *Grow-Lux, Plant-Gro* and *Naturescent*. They are, nevertheless, more expensive in spite of their greater operating efficiency.

Fluorescent tubes emit less light at the ends, so remember to keep your trays toward the middle, or rotate the end trays to the middle every day.

Materials You'll Need

All you really need is your seed, containers, the planting medium, fertilizer, and a place for all this, plus water, light and the right temperatures for growing. Beyond that, it's a matter of the crops you've chosen, the time you want to spend, and how much you want to invest.

Not all plants are good indoor starters, as you'll see when you go through the vegetable, herb and flower listings; some don't like to be transplanted at all and their seeds must be sown directly into the garden (called direct-seeding). Others can only comfortably be transplanted once, from indoor starting medium to garden; still others transplant readily, and can be sown with many other seeds in large open trays (called flats), then transplanted from there to individual containers and from there into the garden. You can look up your crop's habits in the listings to see what (if any) containers you'll need, and a list appears in this chapter of plants disliking transplantation. Containers also come in different sizes, and you can expect the 6-week-old seedling ready for the garden to be proportionate to the mature plant you know: that is, a parsley seedling is smaller than a lettuce seedling so stock up accordingly.

PLANTING CONTAINERS. This is wide open. You can literally use any container large enough to hold a couple of inches of planting medium with a hole or two in the bottom for drainage. For years, I sowed seed in flats I made from scrap lumber and then transplanted the seedlings into styrofoam cups of various sizes (to which I had unlimited access). As gardening became more popular, excellent and inexpensive seedpots and containers became available, and I have since moved on to them.

One of my favorites is peat pellets, which are a growing container and planting medium in one. Sold under the name Jiffy pellets, they are made of peat compressed to the size of a fifty-cent piece. When soaked in water, the pellets expand to seven times their original size and are surrounded by netting that holds the peat in place, forming a self-contained little seedpot. They are especially good for large seeds like melons, cucumbers and squashes. When the seedlings are ready you can put them—plant, pot and all—directly into the garden. Some gardeners prefer to cut away the netting that holds the peat in place, but it soon disintegrates underground, allowing the plant roots to expand freely.

Fiber cubes are similar to peat pellets in that they are just right for large seeds and can be transplanted, plant and cube together, without having to disturb any roots.

Individual peat pots are also good for single-seed planting, but they tend to suck the moisture rapidly from the planting medium, and so must be kept well-watered.

Plastic containers similar to ice-cube trays with four or six planting compartments, known as *four-packs* and *six-packs,* are excellent for starting plants with medium and large seeds. When the seedling is ready to be transplanted, you simply press up from the bottom of each cell in the pack, and a perfectly formed root-and-soil mass will emerge. Unlike peat pots and pellets, these plastic cell-packs can be used again and again.

Plastic trays (flats) with holes in the bottom are best for sowing small seeds. When the seedlings emerge, you'll transplant them to individual containers (see "Transplanting from Flats to Containers" on page 27)—usually six-packs are a good size.

A *holding tray* is always desirable under your collections of containers. It keeps things organized.

PLANTING MIXES. If you use anything beside the self-contained peat pellets or fiber cubes, you will need a planting medium. Unfortunately, garden soil, even very fine garden soil, does not make a good medium for starting seeds indoors. For one thing, it has weed seeds in it; and for another it may even host some disease organisms detrimental to young seedlings. (It was common practice some years back to sterilize one's own garden soil by baking it in the oven. Considering the few dollars saved, the chore was smelly and unpleasant.)

These days, sterilized planting mixes which contain peat and perlite or vermiculite are unsurpassed for seed-starting. They are light, retain large quantities of moisture while still being well-drained, and never crust over. There was a time when I mixed my own by a formula calling for coarsely milled peat moss and vermiculite in equal amounts, plus a handful of ground limestone and a sprinkling of bone meal. Now I buy one 25-pound bag of a blend called Pro-mix, and find it more than enough for all my indoor planting needs.

OTHER SUPPLIES. Plastic bags (the tall kitchen size) to cover seed flats, short row markers and a permanent-ink marking pen for labeling, and an old spoon or fork to handle young transplants.

SOWING YOUR SEEDS

When to Start

You can figure out when to start most plants simply by counting backward six weeks from the time when conditions will be right for their outdoor survival, given in the listings in Part 2. Six-week-old seedlings are the right age to set out; they're young, vigorous and eager to get growing.

Naturally, there are exceptions. Some seeds, such as celery, parsnips, and Begonias, take up to three weeks or more to germinate, even under ideal conditions, and they must be started earlier—up to nine weeks before planting out. Onions can be started from seed indoors as early as you like; if

---

HASTENING SEED GERMINATION

Soak slow-germinating seeds like carrots, parsley and parsnip with water for a day to speed up the sprouting process a bit. To get your root crops going record-fast, use hot tea to begin with and then after the soak, dry your seeds until they can be separated from each other and sow as usual. Water deeply but gently, then cover each row with a board. I'm not sure why this works—probably insures darkness—but, as promised by the gardener who passed the trick along, my parsnips were up in 13 days. A record indeed.

---

they get too leggy in their containers, just shear them with a scissor. All the while, their root systems will be getting larger and stronger.

At the other end of the scale are melons and other *cucurbitaceae* (cucumbers, squash and pumpkins), which grow so quickly from seed started indoors that they require only three to four weeks' lead on the outdoor growing season.

How to Sow

The first thing you must do is organize all your materials: planting mix, planting containers, seed packets and—be sure not to forget these—labels or labelling devices. When you sit down at your station on this all-important planting day, you will be bristling with energy. Don't be tempted to skip labelling to save time—you'll regret it later when faced with scores of identical-looking planting containers.

Make sure the labels are nearby. Whatever you use is fine. And remember to use a marking pen whose ink is not water soluble. The humid conditions will make the ink run—I guarantee it—with predictable results.

STEP 1. Moisten your soil mix. Don't get it so wet you've got to wring it out; just make sure it's uniformly moist. You can do this by adding water directly to the plastic bag it's in, or you can moisten it in batches in another bag or box of some kind.

STEP 2. Fill your planting containers with the soil to within ½-inch of the top.

STEP 3. Level off the soil. In a flat, you can use a small board to do the job; in smaller containers you can use your fingers. The object is to remove crevices in the soil into which a seed could fall below its ideal germinating depth.

HANDLING VERY SMALL SEEDS

Whatever containers you use, planting tiny seeds with any sort of precision is almost impossible. But here are two tricks which might make the process a little simpler. Try mixing the seeds with a few tablespoons of clean sand and then spreading the mixture as evenly as you can over the soil surface. Or you can place the mixture into a salt shaker and tap out the contents onto the soil. You can try a fine tweezer, but that generally works best with slightly larger seeds.

Use a salt shaker to distribute small seeds.

STEP 4. When seeding a flat, you may wish to plant in rows. Make the furrows by laying a pencil onto the soil and pressing it in to the appropriate depth. This also creates a uniform planting surface for the seeds. Otherwise, spread the seeds as thinly and evenly as possible over the soil surface, and then press them gently into the soil with a board or your fingers. For seeding in small individual containers, plant 2 or 3 seeds, and press gently into the soil with fingers. Label each container and then set them in some sort of planting tray; this will eliminate clutter and pandemonium.

STEP 5. Some seeds, especially flower seeds, require light in order to germinate successfully, so check before you proceed with this step. If they don't require light, cover the seeds with additional soil, remembering that they should be buried no deeper than 3 to 4 times their own diameter. That generally translates into a depth of ¼- to ½-inch. NOTE: If you're using peat pellets press one or two seeds into each moistened pot, and pinch the top to cover the seeds with peat.

STEP 6. If you're using containers, group together plants with similar germinating periods, and then place each flat or tray of containers in a plastic bag and seal with a wire twist to keep in moisture. If you make bag-mates out of slow and fast germinators, you'll get into trouble. There should be sufficient air in the bag to allow for successful germination, but because there is a tendency for mold to form, you might want to poke 2 or 3 holes in the bag to allow for a bit of circulation.

STEP 7. Put the flats or trays in a warm place—somewhere that remains consistently in the neighborhood of 70° to 75°F,

such as the top of a refrigerator or not far from a wood stove. Don't put them on the floor where they will be subject to drafts; nor should you place them on a windowsill, no matter how sunny. The nighttime temperatures fluctuate too widely there.

STEP 8. Inspect the flats and trays every day until the seeds have germinated. This is important, because once sprouted, they will start stretching toward the light. Kept in the dark too long, they'll become a tangle of white threads that are beyond help, and you'll have to start all over again. Check them every day; and get them under lights as soon as they have germinated. If you can time it right, it is ideal to get them under light even before the cotyledons have fully emerged.

CARE OF SEEDLINGS

Once germinated, seedlings require the right amounts of light, temperature, water, space and nutrients if they are to become healthy garden plants.

Light

From the moment they germinate, young plants seek light. They'll go to great lengths to get it too. A young seedling kept in a dark corner will literally try to stretch itself over to the light coming in a nearby window. The result is disastrous, since plants do not recover from this "legginess"—having a weakened and overextended, or "leggy," stem.

Newly emerged seedlings require 12 to 16 hours of light each day, generally from a height of about three inches over their heads. Fluorescent or grow lights are best (see page 24), though a sunny windowsill will also work. There is not much room there; but if you have only a limited number of plants, you certainly can use a windowsill with certain provisos:

1. The window must face south or southwest.
2. When plants begin to "lean" in the direction of the sun, they should be turned around. In another hour or so they will be quite erect—until they start leaning again.
3. Move plants back a bit at night or they could suffer setbacks from drafty windows.

One final word about light. Your plants must have a period of eight hours or so without it. The reason: they process their food and grow in the darkness. Never give them more than 16 hours of light each day.

Temperature and Humidity

"Start seeds warm, grow seedlings cool." This pithy quote from Nancy Bubel's *Seedstarter's Handbook* is well worth remembering. Most plants will grow perfectly well at about 60° to 70°. Higher temperatures often result in weak and spindly plants that are rarely able to survive well outdoors. Nighttime temperatures, that is, when the plants are in darkness, can be adjusted downward by about 10 degrees, and the plants will thrive.

If any source of direct heat is nearby, like a radiator, moisture will quickly evaporate and fall below the minimum 30% required by your plants. Move your trays to a better spot.

Watering

Many flower and vegetable seedlings are particularly sensitive to dry conditions. Some, like coleus and begonias, may wilt and die if they experience dry conditions for even a couple of hours. So once your plants are up, feel the soil often—and

that goes double for peat pots, since they tend to dry out quickly—and water as often as you think necessary.

Since young seedlings are very delicate, you should not do any overhead watering for quite a while or the plants may collapse under the deluge. The best method is either to "bottom-water" by placing trays (make sure there are holes in the bottom) in basins filled with water until moisture is drawn up and the soil surface darkens. Somewhat more work, but equally effective, is overhead misting until the soil glistens. Misting must be done more frequently than bottom-watering. In either case, check the soil every day.

Thinning

Whether you've planted in flats or in individual pots or containers, new seedlings will require additional space to grow as soon as their first "true" leaves appear—the first pair after the cotyledons. You'll do this by thinning—cutting away neighboring competitive plants to give the remaining ones the space they need. Thinning must be done swiftly and mercilessly throughout the growing process for the ultimate good of your garden, starting right here at the beginning. Since roots of neighboring plants get tangled up with each other and wrap around the same bits of soil, never pull out unwanted seedlings. This will damage the roots of the remaining plants. Rather, snip the seedlings off at soil level with a pair of scissors.

Transplanting from Flats to Containers

If you have done all your planting in individual containers (such as six-packs, peat-pots, or Jiffy pellets) and timed the plantings according to our earlier discussion, you will not

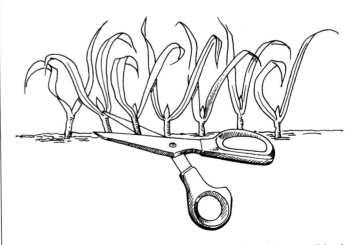

Thinning is always done by snipping the unwanted seedlings at soil level.

SEEDLINGS THAT DON'T TRANSPLANT WELL

Some seedlings must never be transplanted from one pot to another because they never seem to quite recover from it. These plants should be grown from seed in individual containers and then set out in the garden at the appropriate time.

Vegetables & Herbs	Flowers
Anise	Blue Lace Flower
Borage	Butter Daisy
Caraway	California Poppy
Carrots	Creeping Zinnia
Chervil	Flax Lupines
Chinese Cabbage	Mignonette
Coriander	Nasturtium
Corn	Phlox (annual)
Cucumbers	Poppy
Dill	Tree Mallow
Fennel	
Melons and Pumpkins	
Parsley	

have to do any intermediate transplanting. Each of your containers holds enough soil to support the vigorous growth of the young seedling until time for it to be hardened off (acclimated slowly to the outdoors) and set out in the garden.

If you have sown any seeds in flats, however, the young plants must be moved into their own individual 4-inch containers when they grow their first true leaves. (Some gardeners prefer to wait until there are four true leaves before transplanting.) In any case, transplanting from flats—whenever you do it—gives plants more room to grow, improves ventilation and stimulates feeder roots which will result in a bushier more vigorous root mass by the time plants must be set out in the garden. Transplanting also forces a gardener into a selection process that, if executed with efficiency, will have an overall positive influence on the quality of the garden.

S T E P 1 . Gather all your materials together: seeded flats, soil mix, planting containers, labels and marking pen, and old spoon or fork.

S T E P 2 . Fill the planting containers half-way with moist soil mix.

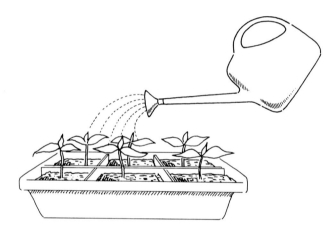

S T E P 3 . Water the soil in the old flat to loosen the seedlings.

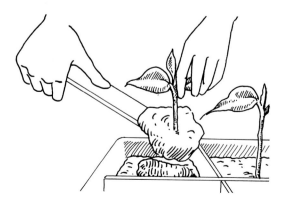

S T E P 4 . Using a flat stick, an old butter knife, or the handle of a fork or spoon—anything that will not tear the

roots of an adjacent plant—gently cut down around and under seedlings and lift them out one at a time. Always hold the seedling meanwhile by its top leaves, never by its delicate stem. A broken stem means a dead plant, while leaves can always grow back.

S T E P 5 . Set the seedling into its new pot, add moist soil to the top, and press firmly in place. If the new soil has been moistened sufficiently, you will not have to water again now. Use your judgment here. If you must water, do so gently or you risk overwhelming the tender plant in its new location.

Seedlings should always be planted slightly deeper than they were in their flats. Some plants, such as tomatoes, cabbage and broccoli, can actually be buried much deeper—right up to their top leaves.

Transplanting sets a plant back a bit, temporarily halting its upward growth and instead encouraging it to grow outward as it establishes a fuller and stronger root system. Every time you transplant, the seedling's root system will increase in size—sometimes to the point of doubling. The more roots a plant has, the greater becomes its ability to draw up nutrients from the soil and to support itself as it grows.

Keep new transplants shaded and cool for at least half a day; if they get droopy, avoid the temptation to water them or put them under intense light. Just give them a chance to recover—which they will, almost invariably.

Fertilizing

Excessive fertilizing can result in leggy seedlings, which is one reason it's best to start with a planting mix rather than a potting soil to which fertilizer may have already been added. This way you can control the amount and type of nutrients your seedlings will have, since the planting mix contains none. You add everything.

I like to use fish emulsion fertilizer at half-strength (the smell is a bit less intense that way) two or three times a week for the first three weeks. I increase the dosage to full strength after that. You can use products available at your garden store, or compost and/or aged manure can be lightly sprinkled on the soil surface, and when you water, their nutrients will be carried down to the plant roots in soluble form—which is the principal way plants can take up nourishment.

HARDENING OFF

"Hardening off" is the process of toughening a plant's cell structure by introducing it gradually to an outdoor environment starting when the seedlings are between four and six

COLD FRAMES AND HOTBEDS FOR HARDENING OFF

A simple cold frame or hotbed, which you can either build or buy, is a definite plus for hardening off spring transplants or direct-seeding under somewhat protected conditions. Each is a rectangular bottomless box with a hinged glass top that tilts at an angle sufficient to catch the rays of the sun on the perpendicular. The cold frame is heated by sunlight, while the hotbed gets additional nighttime heat from an electrical cable or fresh stable manure placed some inches below the soil surface.

Southern exposure is a must, as is protection against strong winds. If the windbreak you devise is also heat-retentive (such as a wall of cement blocks painted black), all the better; it will release its stored heat during the night. Rake up soil around the sides to protect the plants from drafts, and if a heavy frost threatens, cover the top with an old blanket.

On cold or windy days, keep the glass lid of your cold frame or hotbed closed.

Conversely, since seedlings may topple in extreme heat, and even in the mid-50's a sunny day can quickly raise the temperature under glass, keep a thermometer in easy view so you can prop the lid open if the temperature rises above 80°F. On balmy days, you can leave the top completely open; just make sure it's secured with a stick or, better yet, a fixed latch of some kind, lest a sudden gust send it and a thousand shards of glass crashing over everything.

A week or so in the cold frame or hotbed is all your seedlings will require to prepare them for the real world of the garden. And during this time, you can be preparing the garden for their imminent arrival.

One final note: seeds can also be started in the soil within the cold frame, but that is generally reserved for mid-summer when the frame offers protection from heat, not cold. The soil must be prepared as for any other seed bed.

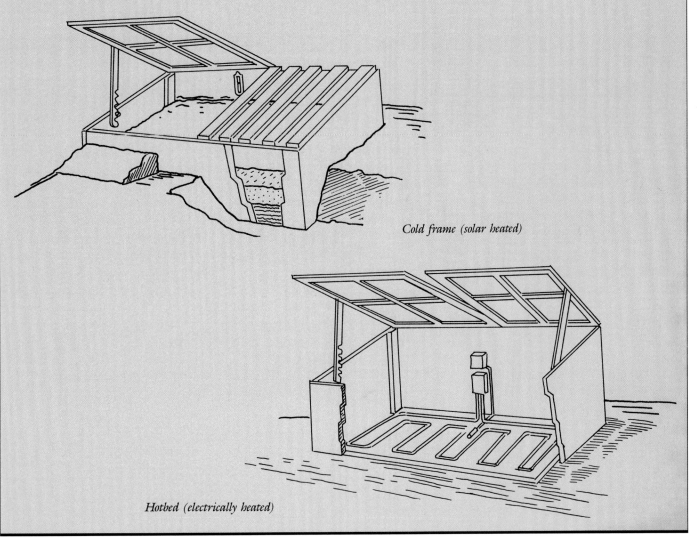

Cold frame (solar heated)

Hotbed (electrically heated)

weeks old. One tried and true technique calls for a week of deprivation before seedlings get their first experience of the outdoors. You cut back on everything except light: gradually discontinue fertilizing, reduce watering, and keep plants quite cool—move them to an unheated room, if possible.

Next, carry the trays outdoors and leave them in a spot where they will get only indirect sunlight. Since strong winds can snap young stems and burn tender leaves (the leaves turn whitish when burned), be sure the spot is sheltered from heavy gusts. Then gradually allow plants more direct sun over three or four days. Bring the trays indoors at night for the first couple of days.

❦ 4 ❦
PLANTING SEEDS AND SEEDLINGS OUTDOORS

By the time your garden soil can be worked in the spring (April in the north; February and March farther south), you will already have planned your garden sites, ordered your seeds, and started many of them indoors. In fact, you should have a few trays of plants hardening off and just about ready to go.

Knowing when the soil can be worked or prepared for planting is a wet/dry question: is the soil dry enough? If tilled or plowed or spaded before spring rains and run-off have been absorbed into the land, soil can harden into masses of unworkable stuff that will reduce the yield of your garden for the entire season. Here's how to check.

Take up a handful of soil and press it into a ball. Now toss it to the ground. If it breaks easily into fairly loose and small clumps, it's dry enough to work. If it tends to hold its shape, or comes apart in large-ish chunks, give it more time. The sandier the soil, the quicker it will dry out in spring; the less coarse clay soils take longer. Here's another dry-enough test the old-timers do: walk in the garden; if the footprints you make are shiny, the soil is still too wet to work.

TILLING THE GARDEN PLOT FOR SPRING PLANTING

If you're working an established garden, the first thing to do is remove all debris from last year—old tomato plants, corn stalks either still standing or on the ground, pumpkin vines, and the like. For the future, you should know that leaving your garden that way from the previous season is bad hygiene. It fosters disease and in some cases harbors the wintering over of certain destructive insect pests. The way to leave your garden in the fall is free of debris and freshly tilled. Even better is to protect and enrich it by sowing a cover crop of annual rye for spring tillage. Now follow Steps 6 through 8 below.

Should you be starting a new plot where only grass has grown before, you'll have a bit more labor. But the pleasure of opening new beds for flowers or food crops is in many ways the sweetest of all. The following directions are for hand-spading; there are separate instructions for starting a new bed with a garden tiller.

Hand-spading a New Plot

STEP 1. Stake out the dimensions of your new plot. Attach string from one stake to the next until the plot is surrounded.

STEP 2. Using the string as a guide, slice along the perimeter of your plot with a sharp D-handled spade, to a depth of 12 inches.

STEP 3. Working from your slice-marks, divide your plot into smaller ones with the spade, and begin the process of skinning off the sod one section at a time. Bend your knees and mind your back. Place the sod in a wheelbarrow or garden cart and dump at the site of your compost pile. (More about compost on page 33)

STEP 4. Turn over all the soil with a spading fork—ideally to a depth of 12 inches. If you're unfamiliar with the process: push the fork, tines down, into the soil with your foot and pry up as much soil as you can—and literally turn it over.

STEP 5. Rake out any remaining sod roots.

STEP 6. Once the ground has been thus opened, you can and should add organic material such as aged manure and compost. If you've got enough on hand to make a 3- to 4-inch blanket, spread it on and then turn it under as deep as it will turn. You can never add too much compost or composted manure, so spread as much as you have. If you've none of your own, you can purchase bags of it at the garden store—an expensive, but beneficial, alternative. A word of caution about fresh manure: it not only contains scads of weed seeds, which are a nuisance, but it also adversely affects the quality of certain root crops—carrots and beets, to name two. If someone is offering you a 2-ton load of fresh manure straight from the barn, by no means turn it down. Have it dumped near the garden and give it time to ripen—6 months to a year is fine, but the longer the better.

STEP 7. Pound any large clods with a rake, and then rake the soil until it is smooth.

STEP 8. Now add any further items to your soil, such as lime, bone meal, and rock powders like greensand and rock phosphate. Follow application directions, and then rake these additives into the top 3 to 4 inches of soil—which is just at the root zone of most garden plants.

Lime is added to the soil to help control the acid-alkaline, or pH, balance. The pH is measured on a 14-point scale with 0 to 6.9 considered acid, 7.0 neutral, and 7.1 to 14 considered alkaline. Most garden flowers and vegetables do best between pH 5.5 and 7.5. Unless the soil is kept within this fairly narrow pH range, certain vital nutrients won't be available to your plants. If you spread fertilizer over acid soil, for example, it can lose almost all its phosphorous to a chemical bond with iron and aluminum already in the soil. So, you really haven't added phosphorous after all, and before long your plants might show deficiency symptoms.

You can buy a simple and inexpensive pH testing kit at most garden stores or through seed catalogues, and get a general idea of what type of soil your garden has. But the best thing to do is have a Department of Agriculture soil test done in the fall, because it can take up to six weeks for results if the labs are busy. If it's spring now, and you can't afford the wait, do it next fall.

TIP: WHEN IN DOUBT, SPREAD LIME. Unless you're gardening in the far west where soils tend to be naturally alkaline, judicious liming will never do your garden soil harm. Lime neutralizes acid soils, adds calcium and magnesium, and improves soil structure. The sandier the soil, the more quickly lime is leached away. Clay soils have a greater storage capacity. Five pounds of lime per 100 square feet in clay soils, and half that much for lighter, sandy soils

---

STARTING A NEW PLOT WITH A TILLER

STEP 1. Stake out the dimensions of your plot as for hand-spading.

STEP 2. The first object is to churn up the sod. Set the tiller depth-guide to no deeper than 3 inches and make a slow pass across the plot, first the width, then the length. If your tiller bucks (known as "porpoising") set the depth-guage even shallower.

STEP 3. Repeat process until all the sod is busted.

STEP 4. Rake out all sod fragments and load them into a cart for your compost pile.

STEP 5. Spread organic material (compost, manure, leaf mold, etc.).

STEP 6. Set the tiller as deep as it will go, and repeat pattern described in Step 2.

STEP 7. Spread soil additives and rake smoothly into the top 3 inches of soil.

---

will raise the pH one unit. A liming every three years is fairly standard.

Popular wisdom calls for waiting seven to ten days after tilling and fertilizing before actually planting. One advantage to waiting a week or so is that it gives you another opportunity to rake before planting, which will kill an untold number of young weeds that have barely germinated. Another is that the soil will have a chance to settle if it's been "fluffed up." If you don't want to wait, don't; no harm will come of planting right away.

Fertilizers

To ensure gardening success, you must be sure your garden soil is capable of providing plants with sufficient nutrients and minerals. These nutrients are provided by what we call fertilizers, of which there are many different kinds.

In the 1960s and 1970s when the environmental movement became popular, controversy raged over the fertilizers we should use in home gardens and on farms. On one side were the "organic" gardeners and farmers devoted to naturally occurring materials; on the other were the users of synthetic, non-natural commercial chemical fertilizers, more or less the same ones used on the nation's farms.

THE USDA SOIL TEST

The Department of Agriculture's report on its test of your soil will provide you with a great deal of information. It will give you a detailed reading on levels of:

Major nutrients: nitrogen (N), phosphorous (P), and potassium (K);

Secondary nutrients: magnesium (Mg), manganese (Mn), copper (Cu);

Trace elements: boron (B), calcium (Ca), iron (Fe), molybdenum (Mo), sulphur (S), and zinc (Zn);

Organic matter: decomposed and partially decomposed plant and animal material which enriches any soil. The test will also give you directions for correcting any deficiencies, along with a pH reading, and how to bring your soil into proper pH range for most garden plants.

Check with your local agricultural Extension Service to have the test performed. You'll be sent a packet which contains all the directions you'll need.

SYNTHETIC FERTILIZERS. When combined with moisture in the soil, synthetic fertilizers rapidly release concentrated nutrients that are almost instantly usable by plants. Plants experience a rush of growth. If you re-apply later in the season as plants are flowering or otherwise heading toward maturity, again they'll surge.

Using synthetic fertilizers, however, can raise as many problems as it solves. Those opposed to them argue that every year millions of tons of topsoil on the country's farms turn to dust and either wash or blow away because the synthetic fertilizers don't begin to replenish the earth in the same way natural organic matter does. These chemicals are basically nothing but a quick "fix"—yet they are the only nutrients added to the soil in exchange for the enormous amount it gives up to the food it is asked to produce. To remain healthy and vigorous, soil needs greater repayment for its labor: it must be given huge amounts of organic matter to restore its spent nutrients. In addition, there is a clear pollution danger to water supplies from the run-off of nitrate salts, a high-percentage of ingredients in most chemical fertilizers.

NATURALLY OCCURRING FERTILIZERS: COMPOST. While unable to do much more than express my fear and anger over the country's eroding farmland and endangered aquifers, I am most definitely in a position to guarantee the sanctity of the little piece of earth entrusted to my care. With a minimum of effort, I make my own fertilizer—*compost*—meaning a mixture of decaying organic matter. Mine is composed of kitchen scraps and garden debris, chicken manure, and an occasional truckload from a neighbor's horse barn. But even without the animal manure, there is always an abundance of materials at hand to make quick compost. And, as you will see a bit later in this chapter, gardeners can even *grow* their own fertilizer in the form of cover crops, or "green manure."

Soil is quite capable of making its own compost, or humus, of rich decayed matter, if it has the materials to work with. In forests and fields, plants die and fall to the ground, along with tons of leaves; and they rot where they fall, forming humus in due course. But if in the garden one persistently removes all plant material (weeds, crops and crop residues), what remains behind to form humus? Nothing. Sooner or later, the soil becomes depleted of its nutrients, and the only thing that will make plants grow then is to add some back, usually in the form of synthetic chemicals.

Gardeners who understand this cycle try to supply their gardens faithfully with organic matter in the form of compost, which is already mixed up and partly decayed, or in the form of fresh kitchen scraps, grass clippings, manures from non-meat-eating animals, shredded leaves, chopped garden debris and more—a process referred to as either sheet composting or trench composting. Or they do both. Once turned into the soil, all this organic matter breaks down and forms humus, full of nutrients that release themselves slowly and constantly to plant roots. The presence in the soil of this decomposed and partially decomposed organic material creates a balanced environment for the soil microbes, earthworms and insects who do the actual work of breaking it down. The more active the soil life, the healthier the soil; the healthier the soil, the healthier the plants which grow upon it; and the healthier the plants, the healthier the creatures who eat them.

LAYOUT OPTIONS

There are many ways to arrange the plants in your garden. Most gardeners plant in straight lines, but you may choose circles, or triangles, or whatever you wish. For years I have maintained a circular flower bed in the middle of a rectangular vegetable garden, and I have experimented with circles of broccoli, and circles of beets, and wagon wheels of Marigolds—just for the fun of it, and of course, to entertain my children. That's part of the fun and creativity of gardening. See pages 36–37 for descriptions of multiple-row, wide-row, diamond and other planting formats.

Though you can certainly use your imagination, gardeners by and large plant vegetables in straight lines simply because vegetables require a good deal of care and straight lines are the easiest to tend. Also, vegetables are food, and many gardeners feel that space set aside for food-growing should be as efficiently planted as possible. They devise methods for

Garden layout option.

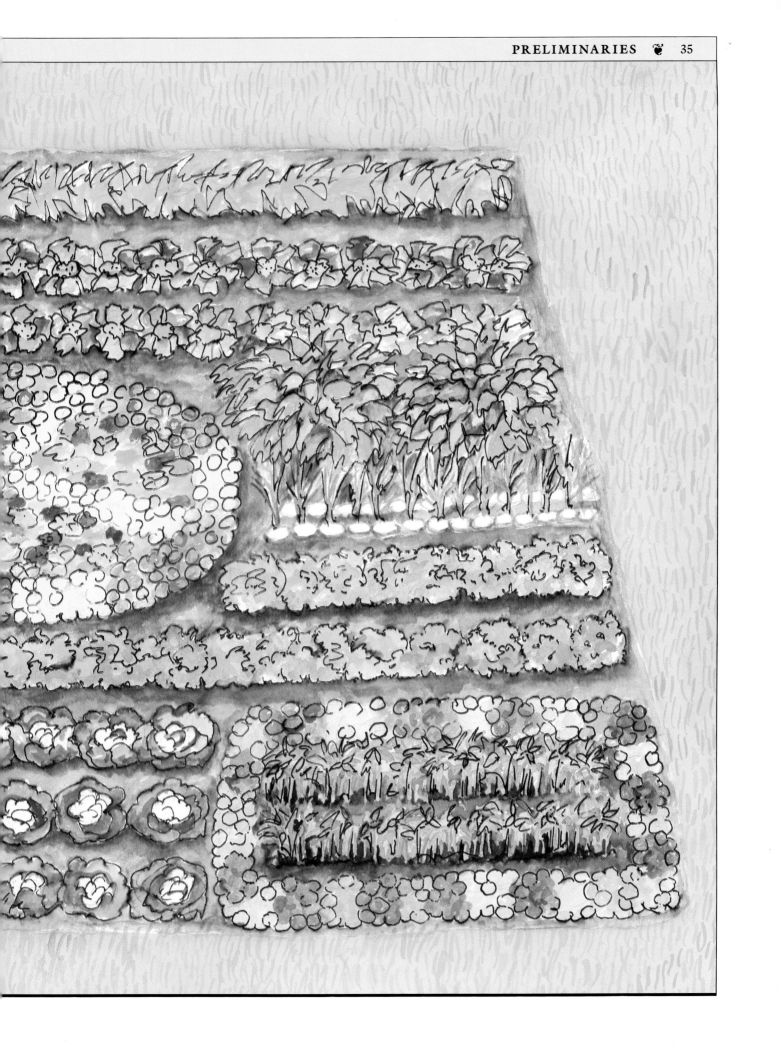

MAKING COMPOST: YOUR OWN NATURAL FERTILIZER

No garden is complete without a compost pile, for no truly serious garden is complete without compost. Entire books have been written on the making of garden compost. They contain fascinating scientific explanations of how the process works: the carbon-to-nitrogen composition ratio of the materials assembled; the microbial action involved, and so forth. One in particular, *Let it Rot* by Stu Campbell, is especially informative and understandable. In fact, the basics of compost-making can be reduced to five simple steps:

THE COMPOST BIN. For best results, the compost pile should be contained in a structure. The container, or bin, as it is commonly known, can be made of almost anything: woven wire fence rolled into a circular cage, concrete blocks, wood pallets, snow fence, and hay bales, for instance. Make your bin big enough to accommodate large amounts of material to be processed. You may even want to have a couple of piles going simultaneously, or to have piles at different stages of completion.

THE INGREDIENTS. Virtually anything is fair game for the compost pile: grass clippings, weeds (without seeds), stable manure, leaves, and the great abundance of material that comes from the average family kitchen, including eggshells, fruit and vegetable parings, stale bread, sour milk and cheese—and much more. You'll quickly notice that some materials (grass clippings and foodstuffs) are much more prone to rapid decomposition than others. Sawdust and wood chips, for example, will take years to fully decompose; for that reason you may wish to exclude them from the pile. Leaves, on the other hand, while tough and fibrous, can be first shredded and then added to the pile—a process which immeasurably hastens the rotting. If a good portion of the materials available to you fall into this fibrous category, their decaying process can be speeded with the use of highly nitrogenous material such as blood meal (available at garden stores) or pulverized dog kibble, available everywhere. Specialized compost activators are advertised all the time for just this purpose. In any case, the ideal pile contains a proper balance of materials.

LAYERING THE PILE. The success of a compost pile depends in part not only on the quality of the materials, but their proximity to one another. There are many layering theories, and one that works well for me starts with a deeply worked floor of soil into which have been plunged 2 six-foot-long sections of plastic pipe to supply air. Now add:

```
6   inches of green matter (grass, shredded leaves, weeds);
2   inches of either fresh stable manure or kitchen scraps;
1   inch of soil to cover;
    a sprinkling of garden lime and rock phosphate;
    a sprinkling of water.
```

Repeat these layers until the pile is 4 feet high.

THE HEAT IS ON. Within a day, the pile will start to heat up. In several days it will start to cook, reaching and stabilizing at about 160°F. At this temperature, the pile of materials begins its transformation to that wonderful black crumbly stuff we gardeners prize so highly.

TURNING THE PILE. After four weeks or so, the pile will have cooled down considerably. Even with the proper amounts of moisture and air, there will be a significant amount of material on the fringes of the pile not yet reached by the heat of decomposition. To get these materials into the heart of the pile where the heat is most intense, the pile must be turned over with a spading fork or a pitchfork and allowed to heat up again. In six weeks, the process will be complete.

TRENCH AND SHEET COMPOSTING. Two somewhat less formal methods are sheet and trench composting. Sheet composting involves spreading fresh organic matter like a sheet over an area and tilling or spading it in immediately. In trench composting, you simply open a furrow or trench with a hoe or spade, pour in the organic matter, and cover with soil. In both cases, soil microbes and earthworms immediately begin their work of breaking down the material.

---

increasing production on a square-foot basis, and take pride in bringing in bountiful harvests of top quality produce.

Flowers, on the other hand, are placed around the property for their visual effect. Unless grown for cutting purposes or future sale, they are rarely arranged in formal rows. Instead, flowers provide a splash of yellow here, red over there beside the walk, a carpet of pinks and purples at the base of the apple tree. Flowers also appear regularly in the vegetable garden, both for aesthetic and practical reasons. A ring of dwarf French Marigolds around a double row of bush beans, for instance, is not only a delectable sight, but serves as a deterrent to the Mexican bean beetle.

Descriptions follow for preparing and direct-seeding various traditional seedbeds. Although the information can also be of use to flower growers, its application is primarily for the efficient planting of vegetables.

Single-row Planting

STEP 1. Once the garden has been thoroughly prepared, rake over the area you wish to plant. A smooth seedbed allows for uniform depth and coverage of seeds—particularly the very small seeds, such as carrots and lettuce—which in turn contributes to even germination.

STEP 2. Drive a stake at each end of the row and stretch a string between them.

STEP 3. The easiest way to make a uniform seed furrow or, "drill" as it is sometimes called, is to lay your rake or hoe directly beneath the string, teeth or blade up, and, with your foot, gently press the length of the handle into the soil. You can also make a drill with the corner of a hoe, but it is almost impossible to achieve uniformity.

STEP 4. Place the seeds in the furrow you've made, and then firm them gently onto the surface with your fingers so each seed makes direct contact with the soil. If you're planting flower seeds which require light for proper germination, this is as far as you go. For vegetable seeds and flower seeds that need darkness, continue to the next step.

STEP 5. Cover the furrow lightly with soil, and gently firm again, either with your hands or with a rake or hoe.

STEP 6. Water gently but thoroughly.

Multiple-row Planting

As we discussed earlier, there is no reason why certain crops have to be planted in rows further apart than the distance recommended for the plants themselves. Three rows of lettuce, for example, will do just as well planted six inches apart as they would planted two feet apart, and a good deal of space will have been saved in the bargain. (You'll still have to leave walkway space between the three-row bands.) The planting techniques for multiple rows is exactly the same as for single rows.

Wide-row and Block Planting

Sowing in broad bands or "wide rows" rather than single-file rows is nothing especially new, although some modern gardeners like to claim it as their own invention. Wide rows are a logical extension of the multiple row, and make extremely efficient use of garden space. The difference between wide-row planting and block planting is based upon spacing within the row, not in the planting space itself. For example, some vegetables, such as leaf lettuce, spinach, peas, chard and chives, do extremely well when crowded in together. These crops are therefore broadcast-seeded in wide rows. Other vegetables which do nicely together in compact areas but prefer a certain minimum distance from each other, such as head lettuce, peppers, root crops, onions and some cabbage-family crops, are block-planted, traditionally in a diamond pattern. In both cases the bed is prepared the same way. A wide row is also excellent for raising a concentrated mass of cutting flowers.

The technique for preparing a wide row is not radically different from preparing any other seedbed. First you must decide how wide it will actually be. Mine are anywhere from eighteen inches to three feet, but I have even tried wide rows up to five feet across—more like beds.

STEP 1. After deciding on a width, stake its outer dimensions and stretch a line all the way around the four stakes.

STEP 2. Standing outside the strings, rake over the area until the seedbed is as smooth as you can make it.

STEP 3. From a height of 2 feet, sprinkle the seeds onto the surface as evenly as possible. If you're working with small seeds, start lower down—about 6 to 12 inches; and if it's windy, even lower yet. For onion and garlic sets, you'll have to push each one into the soil to its full depth.

STEP 4. Firm the seeds in place with your hand or the back of a hoe.

USING THE DIAMOND PATTERN FOR BLOCK PLANTING

The diamond pattern makes for efficient block planting. First, an appropriate spacing is determined between plants, such as 10 inches from the center of one planting hole to another for loose-head lettuce, in a bed to be 30 inches wide. Notice how the 3-4-3 pattern creates diamond shapes all across the bed. Center distances can be as little as 2 inches for carrots, or as much as 18 inches for broccoli. See individual listings for appropriate spacing.

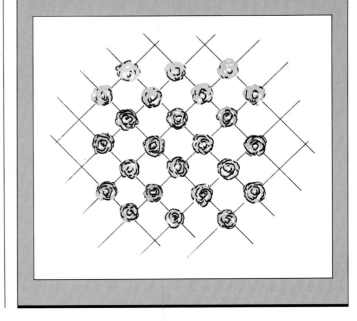

STEP 5. Cover the seeds with soil and firm them again, using the back of a rake or hoe, unless planting small seed, where it is best to sprinkle the soil cover by hand. If your soil is on the heavy side, cover the seeds with a sprinkling of compost or planting mix to prevent crusting over. For large seeds like peas and beans, you can rake up covering soil from the sides of your broad row, and then firm.

STEP 6. Water gently but thoroughly.

Raised Beds

I've been working on the same garden plot for thirteen years. And though I've tilled under many thousands of pounds of organic matter in the form of manure, compost, leaves, grass clippings and the like, my garden soil remains fundamentally clay; which is to say, it could have better drainage. Raised beds are a common solution, because when soil is mounded as it is for raised beds, it tends to compact less, allowing easier passage of water and air.

As with everything else, not all raised beds are the same. Prepared correctly, the Biodynamic French Intensive bed, also known as the double-dug bed, will out-produce any other plot. But the preparation is lengthy and strenuous; it involves deep digging and moving large quantities of soil, and not many gardeners have the time or the backs for it.

As a compromise, you might want to try a simpler kind of raised bed:

STEP 1. Rake up a mound of freshly tilled earth about 8 inches high, 12 inches wide at the base, and as long as you'd like it to be. (Of course, you can also make it as wide as you'd like. I used a 12-inch width only for purposes of this explanation.)

STEP 2. With the back of the rake, square off the top of the bed as smoothly as you can, and create a bit of a lip all the way around. This will serve to hold water.

STEP 3. Plant seed as you would for wide rows or block plantings.

STEP 4. Water thoroughly.

TRANSPLANTING SEEDLINGS INTO THE GARDEN

Once seedlings have been thoroughly hardened off, they are ready to be transplanted into the garden. These are exciting moments, as bare rows and beds suddenly become alive with vigorous young plants. Your enthusiasm must be tempered with caution, however, for removing a pot-bound plant from its container, even a plant that has been thoroughly hardened off, exposes its roots to light and air and can deliver a shock of sorts. Your job is to reduce the potential for danger by making conditions for transplanting the best possible. Here are some guidelines for safe, effective transplanting:

STEP 1. If at all possible, do your transplanting on a cool, cloudy, windless day.

STEP 2. Prepare your planting holes or furrows in advance so they are ready to accept the transplants. Dig them about 8 inches deep and twice as wide as they need to be. Half-fill each hole with a couple of handfuls of compost or aged manure, and an equal amount of soil. Add water so the soil-compost mixture becomes a muddy slurry.

STEP 3. Water flats and containers thoroughly before removing plants. The wetter the potting soil the less chance plant roots will be exposed to the drying effects of the air; but don't make the soil so wet that it washes away and lays the roots bare.

STEP 4. Next, placing your hand across the top of the container (spreading your fingers as necessary to accommodate the seedling), turn the pot upside down, tap the bottom a time or two, and the whole root ball will drop into your palm. If you've planted several seedlings in the same pot, or perhaps if you've bought a pot of plants from the garden nursery with several seedlings in it, you'll see the roots are intertwined. Pry them apart gently and patiently; do *not* cut them with a knife.

STEP 5. As a rule of thumb, most transplants should be set about an inch or so deeper into their permanent places than they stood in their last containers. (Some plants— tomatoes, head-lettuce, onions, the cabbage family—require a bit of pruning beforehand. See individual listings for specifics.) Set the plants accordingly into their muddy holes and, holding them steady, fill in the holes with soil and firm the plants solidly into place. The plants will sink slightly, but that is normal.

STEP 6. Water thoroughly and continuously for two weeks, or until plants are established.

STEP 7. Protect seedlings against frost, wind or sun damage with hot caps, cloches (available at gardening shops), or other makeshift protective devices. Tender plants, such as tomatoes, peppers, eggplants and the vine family of crops, are especially vulnerable to wind and cold.

CARE OF THE GARDEN PLANTS

Thinning the Seedbeds

Thinning represents a gardening paradox: You wait patiently for a crop to germinate, and no sooner do the plants appear than you are obliged to ruthlessly uproot a good percentage of them. I have never overcome my ambivalence regarding this chore, however necessary I understand it to be.

The fact is, however, that most garden crops planted from seed need thinning—especially carrots, lettuce, spinach and radishes, which are easy to sow too thickly. Left unthinned, these crops can become a crowded mass of worthless, stunted, bug-infested plants. So kneel down beside the row with a pair of sharp scissors and carefully thin out your planting, following spacing directions, if any, as given in the listings, or until the outer leaves of one plant barely touch the next. Work slowly to avoid damaging the plants that will remain and do not pull out unwanted plants; cutting them at the base with the scissors is the better method.

You should probably thin more than once: first, almost immediately after seedlings appear, and a time or two again as the weeks pass. These later thinnings often produce tasty young edibles, as in the case of carrots, leaf lettuce, spinach, chard, collards, radish and beets.

Watering

Many gardeners seriously underestimate the water needs of their crops. Water is a critical life-source for plants; it brings needed moisture for plant tissue, and is also the medium in which nutrients are dissolved and made available to plant roots. A steady, moderate supply makes plants grow; shortages create stress, sudden stoppage of growth, and even death.

Knowing when and how much to water are partially functions of the kind of soil you have. Water drains quickly from porous, sandy soils, and tends to collect in compact clay soils. In the first instance, plants may wilt or even die from lack of water. In the second, plants can suffer in saturated overwatered soil for lack of air: Their roots can rot, their fruit bloat and even burst, and they will soon become the target of water-loving pests and water-borne diseases.

Of course, these are rare extremes, and such problem soils can be improved over time by repeatedly mixing in large amounts of compost or raw organic matter. Building raised beds, which can be done immediately, also helps relieve poor drainage.

So the first step in establishing an effective watering schedule is to become familiar with your own garden soil. Study it after a soaking rain. How long does it hold moisture in the top three or four inches? Do puddles form anywhere? For how long? It is precisely this sort of hands-on knowledge that begins the process of making you into an excellent gardener.

HOW TO WATER. There is really only one cardinal rule: roots grow where the water is, so always water deeply. Shallow waterings, even if frequently done, discourage plant roots from diving deeper into the soil where moisture lingers, and ultimately cause the formation of skimpy root systems and skimpy plants.

Generally speaking, if you water your garden with a plain hose, you will succeed only in generating the illusion that you have delivered adequate moisture; in fact what you've probably done is break the cardinal rule. To eventually get enough water to the root zones of your plants, you will have to actually stand in the garden for an hour or more. The best method for hose-type watering is to attach a water-wand or water-break device to the end of your hose, which allows for controlled watering of individual plants without uprooting them as they would be from a sudden blast from a hose nozzle.

Another option is to set a sprinkler or sprinklers in the garden, which will sooner or later provide enough water without demanding your constant attention. Many types are available, such as those with timers and in-line fertilizer attachments. They do a good job (despite the water lost through evaporation before it ever hits the ground), but need to be moved around to provide complete coverage.

For the garden's sake, the best watering device is the drip irrigation hose, not yet in wide use but available in catalogues and stores at reasonable cost. One design features a hose of porous material through which the water leaches out ever so slowly; another popular type has holes every couple of feet which let water trickle out. Both do an excellent job of bringing water to the root zones of your plants. For small gardens the process simply involves attaching the hose to a water source and laying it up and down the length of your walkways. For larger gardens, you will have to move it once or more, and may attach it to lengths of less-expensive hose to reach distant rows. Measure your walkways to determine how many feet of hose you'll need. Generally, a single source will comfortably push water out of about 300 feet of hose. If you have to cover more than that, consider installing a y-valve at the spigot which turns it into two openings that can separately service two 300-foot lengths of drip hose.

Lacking a hose of any kind, a final and effective option is a watering can. It takes work, going and back and forth to your water supply, but the job of delivering a deep supply of moisture to the root zones can be effectively accomplished by just standing there and patiently and gently raining the water into the soil.

WHEN TO WATER. Never wait until your plants show the effects of deprivation before watering. If you do, you may have waited too long. Monitor soil conditions carefully during hot weather by grabbing a handful of soil from the garden and squeezing it in your fist. If it binds together, there is enough moisture for your plants, if it falls apart, start watering.

The cool hours of the morning are ideal for watering, as less evaporation is likely to occur. Avoid watering in the evening as the cool, moist conditions tend to encourage the spread of disease organisms.

Weeding and Mulching

You must learn to live with weeds when you become a gardener. It doesn't mean you let them run wild; that, in fact, you must not do, for weeds will vie with your flowers and vegetables for limited nutrients and moisture in the soil. And you should not let them come to seed for obvious reasons. At the same time, you mustn't let them drive you crazy, for they are a fact of life.

By and large weeds are easy to control. You can hand-pull them, or use any number of mechanical cultivators from hoes to garden tillers to get at them. But almost invariably they will reappear. The chore of weeding, therefore, must be a daily one, or weeds will pile up on you faster than you might imagine. Soon your garden becomes unsightly, and eventually unproductive if the weeds actually gain an upper hand on the flowers and vegetables.

I take considerable pleasure in weeding my garden. It gets me down close to the soil where a great deal goes on, and from which much can be learned. Weeding is also that wonderful sort of mindless work that allows the spirit to wander where it will in quest of answers larger than whether or not the weeding gets finished; although, ironically, before you know it, it does. And the garden looks lovely.

Blanketing the exposed soil with some sort of material that prevents weeds from emerging is called mulching. Mulching materials include: grass clippings, seedless hay or straw, wood chips, corn cobs, cocoa hulls, leaf mold, newspapers, pine needles, black plastic, aluminum foil and even roofing shingles. I find plastic and the like to be visually unpleasing, and so, with certain exceptions, I avoid those materials in spite of their touted effectiveness, keeping instead to the natural products—generally grass clippings and straw—in my garden. There's nothing wrong with cocoa hulls; they're beautiful and they decompose readily, but they're expensive.

Some gardeners mulch over every bit of visible soil—walkways and planting beds alike—right up to the stems of their plants. I prefer to mulch just my garden paths, for I love to see the colors of my plants against the dark brown of the garden soil.

Beyond smothering weeds (some will always grow through even the thickest layer anyway), mulching keeps the soil cool and conserves moisture by preventing large-scale evaporation. And at the end of the season, the mulch will have decomposed somewhat, adding precious organic matter to the soil.

For a successful mulch, you should apply a layer of organic materials about eight inches thick, if you have enough, or as near as you can get to that amount. Wait until late spring when the soil has warmed thoroughly, or the insulating qualities of your mulch will keep the soil too cool, a definite disadvantage for heat-loving plants like tomatoes, eggplants and vine crops. In fact, I will place a black inorganic mulch like plastic around these heat-lovers; the black of the plastic sheeting absorbs heat and transfers it to the soil beneath, while at the same time keeping moisture in and weeds down. Before long the plants grow large, and the plastic becomes dusty, and only I can tell the ugly stuff is really there.

PEST AND DISEASE CONTROL

While you are watching your garden grow in anticipation, others with less patience are also watching. We've already discussed fencing to keep out animal pests. Birds are a different challenge. A mixed blessing, they eat zillions of flying insects, but they will also eat your berries and gobble your corn seed. A solution is to spread cheesecloth over your strawberries or blueberries as they ripen, and treat your corn seed with a non-toxic repellent. Old standby anti-bird tactics such as pie tins dangling from string, bottles sunk in the

GROWING GREEN MANURE

An excellent way to provide large amounts of organic matter for your soil is to grow it exclusively for that purpose. You can sow specialized cover crops such as rye, buckwheat, oats, and alfalfa in the planting beds when other crop residues have been cleared. Called green manure when used this way, the crops attain a certain amount of growth and are then turned under into the soil, which they leave richer in nitrogen as a result. Annual rye is a good choice for home gardeners, as it germinates within a week, provides a thick winter cover against erosion, and can be turned into the soil first thing in spring.

Green manure crops also improve the general condition of the soil, and thereby its ability to hold moisture and nutrients. A further benefit of their thick, lush growth is that it tends to smother both annual and perennial weeds.

GARDEN WEEDS

Garden weeds fall into five basic categories:

Lamb's quarters

ANNUAL BROADLEAF WEEDS. Pigweed, Ragweed, Mustard and Lamb's Quarters. They produce scads of seeds, if you let them, so be on guard. Still, they are fairly easy to control.

Dandelion

PERENNIAL BROADLEAF WEEDS. Dandelions, Chicory, Plantain, Thistle, Dock and Sorrel. These weeds have deep tap roots, any piece of which will start another weed plant. So when you pull a root, pull it all.

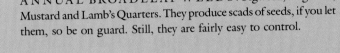

Chickweed

CREEPING WEEDS. Chickweed, Knotweed and Clover. These are tough to deal with because it's hard to pull them by hand. What you don't get by the root will come back again.

ANNUAL GRASSES. Crabgrass, Goosegrass, and a variety of others that come from seedy hay laid as mulch, or windborne from nearby fields. They produce lots of seeds and, once established, are hard to get rid of.

Crabgrass

PERENNIAL GRASSES. Quack Grass, Bermuda Grass, Nut Grass and Bindweed. These are difficult to control because, unless entirely uprooted, they will return again and again.

Quack grass

ground that make weird whooing noises, battery-operated radios, scarecrows, and rubber snakes are all mainly a source of curiosity to the birds in my neck of the woods, but maybe they'll work to keep the birds away from your garden.

If rabbits are a bother, try this old-timer's remedy. Drive 12-inch stakes into the ground around your beans, peas, lettuce—wherever the rabbits seem to be doing the most harm. Next, tie heavy jute string from one stake to the next until the plots are enclosed. With a small barbecue brush, apply a thick coating of lard or congealed fat from cooking bacon or ham. According to practitioners of this trick, rabbits will turn away from the tenderest garden morsels rather than chancing contact with the grease.

It is not surprising that new gardeners examining the array of sprays and dusts on garden-store shelves, conclude that gardening would be impossible but for the grace of lethal chemicals. Not so, in my experience.

Of every ten living things on this planet visible to the naked eye, eight are insects. Without insects, pollination of many, many plants would never take place. Insects are so vital in the food chain, that, without them, life on earth would be incalculably altered.

Why, then, are we schooled to kill them whenever they show up in our gardens? We have been led to believe that garden bugs are intent upon destroying everything in sight and we have to get them first. What happens, anyway, if insects actually get to a plant or two? They may make a few holes, or suck some plant juice, or even kill a plant. It's not the end of the world, because just as the weakest caribou draws the wolves, leaving the herd somewhat stronger in the end for its loss, so, too, does the weakest plant in a row attract disease and pests, allowing the healthy plants to continue their growth unchecked.

I'm not advocating that we allow insects to have their way with our hard-earned plants. The ones which actually damage crops should be eliminated, and there are many control techniques for this which are safe, effective, and cost little. On the other hand, chemical insecticides are toxic, expensive, and their hazards well-documented. If you give a little serious attention to your soil's condition and garden hygiene, you will never experience infestations you cannot handle immediately and effectively.

Soil and Planting Management

What makes for a healthy garden is not an arsenal of herbicides and insecticides, but healthy soil, made so by the generous addition of organic matter. When it comes to pest control, then, prevention is clearly the first line of defense: if you can keep the pests from coming around in the first place, you won't have to kill them. And if they do, when your plants are strong and healthy, they'll resist attack better. So your first step must be to establish an ongoing soil-building program as the foundation for healthy plants.

CROP ROTATION. Other defenses are based on information and experience. For example, many insect pests and disease organisms are crop-specific; that is, they like only certain plants (e.g., cabbage worm, Colorado potato bug, bean rust and so forth). They'll search out and find their target, and then take shelter—even over winter, expecting that the preferred food source will be in the very same spot next year. But clever gardeners move their crops, from one year to the next, creating what Louise Riotte called a "floating crop game." This practice is called crop rotation; and, since it's hard to remember where you put the carrots last year, save your garden charts from year to year for reference and successful planning.

GARDEN HYGIENE. Removing all garden debris that could provide pests and disease organisms with a place to spend the winter will go a long way toward foiling marauders. Throw everything—except weed seeds—into the compost pile where it will eventually do some good. Another garden hygiene measure involves keeping weeds and tall grass surrounding the garden cut short; in this manner you will eliminate breeding and hiding places for insects and other animal pests.

CROP LOCATION. As described in "Companion Planting" on page 10 and "Drawing Up Your Plan," page 10, putting your plant near others which repel the insects it attracts is one ploy, and planting the same crops in more than one spot, as insurance, is another. Pests may attack only one stand and spare the other.

Creating a varied environment in the garden can also help reduce pest damage. Don't put all the corn, or all the cabbage, or tomatoes, or whatever in just one location. Mix your crops: a few cabbage plants here, near the beans, and then a few way over next to the onions. So if pests hit these plants, perhaps those near the onions will be spared.

DISEASE-RESISTANT VARIETIES. As described earlier, plant breeders have actually succeeded in developing varieties of flowers and vegetables impervious to disease or insect attack. So another important step is to plant resistant varieties whenever possible. The catalogues indicate which are their resistant offerings.

SEEDING OUT OF PHASE. Planting crops a little earlier or even a bit later than you normally would is a trick that gets your plants up and growing, but out of phase with the normal breeding cycle of certain harmful insects. When the insects hatch out, their host plants are either not yet out of

INSECT PESTS AND CONTROL MEASURES

This chart covers the most active insect pests in vegetable gardens. Generally, flowers are not as vulnerable to serious infestation as vegetables, but many of these insects do attack flower plants from time to time.

See flower listings for specific insect pests and diseases, and use both this and the disease chart that follows for help with all plants.

INSECT	PLANTS AFFECTED	SYMPTOMS	CONTROL MEASURES
Aphids	Artichokes, peas, cucumber, lettuce, melons, squash	Spindly, pale top leaves and stems. Leaves curl and yellow. Yields reduced.	Gently rub them off leaves, or spray with a hose. Trap using yellow pans filled with soapy water. Aluminum reflectors beneath plants inhibit them from landing. Ladybugs, lacewing flies and parasitic wasps prey on aphids.
Bean weevil	Pole bean, lima bean	Eggs laid in holes chewed by adults along pod seams. Larva emerge when beans are in storage.	Dusting with lime or spraying with lime water (see recipe on page 49) will help keep bugs at bay. Affected plants may be cured by hanging on stakes for six weeks.
Cabbage looper	Crucifers, okra	Cabbage-family leaves eaten, usually from the edges. But holes can appear in leaf center as well. Looper droppings look like poppy seeds, which you can easily see on the soil.	Try *bacillae thuringiensis* (BT), sold as Dipel or Thurecide, which works well on all caterpillar pests. Handpicking is also effective.
Cabbage worm	Crucifers	Like the looper, the cabbage worm (*aka* imported)—the young of the ubiquitous white cabbage butterfly—feeds voraciously on leaves of cabbage-family crops and leaves its black pin-headed droppings nearby as evidence.	Cover plants with netting to keep butterfly from laying eggs. Pick off egg clusters. Handpick worms. Sprinkle wet plants with lime, salt, wood ashes, or rye flour. Use BT spray or dust.
Carrot root fly	Carrot	The carrot root fly's larvae tunnel into the carrot roots, leaving a rust-colored trail of excrement. Plants may be stunted, and roots either unsightly or laid open to rot.	Rotate crops; skip early planting; plant used tea leaves along with seed to discourage maggots. Plant onions and leeks nearby for deterrent value.
Carrot worm	Carrot, parsley, salsify, parsnips, dill, celeriac, celery	Eats carrot, parsley and celery foliage	Handpicking in the early morning is effective, as is BT dust or spray.
Colorado potato beetle	Potato	Pinkish humpbacked larvae with black spots chew ravenously on foliage, eventually stripping leaves if left unchecked.	Handpick egg clusters from undersides of leaves; also handpick larvae.
Corn earworm	Sweet corn, popcorn, tomatoes	Eat their way into corn ears from the tip.	Spray BT. With eyedropper apply several drops of mineral oil to silks as soon as they start to turn brown. This is also a good time to trim the silks, as moths prefer to lay eggs in only long silk.
Cutworm	Eggplant, crucifers, lettuce, tomato	Cut young plants off at soil level, generally right after germination or transplanting.	Apply 2-inch newspaper collar around transplant stems. Small bean plants can be protected by bottomless paper cups placed into the soil. Handpicking is effective; pull soil back from plant stems to uncover. Check higher up on plants for certain varieties.

INSECT	PLANTS AFFECTED	SYMPTOMS	CONTROL MEASURES
Flea beetle	Horseradish, tomato, potato, eggplant	Riddle foliage with tiny holes, virtually skeletonizing them. Young plants especially vulnerable.	Cultivation destroys eggs in soil. Dust with lime or wood ashes, and keep garden free of weeds. Spray with home brews of garlic/pepper/water.
Leafhopper	Crucifers, lettuce, spinach, celery	Many varieties, but all are sucking insects that hop away when suddenly disturbed. They spread yellows virus to plants, resulting in curled crinkled leaves. See chart, page 47.	Keep garden free of debris; plant resistant varieties. Destroy affected plants.
Leaf miner	Spinach, Swiss chard	Leaves are tunneled and blistered, with blotchy appearance. Plant growth may be stunted.	Cover planting with cheesecloth to deter fly from laying eggs. Scrape off egg cases. Scissor off affected leaf parts, and destroy. Cultivation kills pupae. Crop rotation is effective. Keep lamb's quarters at some distance as it attracts leaf miners.
Mexican bean beetle	Beans	Fuzzy yellow larvae eat and ultimately skeletonize leaves from below. Pods and stems may also be damaged.	Plant resistant varieties. Plant a bit earlier than normal. Intercrop potatoes with beans. Handpick egg clusters. Introduce praying mantis (to feed on this pest).
Onion maggot	Onion, garlic, leek	Feeds in lower portion of onion bulb or stem. Plants may die from destruction of underground parts. Stored onions soon show signs of decay. White varieties most vulnerable.	Dust around plants with lime, wood ashes. Spray with garlic/onion home brew.
Red spider mite	Peas	Mealy cobwebs on undersides of leaves. Mites suck juices until leaves drop.	Hose mites off with strong spray twice daily for a week after they appear, this disrupts rapid breeding cycle. Remove webs by hand. Introduce ladybugs and lacewing flies. Marigolds attract mites, so grow them away from peas.
Squash bug	Squash, melons, cucumber, pumpkin	Several varieties, all of which suck plant juices; runners wilt, dry up and die.	Handpick eggs and insects. Can also be trapped beneath boards. Dust around plants with wood ashes mixed with lime. Keep garden free of crop debris to prevent insects from overwintering.
Squash vine borer	Squash, melons, cucumber, pumpkin	Larvae hatch out on stems, and burrow in. Stems wilt and die. Look for small entry holes.	At entry point, slice into section where wilt has begun and remove borer, then bind stem with twist-tie. Garlic/onion spray repels moth from laying eggs. Remove spent vines after harvest to prevent borers overwintering.
Striped cucumber beetle	Squash, melons, cucumber, pumpkin	Young foliage eaten from beneath. Larvae burrow down in roots, and may destroy entire root system. Also spread bacterial wilt and cucumber mosaic disease (see Diseases chart for symptoms).	Plant later than normal. Cover young plants with screen or netting to keep beetles from landing. Introduce braconid wasps and tachnid flies for predatory control. Sprinkle leaves with wood ashes, or spray with lime water. (See page 49).

INSECT	PLANTS AFFECTED	SYMPTOMS	CONTROL MEASURES
Thrips	Onion	White blotches on onion tails; tips of leaves wither and turn brown.	Plant resistant varieties. Spray undersides of leaves with hard stream of water. Shake plant over piece of white paper and the culprits will fall out. Catch and destroy.
Tomato fruitworm	Tomato, sweet corn	Larvae first feed on foliage, then bore holes in fruit.	See corn earworm.
Tomato hornworm	Tomato	Large green well-camouflaged caterpillars feed greedily on nightshade foliage. Check beneath plants for droppings.	Handpick fat caterpillars off curled leaves. If they have whitish humped sections, leave them alone: the humps are parasitic wasp pupae. Introduce braconid and trichogamma wasps for predatory control. Also use BT spray.

PLANT DISEASES AND CONTROL MEASURES

DISEASE	CROPS AFFECTED	SYMPTOMS	CONTROL MEASURES
Anthracnose	Beans, cucurbits (vine crops), nightshades	Circular reddish brown or black sunken spots on leaves, stems, pods.	Practice 2-year rotation. Don't work in garden when it's wet. Don't plant peppers near beans. Pull up and burn affected plants.
Black leg	Crucifers	Lower stem blackens all the way around. Young plants yellow, wilt and die.	Rotate crops. Remove garden debris. Before planting, treat seed with hot water (122°F) for 20 minutes. Use resistant varieties.
Black rot	Crucifers	Blackened veins. Stems show a blackened ring when sliced across. Leaves yellow and drop. Bacteria live in soil and seed.	Same as for black leg.
Blight, early and late	Tomatoes, potatoes	Small, irregular dark brown spots, sometimes with target markings. Tomatoes may sunscald and show leathery spots near stem. Infected potatoes may rot in storage.	Use certified seed potato and resistant varieties. Rotate crops, and remove residues after harvest. Spray plants with late blight with Burgundy mixture.
Blossom end rot	Tomatoes, peppers	Dark sunken spots on blossom end of fruits.	Keep water supply constant, especially during dry weather. Additional liming may also help. Cut away affected fruit parts; the remainder is perfectly edible.
Club root	Crucifers	Plant roots become enlarged or "clubbed," and crack or rot. Affected plants may wilt during day but recover at night. Young plants generally die; reduced yields on established plants.	Practice 4-year crop rotation if you've had trouble in the past. Add lime to soil to discourage acid-loving organisms.

DISEASE	CROPS AFFECTED	SYMPTOMS	CONTROL MEASURES
Damping off	Beans, peas, lettuce, tomatoes	Seedlings don't emerge, or, if they do, often wilt and topple over. Stems show constriction just below soil line.	Use sterile soil mixes for starting seeds indoors. Avoid crowding and overwatering plants. Maintain good air circulation in seedbed.
Leaf spot	Beets, Swiss chard	Leaves become dotted with small, tannish spots with purplish borders. Leaves may drop later in season.	Same as for anthracnose.
Mildew, downy	Cucumbers, melons, some greens	Yellowish or brownish spots on older leaves. Leaves dry, curl and die. Fruits are unaffected. Disease is spread by windborne spores.	Thin plants to improve air circulation and high humidity build-up. Remove diseased foliage and burn. Spray home brew mixture of 2 ounces horsetail herb (available in natural food stores) in 1 gallon water. Repeat often. Old practice of sulfur spray may injure cucumbers and melons. Remove all crop residues. Plant resistant varieties.
Mildew, powdery	Cucurbits, beans, strawberries	Powdery white growth on stems, top and bottom leaf surfaces, and occasionally on fruit. Leaves often turn yellow or brown and overall fruiting is reduced.	Same as for downy mildew.
Mosaic	Beans, tomatoes, cucurbits, peppers, celery	Leaves are mottled and curled, become yellow and die. Cucumbers become misshapen and warty. Bean and tomato plants become stunted.	Grow resistant varieties. Control disease-carrying aphids (see aphids, page 43). Keep tall weeds or grass down around garden. Smokers should neither smoke nor handle tomato or pepper plants because they can transmit a mosaic disease (deadly to the nightshade family). Remove and burn affected plants immediately as they cannot be saved.
Pink root	Onions, shallots	Roots turn pink, shrivel and die. Newly formed roots also become infected, reducing overall bulb size.	Plant resistant varieties.
Rust	Asparagus, beans	Small reddish or dark brown powdery blisters on all plant parts. Plants generally do not survive.	Plant resistant varieties. Remove and burn affected plant parts, and disinfect the clippers before using on other plants.
Scab	Potatoes	Rough, corky, pitted and raised spots on potato tubers. Fungus is soil-borne and resides in seed potatoes.	Don't plant potatoes where scab has been a problem. Don't lime, spread wood ashes or fresh manure in potato patch. Keep pH between 5.5 and 6.0. Plant resistant varieties.
Smut	Sweet corn	White galls and outgrowths on stalks, ears and tassels. Galls dry, burst open and release powdery black spores.	Pick off and burn [young] galls; *never* put them in the compost. Don't plant corn where smut has been a problem within previous three years.

DISEASE	CROPS AFFECTED	SYMPTOMS	CONTROL MEASURES
Wilt, bacterial	Cucurbits	Runners wilt, and eventually much of the plant shrivels. Disease organisms live in intestinal tract of overwintering striped cucumber beetles. Young plants are most susceptible.	Control of striped cucumber beetles is vital (see page 44). Protect emerging plants with hotcaps (available in garden stores) or other devices to keep beetles from landing, but beware of overheating plants.
Wilt, fusarium and verticillium	Tomato, eggplant, watermelon, cantaloupe, peas,	Gradual yellowing and wilting of foliage, beginning with lower leaves. Stems turn brown and then die. Tomatoes on stricken plants will be sunburned as foliage drops.	Plant resistant varieties. Practice 3-year rotation, and do not save seed from affected plants.
Yellows	Cabbage, lettuce, spinach, celery	Foliage turns yellow, and plants become stunted, rarely forming heads. Disease is spread by leafhoppers.	Control leafhoppers (see page 44).

the ground or sufficiently established to resist a few nibbles here and there.

Handpicking Insects

I attend to most of the insect control in my garden by wandering through it with a coffee can half-filled with hot water. If I see a bug, larva, or egg case on a leaf or stem—or wherever it tries to hide itself—I snatch it off and toss it into the can. I then feed the collected bugs to my chickens. Many gardeners who have no further use for the bugs drown them in kerosene instead. If you're squeamish about handpicking, just use gloves.

I've learned more or less which insects to look for on which plants, but strangers still show up from time to time. I look them up on a chart—which is what I suggest you do too, (charts are provided on pages 43–45). Just make sure you don't drown any ladybugs; one of these pretty beetles is capable of gorging on thousands of plant-destroying aphids every day.

Trapping Insects

Another method for handling certain insects is to lure them into traps. If you have slugs in your lettuce, for instance, lay boards alongside the rows on a warm day; and then, in late afternoon, lift them and dispose of any slugs that have gathered to escape the heat. A small dish of beer, thin strands of yeasty dough, and large cabbage leaves strewn here and there are also said to attract slugs. Commercial traps which lure insects with sex hormones are reported to be very effective against Japanese beetles. For flying insects, electrical zappers are available at almost every garden store but they can be too effective, killing every insect that flies into their grids—including many which are beneficial to your garden.

Biological Control of Insects

Lacewing flies, broconid wasps, trichogamma wasps and more, are capable of devouring hundreds of insect pests every day. You can actually buy them, usually by the pint. A pint container, for example, will hold 8,000 to 10,000 ladybugs, enough for 2,000 square feet of garden.

You can also buy powdered disease organisms known as *bacillae thuringiensis (BT)*, which kill certain harmful insects when sprayed or dusted on affected plants. These organisms are sold under the product names Dipel and Thurecide.

Brews and Concoctions

Based on the accepted notion that most insects will avoid strong odors, gardeners have developed and handed down dozens of recipes for foul-smelling repellant sprays which they swear are effective. Most consist of varying proportions of garlic, onion, hot pepper, and water. Some even have a little soap in the mixture. The ingredients are always blended together, carefully strained, poured into a sprayer and applied to affected plants or as a preventive measure to susceptible plants. If you use one, reapply often, especially after a rain.

CALENDAR OF GARDEN ACTIVITIES BY SEASON

These short lists for each season are reminders of tasks to be accomplished over the year even when the garden itself may lie dormant. Note that some of them can be done in late winter in warmer climates but must wait for early spring farther north.

WINTER ❦ *December 21-March 20*

Send away for seed catalogues
Plan vegetable, herb, flower gardens
Order seeds and other growing stock (root crowns for asparagus, sets for onions and the like)
Set up indoor planting station
Assemble supplies for indoor planting (containers, markers, soil mixes, plastic bags and the like)
Early winter: sow seeds for earliest plants indoors
Late winter: start later plants and, as soon as nature permits, sow hardy seeds outdoors

SPRING ❦ *March 21-June 20*

Remove winter mulches from garden
Test soil if not already done in fall
Add nutrients, additives, compost as needed and till when soil is dry enough
Early spring: direct-sow beets, carrots, onion sets, peas, radishes
    set out hardy seedlings you started indoors in the vegetable garden (broccoli, cabbage, chives, onions); and flower garden (Begonias, Foxglove)
Late spring: direct-sow all other seeds
Begin new compost pile

SUMMER ❦ *June 21 - September 20*

Throughout: care of garden, watering, weeding, thinning
Stake tall flowers and tomatoes
Sidedress and topdress crops as needed
Deadhead all flowers
Sow succession plantings
Maintain compost pile
Prune where necessary
Sow annual ryegrass in bare patches as crops are harvested and flowers die off

FALL ❦ *September 21 - December 20*

Protect remaining crops from early and late frosts as much as possible
Test soil if this is your first garden
Mulch perennials
Clean up garden and turn under residues and annual rye
Sharpen and oil garden tools and store in dry protected spot

Lime water is a favorite of mine for combatting the ubiquitous flea beetle and striped cucumber beetle: add a cup of garden lime to a quart of water, let it settle, put it into a sprayer, and shoot it onto the leaves of nightshades and cucurbits (vine crops). It leaves a powdery white finish when dry. Apply often, and always after it rains.

Some years ago, there was much written about a spray made by grinding up the bodies of offending insects with a little water and letting them steep into an essence. This frothy liquid was then diluted and sprayed on susceptible plants, whereupon it presumably sent would-be marauders running for their lives. I'm not sure how effective the concoction was, and I haven't heard much about it recently, but the idea reminds me of scaring birds away by hanging a dead crow at the entrance to your corn patch. From my experience, sometimes this works, sometimes it doesn't.

There are, however, two extremely effective sprays for killing disease organisms, especially early and late blight: *Bordeaux Mixture,* for susceptible plants, and *Burgundy Mixture,* for those already stricken. Although they are available at most garden stores, I will include here John Seymour's recipes from *The Self-Sufficient Gardener,* where I first learned of them in case you want to prepare them yourself.

BORDEAUX MIXTURE	BURGUNDY MIXTURE
8 ounces copper sulfate	8 ounces copper sulfate
6 gallons water	6 gallons water
5 ounces quicklime	5 ounces washing soda (Tide, Bold, etc.)

Mix copper sulfate and all but a few ounces of water until thoroughly dissolved. Mix quicklime (or washing soda) with a bit of water to make a "cream." Pour the cream through a sieve directly into the copper sulfate mixture. If a steel knife comes out of the mixture with copper coating, add a bit more cream. Spray affected plants regularly. *Burgundy Mixture* is the same formula but with washing soda instead of lime.

PART 2

The Plant Listings

HOW TO USE THE LISTINGS

❧ VEGETABLES ❧ HERBS ❧

FLOWERS

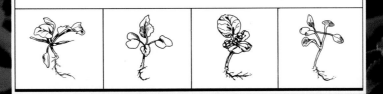

*Pink Zinnias elegantly line this
simple garden fence.*

❧ 5 ❧
HOW TO USE
THE LISTINGS

TOPICS USED IN
ALL LISTINGS

We've finally come to the good part: the descriptions of individual vegetables, herbs and flowers, along with instructions for growing each successfully. For each cultivar you'll find a photograph of the mature plant, a drawing of the plant as a newly emerged seedling, and a panel of information on how to grow it from the time you sow seed all the way through harvest. A brief discussion here of the topics covered in the panels will help you use them more effectively. Topics which apply only to flowers—color, size of bloom, and so on—are grouped at the end of the discussion.

At the head of each entry will be the common name of the plant, the name you're likely to know it by. In the flower listings, Latin names are also given (some catalogues list their offerings by Latin name) as are alternate common names.

DEGREE OF DIFFICULTY. A variety of phrases such as "quite simple," "moderately easy," "very temperamental," will indicate the level of difficulty you're likely to experience in bringing in the crop (or blooms) successfully. A designation of "extremely difficult" or similar expression should only be taken as a challenge: don't be scared off by anything you read here.

TEMPERATURE (FROST) TOLERANCE. Here you will learn whether a plant is vulnerable to frost damage: "hardy" can tolerate frost; "semi-hardy" can take a light kiss of frost; "tender" will be killed by even the lightest frost. Frost tolerance also refers to the ability of a perennial to winter over successfully. The zone map on page 138 indicates where plants will survive the winter. A plant's ability to survive intense heat will also be discussed here.

WHEN TO SOW INDOORS. This is given in number of weeks before last expected frost. Use the zone map on page 138 to determine the dates for your area.

DAYS TO GERMINATION. The approximate number of days, at about 70°F, it will take the seeds to sprout.

WHEN TO SOW OUTDOORS OR SET TRANSPLANTS. The directions will generally be keyed to soil temperature or last expected frost. You can expect to see such phrases as "when the soil is thoroughly warm," or "as soon as the soil can be worked in early spring."

DEPTH OF SEED. This is simply the planting depth for vegetable seeds. The rule of thumb is never to plant a seed deeper than 3 to 4 times its own diameter, but even that varies with time of season and condition of soil. This category does not appear in the flower listings because most flower seeds are quite small and must be only barely covered with soil. Quite a number require light for successful germination and no soil cover at all.

DISTANCE BETWEEN PLANTS. Just what it says. Distance between rows, however, is usually not given since rows are generally laid out for ease of cultivation—how much walking space you need, how far over you can lean to cultivate a row, would determine the widths of your rows and walkways. If you're uncomfortable about guessing, check your seed packet for recommended distances.

SOIL CONDITIONS. The degree of fertility, quality of tilth, and optimum pH range for vegetables under which the plant is likely to thrive. "Reasonably rich, well-drained soil with pH of 6.0–6.8" is what you're apt to find under this heading. Keep in mind that the information provided here relates to ideal conditions, and only rarely are such conditions available. If a flower or vegetable appeals to you, try it in spite of less-than-perfect conditions. If sunlight is adequate, chances are you'll do quite well, especially if you've nourished the soil.

SUNLIGHT REQUIREMENTS. The amount of daily sunshine required for a successful crop. Most vegetables and flowers do best in full sunshine, but will get along with 6 hours, provided the balance of the day is not spent in deep shade. When appropriate, shade requirements will also be discussed here—certain flowers demand a good deal of it.

WATERING. Most plants require a moderate supply of water—approximately one inch per week. This will appear for each plant unless otherwise specified.

SIDEDRESSING. Most vegetable crops require a boost of nutrients during the growing season—generally as they approach maturity. This supplemental feeding, usually laid down beside a plant, is called a sidedressing. The side-dressing recommended here will be either an organic fertilizer such as compost or manure, or a "tea" made by steeping either of those materials in water for several days. While synthetic fertilizers supply nutrients, they do little in the way of conditioning the soil. Flowers only occasionally require sidedressing, so it appears there under SPECIAL NOTES.

DAYS TO FIRST HARVEST. This is hard to pinpoint, so information is always given in a range. Some varieties of tomato, for instance, will produce ripe fruit only 60 days from transplanting, while others may take as long as 80 days. An entry slot of "60–80" should be read as: "Between 60 and 80 days, depending upon variety." The category has been omitted entirely for certain herbs where it is really a judgment call as to when a plant is mature enough to withstand a light harvest. Instead you'll see "harvest as soon as leaves can be handled," or "when plants are 6″ tall," or similar advice. Use your judgment, and harvest early only from vigorous plants.

HARVESTING TIPS. Once they begin, most flowers and vegetables will continue producing over a period of weeks. To keep certain vegetable plants productive (especially peas, beans, summer squashes, cucumbers, leaf crops), it is wise to harvest while the food is young. This is certainly the case with summer squash, zucchini, peas and beans. Frequent harvesting triggers blossom-set, which in turn, creates larger yields. In flower gardening, the practice of removing spent blooms is called dead-heading. Specific instructions for harvesting each crop will appear here.

VARIETIES. It is impossible to list all of the best or most popular varieties of garden vegetables and flowers. I have included several in the vegetable listings with which I have had success, but there are scores of others available through the many excellent seed houses listed on pages 229–236. The task of choosing specific flower varieties is even more difficult, because of individual ideas about color, texture and purpose. So only exceptional flower cultivars are mentioned in this slot.

PESTS AND DISEASES. The various insect pests and plant diseases that affect certain vegetable crops. The flower listings do not include this category because so few garden flowers are ever the focus of serious infestation. If a certain flower is susceptible, you will find mention of its attackers under SPECIAL NOTES.

SPECIAL NOTES. This is a catchall for information you should know about a given plant that doesn't fall into one of the other categories. Occasionally, you will also find directions here for fertilizing flowers.

THESE TOPICS ARE IN FLOWER LISTINGS ONLY

USES. Here you will learn what the flower is best suited for: beds, borders, cutting gardens, rock gardens, containers, indoor growing, ground cover and the like. If a flower is especially good for drying, that will also be noted here.

HEIGHT. As flower beds and borders are a tapestry of plants grown closely together, it is vital for gardeners to know the potential height of each variety. Plots can then be laid out with the tallest plants in the rear (in the case of borders) or the center (in the case of island beds) so that shorter plants will receive their full dose of sunlight. Plant heights are typically given in a range, such as 6″–10″ or 18″–24″, which takes into account several varieties of a given flower, and the probability that a variety will grow differently in any given garden.

COLORS. Most gardeners give color serious consideration when planning their flower beds, so a complete list of colors available for the cultivar is given here.

SIZE OF BLOOM. It is often difficult to tell from pictures of flowers exactly how large their blooms are. For gardeners unfamiliar with certain varieties, this entry provides a sense of scale or weight which is helpful for envisioning how a flower will appear beside its neighbors.

BLOOMING SEASON. This refers to the time period over which you can expect a flower to bloom. Designations are made by season rather than by month. A typical entry might read: "Flowers profusely from mid-spring until frost."

❦ 6 ❦
VEGETABLES

I t often comes as a surprise to beginning gardeners that the diverse population of plant life in the vegetable garden can be traced to a rather small group of botanical families. Discovering that down at the seed level the radish and cabbage are related cousins or that tomatoes and potatoes are from the same tribe lends insight into why such seemingly unrelated vegetables grow as they do, attract the same insects, and are prone to the same diseases.

Plants traditionally cultivated for food—what we usually mean by "vegetables"—are in the *Spermatophyta* division of the plant kingdom. Within this classification are the angiosperms, flowering plants that contain seeds enclosed in an ovary borne by a flower. The angiosperms are further divided into the monocotyledons (or monocots) and dicotyledons (dicots) we discussed in chapter 2, which include the families of those vegetables you will recognize instantly.

The basic difference between monocots and dicots is not so much that monocots have a single seed leaf and the dicots have two, but rather the way the two classes of plants actually grow. Monocots (which include the onion and corn families) grow upwards from the base of their leaves, while dicots, which represent 90 percent of the vegetable garden, grow outward from the edges of theirs.

Each family of plants, their members—along with page references for a complete picture of each—their common culture, and some of their common problems are discussed below. The monocots are first.

MONOCOTYLEDONS

Amaryllus Family (amaryllidaceae)

GENERAL CULTURE. The members of this family can all be grown from seed, though some—particularly onions, garlic and shallots—are frequently grown from "sets," small dormant bulbs grown the previous season. Leeks and chives are generally started indoors and set out early in the season. Chives, which are grown exclusively for their green tails, can also be propagated by division. (See Propagation, page 114.)

Onions, leeks, garlic and shallots are valued for the bulbs which form as the leaf bases thicken over the course of the growing season. To expand to their maximum, these plants require well-worked, loose and rich soil. Onions prefer to have their shoulders out of the ground as they grow, so plant sets or seedlings shallow, and brush surface soil away as the bulbs start to thicken.

When the tops turn brown and fall over, it's the end of the growing season for this family of vegetables. This is the time to dig up your onions, garlic and shallots, and cure them in cool, dry conditions (on a wood pallet in partial shade, or some such place) for about a week. Then bag them in mesh sacks, and store them where it's consistently dry and cool, but doesn't freeze. Under such conditions they should last until next spring.

Leeks continue to grow until late in the fall. Some gardeners mulch the soil heavily around leeks to prevent the soil from freezing, and extend their harvest for many weeks into the winter, or until deep snow makes foraging too difficult. In mild climates, mulching is not necessary, and the crop can remain stored in the ground indefinitely.

PESTS AND DISEASES. Thrips, root maggots; neck rot, pink root, mildew, bottom rot. See Chart, page 43–47, for control measures.

Grass Family (gramineae)

GENERAL CULTURE. The family gramineae is considerably larger than the above list would indicate; it also includes all the other cereal crops (oats, barley, rye, wheat, rice). They aren't listed here because they rarely appear in the vegetable patch.

Sweet corn (popcorn too, for that matter) is an annual grass that develops tender-skinned seeds (the kernels) at maturity. The so-called "ear" (see illustration) is the female portion of the plant; its protruding strings or silk receive dust-like pollen particles from the tassel or male portion atop the plant. Each pollinated silk strand represents two seeds, which accounts for the little-known fact that every ear of corn has an even number of kernels.

Because corn is wind-pollinated, growing it in blocks of short rows rather than in one or two long rows will improve the stand. Since cross-pollination of different types of corn (e.g. sweet corn, popcorn, yellow corn, white corn) can affect both taste and color, different types should be planted either three hundred yards, or several weeks, apart. Watch out for your neighbors' corn as well.

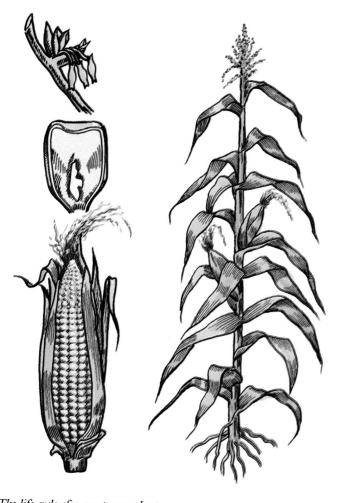

The life cycle of a sweet corn plant

PESTS AND DISEASES. Corn earworm, European corn borer, corn sap beetles, Southern corn rootworms, corn root aphid, corn flea beetles, wireworms, seed corn maggots; Stewart's bacterial wilt, root rot, corn smut, Southern corn leaf blight. See Chart, page 43–47, for control measures.

DICOTYLEDONS

Goosefoot Family (chenopodiaceae)

Beets, page 73
Chard, page 80
Spinach, page 102

GENERAL CULTURE. This family of plants is originally from the seashore. Like plants native to arid zones, they show a tendency to conserve fresh water, which they accomplish by growing thick meaty roots which can penetrate the soil to a depth of ten feet or more.

Also peculiar to this family is the way it bears seeds in clusters or "corms." Spinach seed comes in packets already separated into individual kernels, but beet and chard are generally available in their original state. This simply means that three or four plants will emerge from each corm, and should be thinned to stand 3 inches apart.

These plants do best in soil enriched by compost, aged manure, and other decomposed organic matter. Avoid using fresh manure in soil where beets are the desired crop, for they will fork and otherwise grow irregularly. On the other hand, my spinach has always done quite nicely in fresh manure.

PESTS AND DISEASES. Aphids, flea beetles; powdery mildew. See Chart, page 43–47, for control measures.

Pea Family (leguminosae)

Broad beans, page 73
Peanuts, page 94
Peas, page 94
Shell beans, page 72
Snap beans, page 71
Soybeans, page 102

GENERAL CULTURE. This extraordinary family of plants has its roots in far corners of the world: Asia, eastern

Europe, Africa, Central and South America. Its members share two principal traits in common: each develops seeds higher in protein than any other vegetable; and each is capable, with the aid of certain specialized bacteria, of converting or "fixing" nitrogen from the air to nodules on their roots—which, in practical terms, means they don't require much fertilizer to produce very well.

English peas, as the ones we know are called, come in standard (taller than 18-inch) varieties which require support, and dwarf varieties which usually do not. The edible-podded, snow peas, and fairly new sugar-snap varieties are quite tall and grow best on chicken wire frames.

Bush beans reach a height of 12 to 24 inches and stop growing because the top stems end in flower clusters. Pole beans, on the other hand, develop blossoms in their leaf axils (where leaf joins stem), which does nothing to check their upward growth—the ostensible horticultural basis for the Jack-and-the-beanstalk legend. Pole beans grow more slowly than bush beans, but generally produce more beans per plant. For a continuous supply of bush beans, succession plantings should be made every two weeks or so. There are both bush and pole varieties of snap beans, wax beans, Italian or flat-podded beans, limas and French Horticultural beans. Dry bean cultivars such as Navy, Pinto and Kidney beans are available only in bush varieties.

PESTS AND DISEASES. Aphids, pea and bean weevil, pea thrip, wireworm, cutworm, Mexican bean beetle; downy mildew, bean rust. See Chart, pages 43–47, for control measures.

Chicken-wire support for climbing peas

INOCULATING LEGUME SEEDS

Beans and peas can't take nitrogen from the air all by themselves. They need the cooperation of a special kind of bacteria called rhizobia. These rhizobia are almost always available in the soil, especially if legumes have been grown there before. But if you want to make sure, you can inoculate your pea and bean seed with special bacteria powder which is available through most seed catalogues and garden stores. Directions are included with the inoculant.

Mustard Family (cruciferae)

GENERAL CULTURE. I would be hard put to find a general culture that applies to every member of this huge and diverse family of garden crops, and so I advise you to consult each entry for specific information. A few common traits are shared by most of them, however: (1) they are all cool-weather crops; (2) all but radish and watercress are biennials, which means they have a two-year life cycle—they store food the first year and produce seeds the second; and (3) with the exception of Brussels sprouts, which take about ninety days, they tend to mature very quickly—enough to allow two plantings of cabbage, cauliflower and broccoli, and several plantings each of kale and collards.

PESTS AND DISEASES. Flea beetle, cabbage moth, cabbage worm, cutworm, cabbage root fly, root maggots; club root, black rot, black leg, yellows. See Chart, page 43–47, for control measures.

Gourd Family (cucurbitaceae)

GENERAL CULTURE. There are two myths about the gourd family: vine crops are difficult to grow successfully and they take up too much room.

All the squashes are in fact easy to raise. And while melons are a little finicky, with proper attention given to soil and moisture conditions, they're no more difficult to grow than a good winter squash. As to the issue of space, many of the standard varieties of winter squash and melons can sprawl and should indeed be planted only when space allows. But the seed industry has responded to this by developing a panoply of bush-type cucumbers, melons, squash, gourds and pumpkins that can grow in much less area than required by the old standbys.

All cucurbits need thoroughly warm, moist soil to germinate and plenty of warm weather to keep their growth unchecked. From the moment the first leaves appear, the vines will lengthen quickly. Plants send down one strong tap root, often descending 2 to 3 feet, and develop an extensive shallow root system within a foot of the surface. These shallow feeder roots supply the plants with most of their nutrients and moisture.

The first vine growth is upward to a height of about one

GLOSSARY OF TERMS RELATED TO GROWING CUCURBITACEAE

Drill: a single row of seeds.
Gynoecious: plants bearing only female flowers.
Hill: a group of seeds in a circular grouping.
Monoecious: plants bearing both male and female flowers.
Mound: a raised circle of soil in which a group of seeds is planted.
Netting: the criss-crossed pattern on the skin of muskmelons.
Ribbing: the contoured ribs of some muskmelon varieties.
Slip: the split in the melon stem that indicates ripeness.
Spines: the warts on the skin of some cucumbers whose sharp needles are said to deter certain pests.

POLLINATING YOUR OWN VINE CROPS

Three simple methods exist for performing pollination.
1. Using a cotton swab, collect the pollen from the male flower and transfer it to the center of the female blossom.
2. Pluck a male flower and press it gently into the center of the female.
3. Pluck male flowers and shake them gently over the females, preferably on a day with no wind.

foot, after which it leans over and begins to crawl. Before long, tendrils form on the vine to anchor them to whatever is handy—fences, trellises, other vegetables, even weeds. These tendrils are what make it possible for gardeners with limited space to grow cucumbers, squash and the smaller melons, by training them on fences and trellises.

The first blossoms appear in about three weeks, and are usually male flowers—the ones that produce pollen. About a week later, often less, the female blossoms appear. You can tell the females by the swelling of the flower stem—actually the beginnings of a fruit. Within 12 hours, bees and other insects accomplish pollination, failing only during prolonged bouts of cool damp weather. If such weather descends when your vine crops blossom, and you want to be sure of pollination, you can see to it yourself.

Harvest all cucumbers, summer squash and zucchini on your vines when they are young so the vines will continue to produce. Search well for them through the thick foliage, because once one or two become full-grown (oversize to us) and develop mature seeds, the plant will stop setting blossoms and fruit—having, as far as it is concerned, accomplished its mission.

Melons and winter squash should be harvested when fully ripe (melon stems split; squash skins become hard—see individual entries for more instructions), while gourds and pumpkins should remain on the vine until the plants are killed by frost.

Pollinating your own vine crops

PASSIVE SOLAR HEAT SPEEDS MELON RIPENING

Heat contributes to the ripening of melons. In the north, getting enough heat as the season winds down can be a problem. Prop your melons on stones, bricks or blocks wrapped in black plastic to draw the heat of the sun. Even on cool evenings, the heat released slowly from the stone or masonry below will keep the ripening process going unabated.

PESTS AND DISEASES. Striped or spotted cucumber beetle, cutworm, aphids, squash vine borer, squash bug; anthracnose, angular leaf spot, bacterial wilt, fusarium wilt, powdery mildew, downy mildew, mosaic, scab. See Chart, page 43–47, for control measures.

Nightshade Family (solanaceae)

Eggplant, page 85
Peppers, page 96
Potatoes, page 97
Tomatoes, page 106

Technically speaking, the tomato, eggplant and bell pepper are really berries, no matter how large they actually get to be. Several hundred years ago, both tomatoes and eggplant were called "apples"—tomato being the love apple (poma amoris). Strangely enough, given its name, the tomato was never considered an aphrodisiac. According to legend, the plant was named by Italian sailors who, upon seeing the exotic fruit for the first time in Morocco, gave it the name *pomo dei Mori,* or "Moor's Apple." When the *pomo dei mori* reached France from Italy, the French apparently misheard, and called it *pomme d'amour,* which means "love apple."

DROUGHT GARDENING

This trick may spell the difference between failure and success for gardeners in areas with limited rainfall when it comes to water-loving crops like eggplant and celery. Roll a few pounds of newspaper together into a roll, tie, and soak in water until the mass is completely waterlogged. Then bury the roll 24" in the soil, cover, and plant your water-lovers directly above it. Like a reservoir, the newspaper roll will release water to the plants' root zones as the surrounding soil dries out.

GENERAL CULTURE. The presence of the poisonous alkaloid solanin in their stems and leaves is what binds the nightshades together as a family. Tomatoes were cultivated largely for decorative use for many centuries because their fruit was thought to be poisonous. The same was thought of potatoes, in which the solanin is inert. It requires direct exposure to sunlight for several days to become activated, during which time the exposed portion of the potato turns green—which is why you must cut away all green-colored parts from a potato before eating it.

Potatoes aside, the other nightshades are tropical, heat-loving plants, and must be set out only in soil that is thoroughly warm. Eggplants demand extremely fertile conditions to perform well, but peppers can react to excessive fertilizer by producing an enormous crop of verdant leaves and hardly a pepper. Tomatoes also perform well under fertile soil conditions, but are not as demanding as eggplant.

PESTS AND DISEASES. Cutworms, flea beetle, aphid, blister beetle, Colorado potato beetle, hornworm, tomato fruitworm, stink bugs; early blight, late blight, leaf spot. See Chart, page 43–47, for control measures.

Composite Family (compositae)

Chicory, page 81
Corn salad, page 83
Dandelion, page 85
Endive, page 86
Jerusalem artichoke, page 88
Head lettuce, page 90
Leaf lettuce, page 90
Salsify, page 101

GENERAL CULTURE. These plants are named for their flowers, which, though they appear to be single blossoms, are really small clusters of blooms. There are two subgroups in the family: the salad group (lettuce, endive, chicory, salsify, dandelions) and the thistle group (Jerusalem artichokes)—names given them by John Seymour, author of *The Self-Sufficient Gardener.* The salads (to which I've taken the liberty of adding corn salad though it is actually in the Valerian family—the only member in the vegetable patch) are all cool-weather, tender-leaved and tender-stemmed annuals, started either from seed or indoor-grown seedlings set out as early as possible. Salsify and some strains of chicory are grown primarily for their roots. Jerusalem artichokes, a perennial, are grown for their flavorful tuberous roots. These plants can be grown directly from seed, from seedlings started indoors, or propagated from cuttings of existing plants in very early spring.

FROST MAPS

AVERAGE DATES
OF LAST
SPRING FROST

June 1-June 30

May 1-May 31

April 1-April 30

March 1-March 31

February 1-February 28

January 1-January 31

AVERAGE DATES
OF FIRST
FALL FROSTS

July 1-July 31

August 1-August 31

September 1-September 30

October 1-October 31

November 1-November 30

December 1-December 31

These dates are for approximation only and can be dramatically different within given areas. For example, the average date of last spring frost in my area of Massachusetts is listed as the 10th of May. The eastern end of town, however, is considerably higher up on the mountain and gardeners there must wait several weeks longer for frost-free nights. And, as fall approaches, killing frosts hit their gardens before they do mine. Check with local nurseries or university extension service for details in your areas.

PREDICTING TOUGH WEATHER

When your root crops grow deeper than normal, be prepared for a severe winter. Likewise, if your fruit trees bear earlier than usual, be forewarned of a difficult winter ahead. When leaves fall from deciduous trees early, a mild winter is in store; but when leaves remain on the branches late into the fall, beware. Finally, look for a rough winter when crows just won't be frightened out of your corn patch. In some areas of the country, it is an unlucky omen for your crops if you see two crows flying together on your left.

PESTS AND DISEASES. Aphids, leaf hoppers, cutworm, slugs; leaf spot, bottom rot. See Chart, page 43–47, for control measures.

Parsley Family (umbelliferae)

Carrot, page 77
Celeriac, page 78
Celery, page 78
Chervil, page 127
Fennel, page 128
Florence fennel, page 128
Hamburg parsley, page 88
Parsley, page 132
Parsnips, page 93

GENERAL CULTURE. The flowers of this interesting family of plants are borne aloft on a radiating rib-like structure, hence their resemblance to an umbrella and their name, *umbelliferae*. They divide fairly evenly among root (carrot, celeriac, hamburg parsley and parsnip) and leaf (parsley, fennel, florence fennel, celery and chervil) crops. And they share in common seeds which refuse to germinate in less than three weeks—with parsnips taking the longest at about 28 days. All sorts of tricks have been tried with varying success to hasten germination, from a soak overnight in fresh water to a 10-minute bath in boiling hot tea.

As a rule, out of this group usually only celery is worth starting indoors, so here are two tips for outdoor seeding of these slow starters: (1) plant fast-sprouting shallow-rooting radish seeds in the same seedbeds to mark the rows, so you won't forget where they are, and (2) cover the seeds lightly with a non-soil medium like vermiculite or a seeding mix to prevent suffocating soil-crusting during the extensive germination period.

PESTS AND DISEASES. Carrot fly, celery leaf miner, celery worms, nematodes; canker, rust. See Chart, page 43–47, for control measures.

Smaller Families

Five other families are represented in the vegetable garden, each with a single entry. The monocot Lily Family (liliaceae), represented by Asparagus, page 70; the Carpetweed Family (aizoaceae), by New Zealand Spinach, page 102; the Mallow Family (malvaceae), by Okra, page 92; the Valerian Family (valerianaceae), by Corn Salad; and the Morning Glory Family (convolvulceae), whose lone but indispensible representative in the garden is the Sweet Potato, page 105.

A Basil-lined path leads the way into this cozy vegetable garden.

Marigolds and Ageratum intermingle with prospering vegetables.

Vegetables planted in single rows
make gardening easy.

ASPARAGUS

Perennial

Asparagus is a heroic but rewarding undertaking: you have to create a special bed for it (See "How to Establish an Asparagus Bed"), and it takes a very long time—usually three years—to  produce its first crop. But it's all worth it if you appreciate this wonderful vegetable. The good news is that as a perennial, the asparagus comes back for a full 6-week harvest, spring after delicious spring.

Instead of seed, gardeners start asparagus with dormant root crowns 2 or 3 years old, which have already put in considerable growing time and greatly hasten the days to first harvest. For the fun of it, however, you might want to try a dozen or so plants from seed, so I'll give directions for both.

- DEGREE OF DIFFICULTY: Requires considerable labor to prepare bed, but once established, demands only minimal attention
- TEMPERATURE TOLERANCE: Best in cool weather
- WHEN TO SOW INDOORS: (For seedlings only) Start in fall, place seedlings under lights, set outdoors in spring
- DAYS TO GERMINATION: (For seedlings only) 14–21
- WHEN TO SET OUT ROOT CROWNS OR SEEDLINGS: As soon as ground is dry enough to be worked easily: spring in the north, fall in the south
- DEPTH OF SEEDS: Bury crowns or seedlings 4″–8″ deep in trench; stagger depth for extended harvest
- DISTANCE BETWEEN PLANTS: 12″–18″ apart within rows; 4′–5′ between rows

---

HOW TO ESTABLISH AN ASPARAGUS BED

STEP 1. Dig a trench 12″ wide and 12–18″ deep for each row. Make rows at least 4′ apart.

STEP 2. Shovel in about 6–7″ of compost or well-rotted manure. If your soil is very heavy clay, add an inch or so of clean builder's sand to the mix.

STEP 3. Form mounds of the compost in the trench, about 6″ diameter, 3″ high, 12–18″ apart (some experts recommend 24″; I've been successful with 12″).

STEP 4. Drape a root crown, or set a seedling, over each mound, making certain the crown or the root of the seedling sits at least 4″ below the soil surface and work down to 6″–7″. If crowns/seedlings are planted at different depths, asparagus shoots will emerge over an extended period in spring (a trick I learned from Dick Raymond years ago).

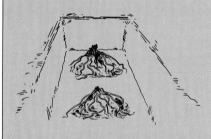

STEP 5. Cover mounds with 2″–3″ of soil; they will still be below surface level of garden.

STEP 6. Complete filling-in process when first shoots appear in spring.

- SOIL CONDITIONS: Well-fertilized, weed-free sandy loam; pH 6.0–8.0
- SUNLIGHT REQUIREMENTS: Full sun
- WATERING: Keep well watered
- SIDEDRESSING: Annual application of manure or compost, about 15 lbs. per 100 sq. ft. of row

---

- DAYS TO FIRST HARVEST: In spring; 2–3 years from planting of crown; 3–4 years from planting of seed
- HARVESTING TIPS: Harvest by cutting the stalks at ground level, but never harvest first year. Let stalks, if any appear, flower and seed. Second year, harvest sparingly, for 1 week only, taking no spears smaller than ¼″ diameter. Third year, harvest liberally for up to 6 weeks
- VARIETIES: Mary Washington, Martha Washington
- PESTS AND DISEASES: Asparagus beetle, rust

BEANS

Annual

According to a Gallup poll, if American gardeners could grow only two vegetables the first would be tomatoes and the second, beans. There is a wide variety in this group—snap beans, broad beans, shell beans, dry beans, soybeans, limas, cowpeas (really beans), garbanzo beans, and a knot of miscellaneous types such as wing beans and yard-longs. Because the culture for each varies, sometimes quite broadly, we will treat the major types on their own.

SNAP BEANS

Snap beans, or green beans, come in both the low bush type and the climbing pole variety.  Both love sun, and won't produce a good crop if deprived of it for much of the day. Snap bean plants produce beautiful blossoms which are pollinated by a bit of wind or a visiting insect. Soon after, slender bean pods appear from the center of the blossoms and begin to enlarge rapidly. Though snap beans are warm weather plants, their blossoms will drop when daytime temperatures are consistently above 85°F. Snap beans are an excellent succession crop, and may be sown every two weeks from late spring through midsummer.

- TEMPERATURE TOLERANCE: Tender
- DEGREE OF DIFFICULTY: Very simple
- WHEN TO SOW INDOORS: Not an indoor starter
- DAYS TO GERMINATION: 10
- WHEN TO SOW OUTDOORS OR SET TRANSPLANTS: After threat of frost
- DEPTH OF SEED: 1"
- DISTANCE BETWEEN PLANTS: 3"–6" in rows and around pole bases
- SOIL CONDITIONS: Well-worked soil rich in organic matter; pH 5.5–7.0
- SUNLIGHT REQUIREMENTS: Full sun
- WATERING: Moderate
- SIDEDRESSING: Unnecessary unless soil extremely poor
- DAYS TO FIRST HARVEST: 45–70
- HARVESTING TIPS: Pick beans immediately and daily when young; keep picking for prolonged harvest
- VARIETIES: *Bush beans:* Bountiful, Tendercrop, Tenderpod, Royal Burgundy, Blue Lake, Golden Wax, Romano; *Pole beans:* Kentucky Wonder, Kentucky Wonder Yellow Wax, Pole Romano
- PESTS AND DISEASES: Bean leaf beetle, Mexican bean beetle, root-knot nematodes; anthracnose, bacterial wilt, mosaic, rust
- SPECIAL NOTES: Stay out of the bean patch after a rain or before the morning dew has evaporated; water is an exceptionally efficient transmitter of disease organisms

SUPPORTING POLE BEANS

I like to grow pole beans on teepees constructed of 4 young hardwood saplings about 2" in diameter and 8'–10' long. If you don't have access to a woodlot, you can use bamboo poles or long tomato stakes available from the garden store.

Draw a 4'-diameter circle in the soil where you intend to plant your pole beans, and drive 4 stakes in around the perimeter about 2' apart, and 3"–4" down. Then lean the poles toward the center so their tops come together to form a teepee frame. Using strong twine or rope, tie the poles together near the top so the structure will withstand strong winds.

Now plant your seeds about 6" apart in a circle around the base of each pole. Next, dig a shallow trench about 3" deep around each circle of seeds, fill to the brim with compost or stable manure, and water the whole area thoroughly. As the plants grow, they will reach out for nutrients and support and find the compost below and poles above—and in about 4 weeks you will see a thing of wonder and beauty in your garden! And, if you're looking for a nice cool place for a few lettuce plants, the interior of the circle is ideal.

_____ *Notes* _____

SHELL BEANS AND DRY BEANS

Shell beans embrace a broad variety of beans whose seeds mature in the pod. They are then picked, shelled (because the pods are fibrous and make terrible eating) and the seeds eaten fresh, that  is, while they are still soft. Limas and a group of beans Southerners call peas (black-eye peas and the like) are so delicious at this stage that they are referred to as butter beans and cream peas respectively. These same beans, when left on the vine until the pods become brown and brittle and the seeds hard as stone, are called dry beans and used mostly for baked beans and soups.

Most beans in this group are available in both bush and pole varieties, and include limas, red and white kidney beans, Pinto beans, French Horticultural and even soybeans. Shell beans require a longer frost-free season than snap beans to reach the edible stage, and have developed a reputation as southern crops, but they can all be grown quite successfully in the north.

- TEMPERATURE TOLERANCE: Tender
- DEGREE OF DIFFICULTY: Simple
- WHEN TO SOW INDOORS: Not an indoor starter
- DAYS TO GERMINATION: 10
- WHEN TO SOW OUTDOORS OR SET TRANSPLANTS: After all threat of frost; pre-soak seeds for an hour or so to aid germination, no longer or they will split; plant with seed-eye down
- DEPTH OF SEED: 1″–1½″
- DISTANCE BETWEEN PLANTS: Bush types: 6″ in rows about 2′ apart (these beans are very bushy). Pole types: 6″ apart around bases of poles or along trellises

- SOIL CONDITIONS: Well-worked, enriched with organic matter; pH 5.5–7.0
- SUNLIGHT REQUIREMENTS: Full sun
- WATERING: Moderate (1″ per week), steady supply
- SIDEDRESSING: Not necessary except in poor soil
- DAYS TO FIRST HARVEST: 75–100
- HARVESTING TIPS: All shell beans can be harvested green (when pods are plump), or allowed to mature and dry on the vine. Lima pods look lumpy when the beans are ripe; when horticultural beans are ripe at the green shell stage, they turn a strawberry shade, while kidney beans turn either white or red, depending on the variety
- VARIETIES: There are scores of excellent varieties, including many heirlooms. Check the list of seed houses, page 229, for catalogues specializing in beans. In the meantime, here are a few of my favorites, chosen for excellent taste and disease resistance. *Limas:* Baby Fordhook, Fordhook 242, King of the Garden (pole); *Shell beans:* Pinto, French Horticultural, Dwarf Horticultural, Red Kidney, White Kidney, Black Turtle, Great Northern; *Southern peas:* Blackeye Peas, Crowder Peas, Cream Peas
- PESTS AND DISEASES: Bean leaf beetle, Mexican bean beetle, root-knot nematodes; anthracnose, bacterial wilt, mosaic, rust
- SPECIAL NOTES: Be careful not to injure plants as you harvest; use two hands, don't yank bean free

ICICLE-TYPE RADISHES HELP BEETS GROW

Many experienced gardeners with heavy clay soil sow seeds of icicle-type radishes along with their beets. As the radishes grow, their cylindical roots dig deep, and when pulled, they loosen and aerate the soil, thus enabling the beet roots nearby to expand into the newly vacant space. This same trick can be done with carrots, turnips—in fact, with all root crops.

BEETS

Annual

Beets are cousins of swiss chard, which may have been the first wild beet without a fleshy root. Beets were first cultivated in the third century, but never really got established in home gardens until the late 19th century. Though beets are usually red there are golden cultivars available too. Expect about a pound of beets per foot of row. Interplant with dwarf beans and onions to save space. Plant where cabbage family grew previously.

- DEGREE OF DIFFICULTY: Extremely easy
- TEMPERATURE TOLERANCE: Do well in hot and cold temperatures, but will not stand severe freezing; sudden extended drops below 50°F may induce seed stalks instead of plump roots
- WHEN TO SOW INDOORS: Not an indoor starter
- DAYS TO GERMINATION: 7–10
- WHEN TO SOW OUTDOORS OR SET TRANSPLANTS: As soon as temperatures consistently above 50°F; sow every 3 weeks for steady supply of young beets
- DEPTH OF SEED: ½″ in loamy soils; 1″ in sandy soils; if drought or crusting likely, cover seed lightly with leaf mold, sand or vermiculite
- DISTANCE BETWEEN PLANTS: Seed consists of several true seeds; thin to 2″–3″ apart
- SOIL CONDITIONS: Loose, sandy loam; pH 6.0–8.0
- SUNLIGHT REQUIREMENTS: Full sun
- WATERING: Moderate, but don't let soil dry out

- SIDEDRESSING: Not necessary if soil reasonably high in organic content; add plenty of compost, rotted manure, or leaf mold at planting time
- DAYS TO FIRST HARVEST: 50–65, depending on variety
- HARVESTING TIPS: Begin when roots quite small, to create growing room for those which remain
- VARIETIES: Detroit Dark Red, Golden Beet, Lutz Green Leaf, Pacemaker II, Cylindra
- PESTS AND DISEASES: European corn borer, cutworm, leafhopper, leaf miner, cabbage maggot

BROAD OR FAVA BEANS

Annual

While all other beans are warm-season crops, Fava beans demand cool conditions and can be planted directly in the garden well before the last expected frost. Sometimes, however, the cool moist soil conditions of early spring can forestall germination for such a long time that the seed will actually rot in the ground before it ever sprouts. For this reason, experienced Fava bean growers either place heat-gathering cloches over the seeds, or start seeds indoors about 6 weeks before setting plants out. Be careful, however, for Favas don't take to transplanting; harden the plants well, and disturb the roots as little as possible when you transplant to the garden.

- TEMPERATURE TOLERANCE: Hardy
- DEGREE OF DIFFICULTY: Simple
- WHEN TO SOW INDOORS: 8–10 weeks before last frost
- DAYS TO GERMINATION: 7–10
- WHEN TO SOW OUTDOORS OR SET TRANSPLANTS: Direct-seed as soon as soil can be worked; set transplants 2–3 weeks before last frost
- DEPTH OF SEED: 2″
- DISTANCE BETWEEN PLANTS: 6″
- SOIL CONDITIONS: Well-worked, enriched with organic matter; pH 6.0–6.8
- SUNLIGHT REQUIREMENTS: Full sun
- WATERING: Steady, moderate supply
- SIDEDRESSING: Apply compost when plants start blossoming
- DAYS TO FIRST HARVEST: 85
- HARVESTING TIPS: Harvest when pods are plump, same as shell beans
- VARIETIES: Long Pod, The Sutton, Broad Improved Long Pod; check specialty seed houses for greater selection
- PESTS AND DISEASES: Aphids; mildew

BROCCOLI

Biennial

Not only one of the most delicious vegetables in the garden, but certainly among the most beautiful, Broccoli developed from various leafy cabbage forms in southern Europe — particularly France and Italy—and was brought to America by immigrants from those countries. Broccoli can be grown from transplants or by direct seeding outdoors. Transplants save 3 weeks of growing time; fall broccoli can be direct-seeded. Set transplants so the stems are almost entirely below ground. Fortify planting holes with compost or aged manure.

- DEGREE OF DIFFICULTY: Very easy
- TEMPERATURE TOLERANCE: Fairly hardy; will stand some frost
- WHEN TO SOW INDOORS: About 6 weeks before last expected frost
- DAYS TO GERMINATION: 7–10
- WHEN TO SOW OUTDOORS OR SET TRANSPLANTS: Soon after last severe frost; wrap stems with newspaper to protect against cutworms; sow seeds for fall crop in midsummer
- DEPTH OF SEED: ¼"–½"
- DISTANCE BETWEEN PLANTS: 12"–18"
- SOIL CONDITIONS: Will do well in most soils; pH 6.0–6.8
- SUNLIGHT REQUIREMENTS: Full sun
- WATERING: Moderate supply, but water young transplants well during hot spells
- SIDEDRESSING: Topdress with compost, water with manure or compost tea
- DAYS TO FIRST HARVEST: 50–85 from transplanting
- HARVESTING TIPS: Harvest first head and 6" of stem before it flowers. In several days, side-heads will begin to form, every bit as good to eat as the larger central heads. Harvest often and plants will produce continuously
- VARIETIES: *Early varieties:* De Cicco, Green Comet, Italian Green Sprouting; *Mid-season and late:* Calabrese, Costal,

Romanesco, Waltham 29; *Mid-spring:* try Floccoli (new broccoli/cauliflower hybrid)
- PESTS AND DISEASES: Aphids, flea beetles, cabbage loopers, cabbage worms; club root, black leg, yellows

BRUSSELS SPROUTS

Biennial

Like broccoli, cabbage, cauliflower, collards and kohlrabi, brussels sprouts belong to the mustard family. They originated in Europe, and were cultivated in Belgium for centuries, presumably near Brussels. In France they're called *petit chou,* or "small cabbage." Except for setting seedlings out somewhat later in the spring than their cousins, brussels sprouts are handled in exactly the same fashion. See Broccoli for details.

- DEGREE OF DIFFICULTY: Fairly simple
- TEMPERATURE TOLERANCE: Hardy; does well in all temperatures; flavor improved by hard frost
- WHEN TO SOW INDOORS: Early spring
- DAYS TO GERMINATION: 7–10
- WHEN TO SOW OUTDOORS OR SET TRANSPLANTS: Sow seeds in cold frames in early spring; set out transplants in mid-spring for fall harvest
- DEPTH OF SEED: ¼"
- DISTANCE BETWEEN PLANTS: 12"–18"
- SOIL CONDITIONS: Moderately fertile soil; pH 6.0–6.8
- SUNLIGHT REQUIREMENTS: Full sun

FALL BROCCOLI

Set transplants for fall broccoli crop between maturing head lettuce or they can follow your early peas. Spacing should be close, about 12", so the soil is shaded by the foliage and kept cool—which broccoli and all its cabbage family cousins like. The best thing about late broccoli, aside from its fabulous taste and its ability to withstand some frost, is that it tends to be fairly worm-free. Somehow the cabbage moths are caught out of cycle, or they lay their eggs elsewhere.

TWO WAYS TO INCREASE BRUSSELS SPROUT PRODUCTION

Since brussels sprouts form above each leaf on the main stalk, commercial growers have devised two methods for increasing leaf production on each plant. The old standby is to snip off the terminal bud at the top of the plant so as to stimulate leaf growth lower down on the stem. The other method is to strip all the leaves from the lower 6 inches of the stem after the plant is well-established; this triggers leaf production higher up on the stem. To avoid the possible spread of disease, never snap off leaves when plant is wet.

- WATERING: Moderate water supply; never let seedlings or transplants dry out
- SIDEDRESSING: When sprouts form, work compost and/or manure into top few inches surrounding stem; water with manure or compost tea
- DAYS TO FIRST HARVEST: 80–90
- HARVESTING TIPS: Break off sprouts as soon as they're about an inch across. New ones will grow in their place. The best-tasting sprouts have been kissed by frost, so let the majority of the crop grow well into the fall. You can even harvest brussels sprouts in the snow. Expect about 1 pound per plant of hybrid stock
- VARIETIES: Catskill, Long Island Improved, Jade Cross, Achilles, Peer Gynt
- PESTS AND DISEASES: Aphids, flea beetles, cabbage loopers, cabbage worms; club root, black leg, yellows

CABBAGE

Biennial

Cabbage leaves were in general use as early as 2000 B.C., but the head type was first reported in the mid-16th century. Cabbage can be green or purple, its leaves smooth or savoyed (curly); heads  are round or pointed, early (60 days) or late (120 days) maturing. Like broccoli and cauliflower, cabbage can be planted quite early for an early crop, in midsummer for a fall crop. For early crop, use transplants grown indoors. Late crop can be direct-seeded in a special bed. Interplant onions and early lettuce with cabbage, but be sure to harvest these when cabbage starts spreading out.

- DEGREE OF DIFFICULTY: Fairly easy, but requires care
- TEMPERATURE TOLERANCE: Does best in cool conditions; tolerates frost but not heat
- WHEN TO SOW INDOORS: 6 weeks before last expected frost
- DAYS TO GERMINATION: 7–10
- WHEN TO SOW OUTDOORS OR SET TRANSPLANTS: Early spring, after last of the severe frosts; set up to top leaves in pre-fertilized holes
- DEPTH OF SEED: ¼″–½″ when direct-seeded for fall crop
- DISTANCE BETWEEN PLANTS: 12″–18″; 8″–12″ in South to keep soil cooler
- SOIL CONDITIONS: Cool soil; pH 6.0–6.8
- SUNLIGHT REQUIREMENTS: Full sun
- WATERING: Moderate supply; don't let young seedlings dry out
- SIDEDRESSING: Topdress with compost or aged manure when heads start to form
- DAYS TO FIRST HARVEST: 60–90
- HARVESTING TIPS: Harvest whenever heads are firm. For multiple heads, cut central head, allowing several leaves to remain. New heads will form at leaf junctures; harvest them when fairly firm. For winter storage, pull up whole plants—head, stem, roots and all. Remove loose outer leaves and store in cool shed or cellar
- VARIETIES: Plant varieties with different maturing dates to extend harvest. Early Jersey Wakefield, Stonehead, Golden Acre, Market Topper; *Disease-resistant red varieties:* Red Danish, Ruby Ball; *Savoy types:* Perfection Drumhead, Savoy King
- PESTS AND DISEASES: Aphids, flea beetles, cabbage loopers, cabbage worms; club root, black legs, yellows

CANTALOUPE

Annual

Also known as a muskmelon, the cantaloupe had its beginnings in Iran and India. It is a member of  the same family as cucumber, squash, pumpkins, gourds and watermelons. There are many types of muskmelon, most notably the smooth-skinned honeydew with green flesh and the white-fleshed casaba. It's sometimes a real trick to get sweet-tasting melons to table. Excessive rain, drought, or more than average cloudiness during ripening can all

Notes

bear on the final quality of the melons. Melons are heavy feeders, so keep the soil well-supplied with compost or rotted manure.

- DEGREE OF DIFFICULTY: Finicky; requires ideal conditions to produce high-quality melons
- TEMPERATURE TOLERANCE: Extremely tender. Grows best 60–85°F.
- WHEN TO SOW INDOORS: 6 weeks before garden soil is thoroughly warmed

PRE-SPROUT SEEDS FIRST

If your growing season is rather short, but you don't have the room indoors to grow melon seedlings of your own, you can still get a jump on the season without settling for nursery-bred plants. The trick, which I learned from master gardener Dick Raymond, is to pre-sprout your seeds before planting them; it works as well with cucumbers, pumpkins, squash—even corn and beans.

1. Soak several sheets of sturdy paper towels in warm water; wring out excess water and lay flat.

2. Spread seeds on half the paper surface.
3. Fold other half over seeds, and then roll this 4 times more into 1" pleats.

4. Roll packet into a warm, moist face towel, and wrap in a plastic bag.
5. Place on top of the refrigerator or some other warm location.
6. Check seeds after several days.
7. Plant sprouted seeds on edge and cover with soil, taking care not to break the sprout.

- DAYS TO GERMINATION: 7–10
- WHEN TO SOW OUTDOORS OR SET TRANSPLANTS: When soil is thoroughly warm
- DEPTH OF SEED: 1"
- DISTANCE BETWEEN PLANTS: 12" apart in rows 4'–6' apart; or set 3–4 plants in hills 4'–6' apart.
- SOIL CONDITIONS: Warm, rich, well-drained; pH 6.0–6.8
- SUNLIGHT REQUIREMENTS: Full sun
- WATERING: Requires steady, moderate water supply during periods of vine and fruit development, but not during ripening period
- SIDEDRESSING: When vines start to crawl, and again when plants begin to set fruit
- DAYS TO FIRST HARVEST: 65–90
- HARVESTING TIPS: Harvest at "full slip" stage, when stem comes easily away from fruit; ripe fruit also changes from green to yellow or tan
- VARIETIES: Choose disease-resistant varieties with appropriate maturity dates for your area. Harper Hybrid, Bush Star, Saticoy, Venus (Honeydew type), Ambrosia, Burpee Hybrid, Sweet 'n' Early, Early Hybrid Crenshaw, Golden Beauty (Casaba), Honeyloupe
- PESTS AND DISEASES: Striped cucumber beetle, vine borer; bacterial wilt, downy mildew, mosaic

CARROTS

Annual

Like all root crops, carrots thrive best in loose, sandy soil. If your soil tends toward the heavy clay type, don't despair; there are several short-rooted varieties you can grow with complete success. Additionally, you can loosen up the top 4"–5" of your soil by working in compost, chopped leaves, or builder's sand before planting, and be sure to cover seed with sand or vermiculite to prevent crusting. Another way to get a standout crop of sweet, well-formed carrots is to plant seeds in a raised bed. See page 38 for directions. Thin out early so main crop stands about 3" apart. Plant with leeks to repel carrot fly.

- DEGREE OF DIFFICULTY: Fairly simple with good deep soil
- TEMPERATURE TOLERANCE: Grows well from early spring to fall; tolerates some frost
- WHEN TO SOW INDOORS: Not an indoor starter
- DAYS TO GERMINATION: 14–21
- WHEN TO SOW OUTDOORS OR SET TRANSPLANTS: As soon as ground can be worked. Sow succession crops every 3 weeks for steady supply of young carrots
- DEPTH OF SEED: ¼"–½"; cover with sand, vermiculite or other artificial planting mix; keep moist
- DISTANCE BETWEEN PLANTS: 1"–2"
- SOIL CONDITIONS: Deep, loose soil; pH 5.5–6.8; for clay or hardpan, use short cultivars or plant in raised beds
- SUNLIGHT REQUIREMENTS: Full sun

- WATERING: Sprinkle seedbeds daily until seeds germinate; moderate supply thereafter
- SIDEDRESSING: Not necessary; apply fertilizer at planting time; avoid incomplete compost or fresh manure, which encourage forked roots
- DAYS TO FIRST HARVEST: 50–75
- HARVESTING TIPS: Begin when roots are thickness of a pencil; this allows remaining roots to grow larger
- VARIETIES: *Short-rooted (3"–4") varieties:* Short 'n' Sweets, French Forcing; *Medium-rooted (5"–7"):* Chantenay, Nantes Half-Longs, Danvers Half-Longs; *Long-rooted (7"–8"):* GoldPak, Imperator
- PESTS AND DISEASES: Carrot rust fly, carrot worm; leaf blight

CAULIFLOWER

Biennial

Cauliflower is one of the more spectacular sights in the vegetable garden. Perhaps because of that, many gardeners fear it takes more expertise to grow those perfect snow-white florets than they possess. This is not true. The trick is to get cauliflower off to a very early start, as it grows best in cool weather. Plants started from seed indoors about 2 months before the last frost, hardened off properly, and set out even as early as 2 weeks before that frost should be quite safe from injury by cold weather. If a hard frost is predicted, cover plants with hot caps or newspaper overnight.

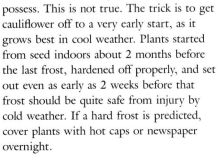

BLANCHING TECHNIQUES

1. *Clothespins:* fasten overhead leaves with spring-loaded clothespins.
2. *Rubber bands:* grasp outer leaves with one hand and slip rubber band gently around the tops.

Fertilize planting holes and sidedress plants when heads start to form. To keep heads white and tender, they must be blanched—the top leaves closed over them to block out sunlight—when they reach 2"–3" across. You can fasten the leaves with rubber bands or clothespins. One technique calls for breaking the spines of outer leaves and folding them over the young heads, but I would avoid wounding the plant needlessly and inviting unwanted disease.

Cauliflower can be planted as a fall crop too. Start seeds outdoors in their own seedling bed about 3 months before first expected frost, and transplant them into permanent rows when they are 2"–3" tall. Space them no further than 12" apart so they create cooling shade for the soil as they grow through the dog days of late summer.

- DEGREE OF DIFFICULTY: Requires hands-on attention for best crop
- TEMPERATURE TOLERANCE: Cool weather crop; tends to suffer in heat spells
- WHEN TO SOW INDOORS: 6–8 weeks before last expected frost
- DAYS TO GERMINATION: 7–10
- WHEN TO SOW OUTDOORS OR SET TRANSPLANTS: As early as possible; don't worry about anything but a hard frost
- DEPTH OF SEED: ¼"
- DISTANCE BETWEEN PLANTS: 12"–14"
- SOIL CONDITIONS: Cool soil; pH 6.5–7.0
- SUNLIGHT REQUIREMENTS: Full sun
- WATERING: Keep seedbed moist; moderate water supply after germination
- SIDEDRESSING: Add compost when heads start to form; water regularly thereafter with compost or manure tea
- DAYS TO FIRST HARVEST: 50–85
- HARVESTING TIPS: Harvest when heads are 6" or more in diameter, but before flower parts begin to separate. Cut stem flush with bottom of head.

- VARIETIES: Use only early-maturing varieties—any of the Snowball cultivars such as Early Snowball and Snow King. Snow King, more heat-tolerant, is better for southern growing. Purple Head, generally found in catalogues under Cauliflower, is really a broccoli and should be grown as such
- PESTS AND DISEASES: Aphids, flea beetles, cabbage loopers, cabbage worms; club root, black leg, yellows

CELERIAC

Annual

A native of Europe and portions of Asia, celeriac is also known as turnip root, celery root and knob celery. It is a close relative of celery, but is grown for its tasty roots rather than its fleshy  stems. According to lovers of pea soup, that dish is incomplete without a hefty slice of celeriac. It goes just as well in other soups, salads or sliced and eaten with dip. The French salad appetizer *celeri remoulade* is strips of this root in a tart mustard sauce. Try a half-dozen plants in a sunny section of your garden.

- DEGREE OF DIFFICULTY: Very easy
- TEMPERATURE TOLERANCE: Wide temperature range; tolerates frost
- WHEN TO SOW INDOORS: 2 months before last severe frost; can be direct-seeded in mild regions
- DAYS TO GERMINATION: 14–21
- WHEN TO SOW OUTDOORS OR SET TRANSPLANTS: Very early in spring

- DEPTH OF SEED: ¼"
- DISTANCE BETWEEN PLANTS: 6"
- SOIL CONDITIONS: Fertile, moist, well-drained; pH 6.0–6.8
- SUNLIGHT REQUIREMENTS: Full sun
- WATERING: Keep seedbed moist; soak rows of transplants thoroughly and keep well-watered during dry spells
- SIDEDRESSING: Unnecessary except in poorest soil
- DAYS TO FIRST HARVEST: 120
- HARVESTING TIPS: Celeriac tastes best after a frost. Roots will be 2"–5" in diameter. They can be stored in the ground where winters are mild. Northern gardeners should dig roots and store them in boxes of sand, sawdust or peatmoss where they will keep well for months
- VARIETIES: Alabaster, Apple, Giant Prague, Large Smooth Prague
- PESTS AND DISEASES: Leaf hoppers, tarnished plant bug; leaf tier, leaf blights, yellows
- SPECIAL NOTES: Some gardeners feel that visible side-shoots should be trimmed to increase root size. This can be done with a knife or garden hoe.

CELERY

Annual

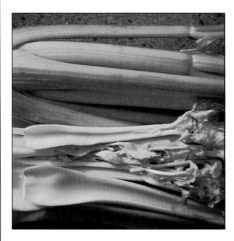

Although celery is far and away among the most difficult vegetables in the garden to grow successfully, I urge you to try a few plants for the  challenge. Conditions must be practically ideal: soil must be well-drained and extremely rich; the plants must be started very early

TECHNIQUES FOR BLANCHING CELERY

Many gardeners like to blanch celery, which is reputed to improve its flavor and lighten its color. Still other avid celery growers like their celery as it is naturally. Still others use self-blanching varieties. If you want to try blanching a few celery plants as they head toward maturity, here are three techniques.

1. Hilling: with a hoe, pull dirt up around entire celery plants; try to avoid getting dirt into the inner portion of the plant as it may cause rotting.

2. Boarding up the rows: simply place one board on each side of your celery row and stake in place to keep the wind from blowing them over.

3. Milk carton method: cut away the bottoms of half-gallon milk cartons and slip one over each plant.

Whichever method you select, the blanching process will be complete in 2–3 weeks, and you can compare the blanched with the unblanched for color and flavor.

from seeds that are hard to handle and slow and temperamental germinators; celery will tolerate neither frost nor very hot temperatures; it must be watered and fed on a regular schedule. And even then, if you do not harvest celery promptly, it will turn woody and unusable. But it is still worth trying.

- DEGREE OF DIFFICULTY: A challenge for even the most experienced
- TEMPERATURE TOLERANCE: Will stand neither frost nor great heat
- WHEN TO SOW INDOORS: 3–4 months before spring planting
- DAYS TO GERMINATION: 14–21
- WHEN TO SOW OUTDOORS OR SET TRANSPLANTS: Can direct-seed in warm regions, or set out fully-hardened transplants on a cloudy day after last expected frost and water well
- DEPTH OF SEED: 1/16″; press lightly into soil or planting medium with thin board or shingle
- DISTANCE BETWEEN PLANTS: Indoors, thin seedlings to 2″ apart; set transplants 6″–12″ outdoors
- SOIL CONDITIONS: Rich, well-drained, deep; add lots of compost before planting
- SUNLIGHT REQUIREMENTS: Full sun
- WATERING: Water thoroughly and often
- SIDEDRESSING: Mulch with compost throughout growing season
- DAYS TO FIRST HARVEST: 110–120
- HARVESTING TIPS: Cut taproot below ground and flush with bottom of stalks. Overmature plants become hard and crack. In mild regions, celery can be overwintered in the ground and will produce seed the following spring
- VARIETIES: Tendercrisp, Summer Pascal, Golden Self-Blanching
- PESTS AND DISEASES: Leaf hoppers, tarnished plant bug; leaf tier, leaf blights, yellows

CELTUCE

Annual

As you may have guessed, celtuce derives its name from both celery and lettuce, and is, in fact, a two-in-one vegetable. Celtuce is believed to have been brought to this country by a missionary just after the Second World War, which accounts for its relative novelty. More and more seed catalogues, however, are carrying it. The crisp celery part, which is actually the seed stalk (this, incidentally, can bolt to a height of almost five feet), is quite mild-flavored, and can be stir-fried, braised, and baked. The leaves resemble romaine or cos lettuce, and stay crispy in salads.

- DEGREE OF DIFFICULTY: Easy as leaf lettuce
- TEMPERATURE TOLERANCE: Cool weather crop
- WHEN TO SOW INDOORS: Not an indoor starter
- DAYS TO GERMINATION: 7–10
- WHEN TO SOW OUTDOORS OR SET TRANSPLANTS: As soon as ground is workable; again in mid-to-late summer for fall crop
- DEPTH OF SEED: 1/4″
- DISTANCE BETWEEN PLANTS: 18″
- SOIL CONDITIONS: Reasonably fertile soil; pH 6.0–6.8
- SUNLIGHT REQUIREMENTS: Full sun
- WATERING: Moderate supply
- SIDEDRESSING: Apply compost about a month after planting
- DAYS TO FIRST HARVEST: 30 for greens; 90 for stalks
- HARVESTING TIPS: Harvest leaves quite young, until they become milky. Harvest

_____ *Notes* _____

stalks when they're 1″ at base; strip leaves and peel outer skin to remove sap tubes. Stalks can be harvested until flowering begins

- VARIETIES: Celtuce
- PESTS AND DISEASES: Generally free of pests and disease

CHARD

Annual

Chard, which comes in both the Swiss green variety and the Ruby red version, is closely related to the beet, but is prized for its succulent thick stalks, not its roots, which are inedible. Because of its adaptability to a wide range of temperatures, chard can be grown all season long. It is a wonderful substitute for cooked spinach.

- DEGREE OF DIFFICULTY: Moderately simple
- TEMPERATURE TOLERANCE: Will stand the frosts of early spring and fall, and tolerate hottest days of summer
- WHEN TO SOW INDOORS: Not an indoor starter
- DAYS TO GERMINATION: 10–14
- WHEN TO SOW OUTDOORS OR SET TRANSPLANTS: In early spring, again in mid or late summer; in South, it grows over the winter
- DEPTH OF SEED: ½″–1″
- DISTANCE BETWEEN PLANTS: 6″–8″
- SOIL CONDITIONS: Rich soil; pH 5.8–6.5
- SUNLIGHT REQUIREMENTS: Full sun

FORCING CHARD ROOTS

Most gardeners know how to force roots indoors during the off-season (see Chicory, page 81); but did you know that chard roots can be forced outdoors in midsummer, to produce small, blanched, tight green buds that are delicious to eat? Cut the plant to within 1″ of the soil, and hill over the stump with several inches of soil. Within a few days you can feel gently for the new bud, and just before it emerges at the surface, cut it.

- WATERING: Moderate supply
- SIDEDRESSING: Apply compost every 2 weeks, water in well
- DAYS TO FIRST HARVEST: 50–60
- HARVESTING TIPS: Try this harvesting trick: cut a few feet of row, or as much as you need, down to within 2″ of the soil. Continue along the row over several days, and the earlier cut sections will begin to grow back. Soon you can start all over again
- VARIETIES: Swiss Chard has green leaves with white stems; Ruby Chard, red stems, and reddish green leaves, does not look out of place in a flower border
- PESTS AND DISEASES: European corn borer, cutworm, leafhopper, leaf miner, cabbage maggot

CHICORY

Annual

Chicory is what you'd call a triple-threat garden crop. Its leaves are used for salads and its roots either for a coffee substitute or to force the gourmet delight known as Belgian or French endive. Most varieties (see special notes below) will grow to a height of 2'–4', so place them where they will not overshadow lower-growing crops.

- DEGREE OF DIFFICULTY: Simple
- TEMPERATURE TOLERANCE: Tolerates frost, but French endive should not be sown until late spring
- WHEN TO SOW INDOORS: Not an indoor starter

FORCING FRENCH ENDIVE

To store chicory roots for midwinter forcing, use roots no less than 1" in diameter and trim all but 2" of tops. Set in cardboard boxes, cover with 6" dry sand, and store at 60°F. After several months, roots are ready to be forced. Cut tips so roots are all 6"–8" long, replace in sand and water the box thoroughly. When the tips of the creamy yellow heads begin to peek through the sand surface (about 3 weeks or so later), they can be cut from the root. Endive can be steamed, sauteed, or used in salads raw.

- DAYS TO GERMINATION: 14
- WHEN TO SOW OUTDOORS OR SET TRANSPLANTS: For greens, as soon as soil can be worked; for endive, when soil is warm
- DEPTH OF SEED: ¼"
- DISTANCE BETWEEN PLANTS: 8" for greens and coffee substitute; 4"–5" for endive
- SOIL CONDITIONS: Deep, friable soil for unimpeded root growth; don't oversupply with organic matter
- SUNLIGHT REQUIREMENTS: Full sun
- WATERING: Moderate supply
- SIDEDRESSING: Not required
- DAYS TO FIRST HARVEST: 60 days for greens; 110 for coffee substitute and endive
- HARVESTING TIPS: Dig roots before frost. For coffee substitute, clean, peel and cut roots into small chunks; then roast and grind
- VARIETIES: *For greens:* San Pasquale, Sugarhat; *For coffee substitute:* Large-rooted Magdeburg; *For endive:* Witloof Chicory
- PESTS AND DISEASES: Aphids, nematodes

CHINESE CABBAGE

Biennial

No gourmet kitchen should be without chinese cabbage, better known as bok choi or pak choi. There is both a leafy variety which looks a little like swiss chard, and a head type which resembles romaine or cos lettuce. The pale, yellow-green leaves have a crisp, nutty flavor that is indispensible for practically all Chinese dishes. Although chinese cabbage does best in cool weather, the first-time grower would be wise to direct-seed it in mid-to-late summer so it comes to maturity in the cool weather of autumn. Another good reason to direct-seed chinese cabbage is that it tends to do poorly when transplanted.

- DEGREE OF DIFFICULTY: Not a problem if soil is adequate
- TEMPERATURE TOLERANCE: Hardy; prefers cool conditions; best as a fall crop
- WHEN TO SOW INDOORS: Not an indoor starter
- DAYS TO GERMINATION: 7–10
- WHEN TO SOW OUTDOORS OR SET TRANSPLANTS: 45 days before first frost for leafy types, 75–80 days for head types; grown as winter crop in the South
- DEPTH OF SEED: ½"
- DISTANCE BETWEEN PLANTS: 8"–12"
- SOIL CONDITIONS: Rich, well-drained, moist
- SUNLIGHT REQUIREMENTS: Full sun
- WATERING: Keep well-watered, starting with seedbed
- SIDEDRESSING: Add nitrogen fertilizer when plants half-grown
- DAYS TO FIRST HARVEST: 45 days for leaf type; 70 days for heads
- HARVESTING TIPS: Harvest leaves as needed; cut heads level with ground, as romaine lettuce
- VARIETIES: *Leafy varieties:* Pak Choi, Crispy Choy; *head varieties:* Michili, Burpee Hybrid, Wongbok
- PESTS AND DISEASES: Aphids, flea beetles, cabbage loopers, cabbage worms; club root, black leg, yellows

COLLARDS

Biennial

Although long considered an exclusively southern crop like okra and black-eyed peas, collards—also known as headless cabbage—have been popular in northern gardens for quite some

time and definitely deserve a spot in yours. Like other cool weather vegetables, collards are sown once for a spring crop, and again for a fall crop; but unlike most greens, they can tolerate the intense heat of summer and still produce excellent results. Get them going indoors quite early for your first crop, or direct-seed as soon as you can work the soil, and then sow again in mid-to-late summer.

- DEGREE OF DIFFICULTY: Quite simple
- TEMPERATURE TOLERANCE: Hardy; prefers cool conditions

- WHEN TO SOW INDOORS: 8 weeks before last frost for spring crop
- DAYS TO GERMINATION: 7–10
- WHEN TO SOW OUTDOORS OR SET TRANSPLANTS: 4–6 weeks before last frost for spring crop; direct-seed mid-to-late summer for fall crop
- DEPTH OF SEED: ¼"
- DISTANCE BETWEEN PLANTS: 6"–8"
- SOIL CONDITIONS: Cool, moderately fertile
- SUNLIGHT REQUIREMENTS: Full sun
- WATERING: Keep well watered
- SIDEDRESSING: Apply fertilizer several weeks after planting
- DAYS TO FIRST HARVEST: 60–80
- HARVESTING TIPS: Three choices: 1) harvest lower leaves as soon as enough to make a meal—others will grow higher on the stalk; 2) Harvest young plant when 8"–10" tall; or 3) Harvest mature plant, cutting at ground level

CORN VARIETIES

Variety	Comments	Variety	Comments
Polar Vee	Does well in cool climates.	Iochief	Strong stalks are wind and drought resistant; heavy yielder.
Earlivee	Dependable early producer.		
Spancross	A dependable, early variety.	Illini X-tra Sweet	Needs warm soil for germination. Stays quite sweet up to 48 hours after harvest. Freezes well.
Golden Midget	Space-saving plant for small gardens or tub planting.		
Black Mexican	Open-pollinated, very hardy corn; ears are white in edible stage and turn blue-black when mature.	Golden Cross Bantam	Good all purpose variety for main crop. Large kernels, good flavor.
		Mainliner EH	A late, extra-sweet variety whose kernels retain their sugar content for a long time after harvest. It does *not* have to be isolated from other sweet corn.
Early Sunglow	Early vigor in cool temperatures.		
Silver Sweet	Bright purple husks.		
Sugar and Gold	Tender, sweet ears produced on short plants. Ideal if you have a short growing season.	Candystick	Slender ear especially good for freezing on the cob.
Early Extra Sweet	Isolate or stagger other corn plantings for best production. Holds sweetness up to 48 hours after harvest.	Bi-Queen	Disease resistance makes this two-colored variety good for southern gardens.
Butter and Sugar	Successive plantings every two weeks yield a steady crop of delicious ears; dependable producer.	Silver Queen	Sweet, slender ears; good for freezing. Resists disease and drought well.
		Country Gentleman	Open-pollinated variety. Irregular kernel arrangement. Good for cream-style corn.
Gurney's Mini-Max	New variety designed to produce large ears on short plants.		
Golden Bantam	Open-pollinated variety; ears mature over a two to three week period.	White Cloud Popcorn	Tall, study plants with high yield of early, hulless, pearl-white kernels. Good flavor.
Hybrid Truckers Favorite	Large ears; good for eating fresh, roasting or freezing.	Popcorn-Purdue 410	Heavy yielder; large cream-colored kernels have good popping action.
Quicksilver	Early white variety bred for its similarity to Silver Queen.	Strawberry Ornamental Popcorn	Small, strawberry-shaped cobs; double purpose—good for popping or decoration.
Seneca Chief	Smooth, tight husks are resistant to insect attacks.	Rainbow Ornamental	Colorful, festive, decorative corn for fall arrangements. Good roadside stand item.
Reid's Yellow Dent	Well adapted to southern soil and weather conditions. Good roasting variety.	Tennessee Red Cob	Southern favorite for roasting. Large, deep-grained ears set on red cobs.

List Courtesy of *Gardens For All*, Burlington, VT.

- VARIETIES: Georgia, Vates
- PESTS AND DISEASES: Aphids, flea beetles, cabbage loopers, cabbage worms; club root, black leg, yellows

---

CORN, SWEET

Annual

How corn grows and produces ears has been explained on page 58. If the ground is warm, and your seed is fresh, you'll have no problem producing a decent stand. Remember to plant in blocks rather than single rows, and if starlings or crows are a problem in your area, treat your seeds with a bird-repellent before planting. Otherwise, you're likely to lose much of your planting immediately after it germinates. Remember, too, that different types of corn (sweet corn, the new extra-sweet varieties, and popcorn) will cross-pollinate, affecting color and flavor, so plant at least 300 feet apart.

- DEGREE OF DIFFICULTY: Quite simple if soil is rich and space sufficient
- TEMPERATURE TOLERANCE: Tender
- WHEN TO SOW INDOORS: Not an indoor starter, but try a couple dozen plants about a month before last frost
- DAYS TO GERMINATION: 10–14 when soil is thoroughly warm
- WHEN TO SOW OUTDOORS OR SET TRANSPLANTS: After all danger of frost
- DEPTH OF SEED: 1″–1½″
- DISTANCE BETWEEN PLANTS: 8″–12″; use wide rows or blocks of short rows
- SOIL CONDITIONS: Rich loam; pH 5.5–7.5

- SUNLIGHT REQUIREMENTS: Full sun
- WATERING: Steady and continuous supply
- SIDEDRESSING: When plants are half-grown, apply 3″ alongside of each row
- DAYS TO FIRST HARVEST: 65–95
- HARVESTING TIPS: Don't pull back husks to determine ripeness of ears, since that attracts birds and insects. Ripe ears are ready for harvest when silk is brown and husks are tight to the tip—about 20 days after silk first appears. Bend the ear downward, twist, and snap off. And remember: sweet corn tastes best if it is harvested just before cooking
- VARIETIES: See "Corn Varieties"
- PESTS AND DISEASES: Flea beetle, European corn borer, cornstalk borer, corn earworm; smut, wilt

---

CORN SALAD

Annual

Corn salad is a tender and delicately flavored green, that has nothing whatever to do with corn. It is speculated that European growers of grain or "corn" discovered this leafy crop growing in their fields. Corn salad is also known as Mache, Fetticus, and Lamb's Lettuce, no doubt owing to its appearance at lambing time in early spring.

A hardy cool-weather crop, corn salad should be direct-seeded as early as the soil can be worked—about the same time you'd plant leaf lettuce—and again in mid-to-late summer for a fall crop. Wide row planting, as with leaf lettuce, is an option.

Notes

_____ *Notes* _____

- DEGREE OF DIFFICULTY: Quite simple
- TEMPERATURE TOLERANCE: Hardy, cool weather crop
- WHEN TO SOW INDOORS: Not an indoor starter
- DAYS TO GERMINATION: 7–10
- WHEN TO SOW OUTDOORS OR SET TRANSPLANTS: As soon as soiled can be worked
- DEPTH OF SEED: ½"
- DISTANCE BETWEEN PLANTS: 3"–4"
- SOIL CONDITIONS: Average loam; pH 5.8–6.5
- SUNLIGHT REQUIREMENTS: Full sun
- WATERING: About one inch per week
- SIDEDRESSING: Responds to nitrogen sidedressing, but not absolutely necessary
- DAYS TO FIRST HARVEST: 30–70
- HARVESTING TIPS: As soon as there is something to eat, pinch individual leaves or cut entire plant to within 2" of ground level (it will grow back)
- VARIETIES: Dark Green Full-Hearted, Large Round-Leaved
- PESTS AND DISEASES: None seem to bother this hardy green

CUCUMBER

Annual

Although cucumbers are by no means the easiest vegetable to raise, no home garden would be complete without at least a few vines—especially now that compact varieties are available which don't sprawl as traditional ones do. Cucumbers are also lightweight enough to be trellised on a fence, which would also free garden space for other cultivars.

If you only have space for one type, try picklers. They are huge producers, as good for slicing into salads as for pickling, and mature quite early. Plant dill in your herb garden as soon as the soil can be worked in spring, so the two crops come in simultaneously—perfect timing for the season's first pickles.

- DEGREE OF DIFFICULTY: Moderately difficult
- TEMPERATURE TOLERANCE: Extremely tender
- WHEN TO SOW INDOORS: 3–4 weeks before setting out; sow in individual containers such as Jiffy pellets so transplants can go directly into the soil without disturbing the roots
- DAYS TO GERMINATION: 7–10
- WHEN TO SOW OUTDOORS OR SET TRANSPLANTS: When soil is warm and all threat of frost past; water well
- DEPTH OF SEED: 1"
- DISTANCE BETWEEN PLANTS: 12" in rows, or 3 plants together in hills spaced 2'–3' apart

MULCHING CUCUMBERS AND OTHER VINE CROPS WITH BLACK PLASTIC

Being tropical by origin, vine crops love heat and moisture. The hotter and moister the soil, the faster they'll grow. Some northern gardeners create these conditions by covering rows with black plastic sheeting. They poke holes in the plastic and set in transplants or direct-seed. Rocks and piles of soil are placed on the plastic to anchor it and protect it from wind. Plastic mulch accomplishes several things at once:

1. It blocks out light and thereby kills weeds;

2. It prevents evaporation of moisture, requiring less watering time for the gardener;

3. It absorbs sunlight, which it converts to heat and transfers to the soil beneath.

- SOIL CONDITIONS: Rich, mellow soil fortified with compost or aged manure
- SUNLIGHT REQUIREMENTS: Full sun
- WATERING: Water deeply and keep soil from drying out below 3"; vines will stop growing if deprived of water
- SIDEDRESSING: Fertilize soil several days before planting, then sidedress when plants are about 10" tall or just before vines begin to spread
- DAYS TO FIRST HARVEST: 55–65
- HARVESTING TIPS: Slicers can be picked at 8", picklers at 4", and gherkins anywhere from 1"–3"; for abundant crops, pick fruit every other day; once a single cucumber matures to the point where hard seeds have developed inside it, the plant stops producing female flowers and new cucumbers
- VARIETIES: Because cucumbers are susceptible to many diseases, it is wise to choose only resistant varieties if you suspect trouble
- PESTS AND DISEASES: Striped and spotted cucumber beetles, cutworms, aphids, vine borers, squash bugs; anthracnose, angular leaf spot, bacterial and fusarium wilt disease, powdery and downy mildew, mosaic, scab

DANDELION

Perennial

Because wild dandelions grow all over the place, people who work hard to get rid of them are sometimes amazed to see packets of cultivated dandelion seeds for sale in garden stores. These tame dandelion varieties are larger and juicier than their wild cousins, and growing in popularity as high-vitamin greens. But they are still perennials, and should be planted in a special section with other perennial food crops, such as rhubarb, horseradish and asparagus. Care should be taken not to let them come to seed.

- DEGREE OF DIFFICULTY: Very easy
- TEMPERATURE TOLERANCE: Hardy
- WHEN TO SOW INDOORS: Not an indoor starter
- DAYS TO GERMINATION: 10–14
- WHEN TO SOW OUTDOORS OR SET TRANSPLANTS: As soon as soil can be worked
- DEPTH OF SEED: ¼"
- DISTANCE BETWEEN PLANTS: 6"–10"
- SOIL CONDITIONS: Any reasonably fertile soil; pH 5.8–6.5
- SUNLIGHT REQUIREMENTS: Full sun
- WATERING: Water well during dry periods
- SIDEDRESSING: Not necessary
- DAYS TO FIRST HARVEST: 60–90
- HARVESTING TIPS: Cut leaves, including a piece of the root-top, when they are 8" high. Plants not harvested in the first season should be harvested early the following spring before leaves get bitter. To reduce bitterness, try blanching: turn flowerpots or milk cartons over plants to

block out the light for 1–2 weeks. See page 78 for further details. Flowers should be harvested when they are yellow and tender, at which time they can be cooked along with the greens or used to make wine

- VARIETIES: Thick Leaved, Improved Thick Leaf
- PESTS AND DISEASES: None; dandelions seem impervious to infestation

EGGPLANT

Annual

This gorgeous vegetable, with its purple blossoms overarching like Victorian lamps, is a treasure to behold in the garden. Originally thought to be the cause of temporary insanity, and hence misnamed *malanzana,* eggplant fresh from the vine is truly a delight.

Eggplant is tricky to grow, however. If daytime temperatures are too high or nighttime temperatures too cool, it may have trouble setting blossoms. Eggplant is also an extremely heavy feeder, and will appreciate a few good handfuls of compost or aged manure in the planting hole and a sidedressing when blossoms appear. Cultivate eggplants gently and not too deeply, as their heat-loving roots are very close to the surface and easy to damage.

- DEGREE OF DIFFICULTY: Moderately difficult
- TEMPERATURE TOLERANCE: Extremely tender

- WHEN TO SOW INDOORS: 4–6 weeks before last frost
- DAYS TO GERMINATION: 7–10
- WHEN TO SOW OUTDOORS OR SET TRANSPLANTS: When ground is thoroughly warm; roofing paper or black plastic on the soil around each plant will capture desirable heat
- DEPTH OF SEED: ¼"–½"
- DISTANCE BETWEEN PLANTS: 12"–16"
- SOIL CONDITIONS: Rich, moist, loamy; pH 5.5–6.5
- SUNLIGHT REQUIREMENTS: Full sun
- WATERING: Never let soil dry out; mulch to conserve moisture
- SIDEDRESSING: When plants start to blossom
- DAYS TO FIRST HARVEST: 65–75
- HARVESTING TIPS: Start picking eggplants anytime after their skins become glossy—no need to wait until they are fully mature. Mature fruit keep fairly well on the vine, but don't leave them too long or they'll get hard
- VARIETIES: Dusky, Black Beauty, Tycoon, Black Magic, Golden Egg, Easter Egg
- PESTS AND DISEASES: Flea beetles, cutworms, Colorado potato beetles

ENDIVE

Annual

Not to be confused with the compact little European vegetable (see Chicory), this endive is a cool-weather lettuce-like plant, somewhat bitter, that does best when it matures in the fall. There

are curly and broad-leafed varieties, the latter a staple of Italian cooking known as escarole, which is wonderful when steamed and served with a spritz of lemon and drizzle of extra virgin olive oil.

- DEGREE OF DIFFICULTY: Very simple
- TEMPERATURE TOLERANCE: Hardy
- WHEN TO SOW INDOORS: Can be started indoors for spring crop, but performs best when started in the cold frame or direct-seeded for fall crop
- DAYS TO GERMINATION: 10–14
- WHEN TO SOW OUTDOORS OR SET TRANSPLANTS: Direct-seed in mid-summer for fall crop
- DEPTH OF SEED: ½"
- DISTANCE BETWEEN PLANTS: 6"
- SOIL CONDITIONS: Average soil; pH 6.0–7.0
- SUNLIGHT REQUIREMENTS: Full sun
- WATERING: Keep soil moist until germination
- SIDEDRESSING: Not necessary
- DAYS TO FIRST HARVEST: 90
- HARVESTING TIPS: Wait until heads are fully formed before cutting. To reduce natural bitterness, you might try blanching: about a week before harvest, tie the outer leaves together over the head of the plant, or simply slip a bottomless milk carton over each plant. See page 78 for further details
- VARIETIES: Green Curled, Broad Leaved Batavian, Florida Deep Heart
- PESTS AND DISEASES: Occasionally: aphids, slugs, nematodes

GARLIC

Annual

Garlic is the essence of good cooking, and is said to promote good health if not good breath. Instead of seed, garlic is grown by planting cloves that look like the ones in your kitchen but are specially cultivated for seeding. For a dollar's worth of these, you can produce several pounds of the best garlic you've ever eaten. Seed bulbs contain up to 15 cloves, each capable of producing a complete bulb, but only the largest will produce large bulbs, so plant accordingly. Try planting garlic in double, triple or even wider rows to save space.

Garlic thrives in soil fortified with aged manure or compost, so lay it on thick. Generally speaking, garlic plants with the largest and greenest tops also have the biggest bulbs beneath the soil, so be sure to sidedress or topdress several times over the course of the season.

- DEGREE OF DIFFICULTY: Fairly simple
- TEMPERATURE TOLERANCE: Hardy

FOR GARLIC LOVERS

For garlic lovers who fear bad breath: one raw green bean, or one spring of parsley eaten after a garlicky meal will, according to tradition, eliminate all traces of the pungent fumes from your breath.

- WHEN TO SOW INDOORS: Not an indoor starter
- DAYS TO GERMINATION: Not applicable
- WHEN TO SOW OUTDOORS OR SET TRANSPLANTS: Set individual cloves the previous fall or as early in spring as possible
- DEPTH OF SEED: Full depth of clove
- DISTANCE BETWEEN PLANTS: 3"–4"
- SOIL CONDITIONS: Rich, well-worked soil; pH 5.8–6.8 for biggest globes
- SUNLIGHT REQUIREMENTS: Full sun
- WATERING: Moderate but steady supply
- SIDEDRESSING: 2 or 3 times during season for large globes
- DAYS TO FIRST HARVEST: 90–100
- HARVESTING TIPS: When tops fall over and die, pull bulbs and dry in sun for several days; store in clay pots with tight-fitting covers for long-lasting quality
- VARIETIES: Try Elephant Garlic for really large yields
- PESTS AND DISEASES: An insect repellant itself, garlic remains safe from attack

GOURDS

Annual

One of the most colorful things about colorful gourds are the names of the varieties: Dipper, Turban, Birdhouse, Bottle, White Egg, and so forth. Gourds are grown more or less the same as all the cucurbits, but since they are grown for ornamental rather than culinary value, care must be taken to safeguard the fruit from damage; fruit left to mature on the

GROW YOUR OWN BATH SPONGES

Luffa gourds are fast-growing gourds that contain a soft, spongy interior. This interior is commercially available in health food and specialty stores as a bath sponge. For really soft sponges, harvest luffa gourds when still green; but if you like the scrub-cloth quality, wait until the gourd's skin has turned yellow and dry. Then simply pull the skin away, and you will have a sponge.

ground can become misshapen. If you want perfectly shaped gourds, grow them along a fence, spaced a foot apart. The tendrils from the vine will grab hold of the fence and the fruits will be safely suspended as they come to maturity. Generally a shovelful of compost or rotted manure beneath the planting is sufficient fertilizer for the season, but sidedressing when vines start to crawl won't hurt.

- DEGREE OF DIFFICULTY: Moderately difficult
- TEMPERATURE TOLERANCE: Extremely tender
- WHEN TO SOW INDOORS: Not an indoor starter
- DAYS TO GERMINATION: 7–10
- WHEN TO SOW OUTDOORS OR SET TRANSPLANTS: Direct-seed or plant pre-sprouted seeds (see page 38) after all danger of frost is past
- DEPTH OF SEED: 1"–1½"
- DISTANCE BETWEEN PLANTS: 2 plants each in hills 4' apart
- SOIL CONDITIONS: Best in sandy loam, but will perform in all types; pH 5.5–6.8
- SUNLIGHT REQUIREMENTS: Full sun
- WATERING: Steady, moderate supply
- SIDEDRESSING: When vines start to crawl, if desired
- DAYS TO FIRST HARVEST: 140–150
- HARVESTING TIPS: Harvest when stems shrivel, not before or gourds will rot. If frost is expected earlier, cover unripe fruit with plastic. Leave 2" stems on harvested fruit, handling it carefully to avoid nicks and bruises. Allow to cure in dry, warm place for 2 weeks. Dipping cured gourds in alcohol is said to insure their keeping qualities

Notes

_____ *Notes* _____

• VARIETIES: Catalogues offer huge numbers of interestingly named and shaped cultivars
• PESTS AND DISEASES: Striped and spotted cucumber beetles, cutworms, aphids, vine borers, squash bugs; anthracnose, angular leaf spot, bacterial and fusarium wilt disease, powdery and downy mildew, mosaic, scab

HAMBURG PARSLEY

Annual

Like parsnips, these delicately-flavored roots are especially good as soup and stew enhancers, but are also delicious eaten raw, steamed, or sautéed as a side dish. The bright green leaves make wonderful garnish. Culture is very similar to carrots and parsley.

• DEGREE OF DIFFICULTY: Fairly simple
• TEMPERATURE TOLERANCE: Hardy
• WHEN TO SOW INDOORS: Not an indoor starter
• DAYS TO GERMINATION: 21–28
• WHEN TO SOW OUTDOORS OR SET TRANSPLANTS: Early spring or mid-summer for fall crop
• DEPTH OF SEED: ¼″
• DISTANCE BETWEEN PLANTS: 6″
• SOIL CONDITIONS: Light, well-worked, deep soil; pH 5.5–7.0
• SUNLIGHT REQUIREMENTS: Full sun
• WATERING: Water only during dry spells
• SIDEDRESSING: Not necessary
• DAYS TO FIRST HARVEST: 90

• HARVESTING TIPS: Although you can harvest these delicious roots when they are still quite young, they are best left in the ground to sweeten following fall's first frosts. They can be heavily mulched and left in the ground over winter or dug up and stored in boxes of sand or sawdust
• VARIETIES: Record, Hamburg
• PESTS AND DISEASES: Slugs seem to be the only pest

JERUSALEM ARTICHOKE

Perennial

This close relative of the sunflower derives its name not from the Holy City but from its family: *Girasol*. The plant has no relation whatever to the many-leafed globe artichokes, and are valued instead for their below-ground tubers. Jerusalem artichokes are an excellent, nearly starch-free substitute for potatoes, and can also be used in stir-fry meals as a double for water chestnuts or steamed and served with butter and parsley.

Jerusalem artichokes are grown from seed-tubers rather than seed. They grow quite tall—usually 6′–8′—so they should be planted on the north or east sides of the garden where they will not cast shade on smaller plants. Better yet, give them their own bed outside the vegetable patch. Then if they start to spread, which they're prone to do, they won't overwhelm the garden. With their tall graceful stalks and brilliant yellow flowers, Jerusalem artichokes make a lovely border.

- DEGREE OF DIFFICULTY: Extremely simple
- TEMPERATURE TOLERANCE: Hardy perennial
- WHEN TO SOW INDOORS: Not an indoor starter
- DAYS TO GERMINATION: 14 days
- WHEN TO SOW OUTDOORS OR SET TRANSPLANTS: Sow seed-tubers as soon as soil can be worked
- DEPTH OF SEED: 2″
- DISTANCE BETWEEN PLANTS: 12″
- SOIL CONDITIONS: Average soil
- SUNLIGHT REQUIREMENTS: Full sun
- WATERING: Moderate
- SIDEDRESSING: Not necessary
- DAYS TO FIRST HARVEST: 125
- HARVESTING TIPS: Dig up tubers in fall after frost has killed the tops of the plants. If you wish, leave a few tubers in the ground for next year's crop, or you will simply have to plant again come spring
- VARIETIES: Improved Mammoth French, Stampede, Red Jerusalem Artichoke
- PESTS AND DISEASES: Only aphids seem to bother this crop

KALE

Biennial

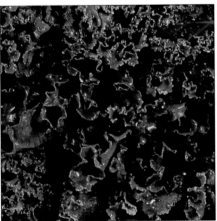

Kale is strictly a cool weather vegetable and must be planted very early for a late harvest in spring or in midsummer for a fall crop. In the South, kale can be planted as late as October

and kept growing right through the winter. Given reasonably fertile soil, a steady supply of moisture and adequate thinning, just a few feet of kale will produce an ample supply of this tangy, nutritious green. Try flowering kale as an ornamental in your flower border.

- DEGREE OF DIFFICULTY: Simple
- TEMPERATURE TOLERANCE: Hardy
- WHEN TO SOW INDOORS: Not an indoor starter
- DAYS TO GERMINATION: 7–10
- WHEN TO SOW OUTDOORS OR SET TRANSPLANTS: Direct-seed in very early spring or in midsummer for a fall crop
- DEPTH OF SEED: ¼″
- DISTANCE BETWEEN PLANTS: 12″–15,″ although some gardeners claim closer spacing (6″) makes for more tender leaves
- SOIL CONDITIONS: Average soil, pH 5.8–7.5
- SUNLIGHT REQUIREMENTS: Full sun
- WATERING: Moderate supply
- SIDEDRESSING: Not necessary
- DAYS TO FIRST HARVEST: 55–65
- HARVESTING TIPS: Center leaves are always more tender than outer leaves and can be picked whenever they're large enough to eat. Whole plants can be harvested at once, and harvest can be extended right through the winter. Being a biennial, kale will resume growth in the spring
- VARIETIES: Siberian Kale, Blue Curled Scotch Kale, Dwarf Blue Curled Vates
- PESTS AND DISEASES: Aphids, flea beetles, cabbage loopers, cabbage worms; club root, black leg, yellows

KOHLRABI

Biennial

The crispy sweet flesh of this enlarged, above-ground, turnip-like tuber is among the most delicious vegetables anywhere. Kohlrabi can be sliced and eaten raw with sour-cream dip, used in Chinese dishes as a water-chestnut substitute, or added to soups. Some people eat it like radishes, smeared with butter and sprinkled with salt.

- DEGREE OF DIFFICULTY: Moderately easy
- TEMPERATURE TOLERANCE: Hardy
- WHEN TO SOW INDOORS: Not usually an indoor starter, but can be started indoors for extremely early transplanting outdoors
- DAYS TO GERMINATION: 10–14
- WHEN TO SOW OUTDOORS OR SET TRANSPLANTS: As early as soil can be worked
- DEPTH OF SEED: ¼″
- DISTANCE BETWEEN PLANTS: 4″–5″
- SOIL CONDITIONS: Fertile, well-worked soil; pH 6.0–7.0
- SUNLIGHT REQUIREMENTS: Full sun
- WATERING: Water frequently
- SIDEDRESSING: Not necessary if soil enriched with compost or other organic matter, but if desired, when stem begins to bulge
- DAYS TO FIRST HARVEST: 50–60
- HARVESTING TIPS: Harvest when 2″–3″ in diameter or plants get woody
- VARIETIES: Early White Vienna, Grand Duke very popular but many other good ones exist
- PESTS AND DISEASES: Sometimes: Japanese beetles

LEEKS

Biennial

It is rumored that Nero always ate leeks before his major orations, which in turn gave rise to the claim that these sweet and succulent stems are excellent for the vocal chords.

Like their onion cousins, leeks can be started indoors quite early—as long as their tops are kept trimmed until transplanting time—or seeded directly in the garden in early spring. Also like onions, leeks do very well in multiple or wide rows. Set transplants or plant seeds outdoors in 4″-deep trenches, covering seeds only with ¼″ of soil. As the plants begin to grow, fill in the trench with soil or, preferably, compost. This process will blanch and sweeten the lower stem—the most highly prized portion of the leek. The green tops, however, are also delicious and can be used as you would scallions.

Try leeks steamed, broiled, braised, or even fried.

- DEGREE OF DIFFICULTY: Requires care for high quality crop
- TEMPERATURE TOLERANCE: Hardy
- WHEN TO SOW INDOORS: 6–8 weeks before last frost
- DAYS TO GERMINATION: 10–14
- WHEN TO SOW OUTDOORS OR SET TRANSPLANTS: 3 weeks before last frost, in 4″ trenches
- DEPTH OF SEED: ¼″
- DISTANCE BETWEEN PLANTS: 2″–3″
- SOIL CONDITIONS: Rich soil; pH 6.0–6.8
- SUNLIGHT REQUIREMENTS: Full sun
- WATERING: Steady, abundant supply; soil can remain moist but not soggy
- SIDEDRESSING: Not necessary if soil rich in organic matter
- DAYS TO FIRST HARVEST: 120
- HARVESTING TIPS: Harvest can be extended into winter if crop heavily mulched
- VARIETIES: Large American Flag (also known as Broad London), Titan
- PESTS AND DISEASES: Generally impervious

LETTUCE

Annual

When I think of the spring garden, I think of salad; and when I think of salad, I envision lettuces. First the loose-leaf lettuces: lovely oak leaf and red leaf and black seeded simpson; then the crisp, ribbed leaves of cos and romaine; the tender buttercrunch; Boston and other loose-heads; and finally the cool, tight crisp-heads like iceberg. As a rule of thumb I counsel beginning gardeners to avoid over-planting, but when it comes to lettuce, I invariably plant far beyond my capacity to consume. I make lettuce salads with all sorts of wonderful dressings and additions; I give huge quantities to friends; I feed it to my chickens; and ultimately I turn batches of it back into the soil.

Lettuce loves cool weather. In fact, when temperatures turn hot, lettuce becomes bitter and then bolts to seed. Plan on an extended spring crop, and then on another for fall.

I like to sow leaf lettuce in wide rows. If you use one, you might try this: mix the contents of several loose-leaf varieties in a single envelope, and then sow as evenly as possible over the entire seedbed. Thin so plants stand about 1″–2″ apart. When the crop starts coming in, you will have every leaf variety represented in that one wide row, and you can just snip what you need for a meal. If you really want a salad-in-one, put a few onion sets in the bed, sprinkle in some radish seeds, a little rocket, and a little spinach. Overcrowding is often the problem in this salad-bed, so thin carefully for success.

Head lettuce requires a bit more attention than leaf varieties, but not much. When seedlings are about 3″–4″ tall, they are ready to be set out, but don't actually transplant them until you've pruned off a couple of the outer leaves. Don't worry about setting back the plant's growth; in fact, by reducing the size of the outer growth in proportion to the roots, you will have contributed to much stronger growth in the long run.

I've always had most success with head lettuce grown on raised beds fortified with lots of compost. The more closely spaced the heads are, the smaller they'll be: for large crisp-head lettuce, plant about 16″ apart; otherwise, space them about 10″ and they'll be the right size to make salad for four. Loose-head types like buttercrunch do nicely 10″–12″ apart, as does cos or romaine.

- DEGREE OF DIFFICULTY: Leaf lettuce and loose-head, quite simple; crisp-head and cos lettuce a little tricky
- TEMPERATURE TOLERANCE: Semi-hardy

VARIETIES OF LETTUCE

Loose-Leaf lettuces: Oak Leaf, Ruby, Red Sails, Black Seeded Simpson, Salad Bowl, Flame

Loose-head lettuces: Buttercrunch, Bibb, Big Boston, Dark Green Boston

Cos or romaine: Parris Island Cos, Paris White Cos, Green Towers

Crisp-head lettuces: Ithaca, Great Lakes, Iceberg, Minetto

- WHEN TO SOW INDOORS: 6 weeks before last frost
- DAYS TO GERMINATION: 10
- WHEN TO SOW OUTDOORS OR SET TRANSPLANTS: Direct-seed in cold frame or special beds such as wide rows; set transplants out after severe frosts are past
- DEPTH OF SEED: ¼″
- DISTANCE BETWEEN PLANTS: Loose-leaf lettuce can be crowded, 1″–2″ apart; head and romaine, 10″–16″ apart
- SOIL CONDITIONS: Rich, loamy, moist; pH 6.0–7.0
- SUNLIGHT REQUIREMENTS: Full sun most of day with a little afternoon shade
- WATERING: Keep well-watered
- SIDEDRESSING: Responds to nitrogen fertilizer
- DAYS TO FIRST HARVEST: 45–90
- HARVESTING TIPS: Leaf lettuce should be sheared to 2″ above ground and allowed to grow back again. If you start early, you should be able to get two complete cuttings from a row before the lettuce turns bitter and bolts to seed. Loose-head types can also be cut in this way, and they'll never actually form heads. Harvest crisp-head types by cutting even with the soil. For cos, you might consider blanching the lovely tapered heads by slipping a bottomless milk carton over the top for 10 days. See page 78 for further details
- VARIETIES: See lists below
- PESTS AND DISEASES: Aphids, cutworms, slugs

MUSTARD

Biennial

Like collards and okra, mustard is thought to be an exclusively southern crop by many new gardeners; but the fact is, this snappy-flavored member of the cabbage family is well-suited to northern growing. Mustard greens are loaded with Vitamin A, C, and all the B group too. They make tangy additions to salad, but can also be steamed lightly and served with lemon.

Mustard seed is extremely small; to make it easier to handle, mix seed with a few teaspoons of sand, and then spread the mixture as evenly as possible in the seedbed. Even then, plants are likely to be crowded when they emerge; thin immediately so that plants are about 4″–6″ apart.

- DEGREE OF DIFFICULTY: Very simple
- TEMPERATURE TOLERANCE: Hardy
- WHEN TO SOW INDOORS: Not an indoor starter
- DAYS TO GERMINATION: 10–14
- WHEN TO SOW OUTDOORS OR SET TRANSPLANTS: 4 weeks before last frost, and/or in late summer for a fall crop
- DEPTH OF SEED: ¼″
- DISTANCE BETWEEN PLANTS: 4″–6″
- SOIL CONDITIONS: Reasonably fertile soil; pH 6.0–6.8
- SUNLIGHT REQUIREMENTS: Full sun
- WATERING: Steady, moderate supply
- SIDEDRESSING: Not necessary if soil contains organic matter
- DAYS TO FIRST HARVEST: 35
- HARVESTING TIPS: Because the flavor of mustard greens is improved by a little

Notes

frost, many gardeners prefer it as a fall crop. Harvest greens whenever there's enough to eat
- VARIETIES: Tendergreen, Green Wave, Fordhook Fancy
- PESTS AND DISEASES: Aphids, flea beetles, cabbage loopers, cabbage worms; club root, black leg, yellows

OKRA

Annual

With its gorgeous hibiscus-like yellow flowers, okra is clearly one of the most beautiful plants in the garden. If you like the flavor of these tender green spineless pods, a few plants will be sufficient, especially if your garden soil is fortified with compost or manure.

Okra seeds are tough and generally need a good 12-hour pre-soak to hasten germination. Some gardeners stick okra seeds in the freezer for a few days before planting, to simulate the end of winter. Poor drainage and sudden temperature changes can create problems for okra at blossom-time, so try planting on raised beds, and then mulch heavily to keep moisture and soil temperature even.

- DEGREE OF DIFFICULTY: Quite simple
- TEMPERATURE TOLERANCE: Tender
- WHEN TO SOW INDOORS: Not usually an indoor starter, but you can try starting in individual containers about a month before the last frost to get an extra early jump on the season

- WHEN TO SOW OUTDOORS OR SET TRANSPLANTS: When ground is warm, and threat of frost past
- DEPTH OF SEED: ½"–1"
- DISTANCE BETWEEN PLANTS: 2' for dwarf varieties; 5' for larger, warm-climate cultivars
- SOIL CONDITIONS: Average, well-drained (try raised beds for improved drainage); pH 6.0–8.0
- SUNLIGHT REQUIREMENTS: Full sun
- WATERING: Moderate
- SIDEDRESSING: Not necessary if soil fairly rich, but if desired, when blossoms first appear
- DAYS TO FIRST HARVEST: 50–60
- HARVESTING TIPS: Unless you've planted a spineless variety (which I recommend), wear gloves and a long-sleeved shirt to avoid skin rashes. Start harvesting when pods are 2" long. Pods of some varieties are meant to be harvested at 6"–8" or more, but I'd pick them younger
- VARIETIES: *Standard:* Clemsen Spineless, Emerald; *Dwarf:* Perkins Spineless, Dwarf Green Long Pod
- PESTS AND DISEASES: Corn earworm, stink bug, imported cabbage worm; southern blight, wilt

ONIONS

Biennial

Besides regular onions, there are bunching onions, which are scallions (also called green onions and spring onions); Egyptian onions, which form little bulbs at the top of their flower spikes, and Welsh onions, fairly uncommon in American gardens. Each has its purpose so choose your varieties accordingly.

If you're planning to grow onions in any quantity, wide, raised beds are best for improved drainage. You have 3 options for starting onions: from "sets"—immature bulbs grown the season before and allowed to remain dormant over winter; from seedlings; and from seed.

Probably the most popular way is from sets. The ideal set size is small, about ¾″ in diameter. Plant sets to their full depth—no more, no less. Since onions so grown are actually in their second year of biennial life, they will want to set seed. To avoid this, watch for a seed stalk that has a Kremlin-dome top to it, and snip it off at the base. The more actively you attend to this chore, the larger your onions will be. This job is unnecessary for onions started from seed or transplants.

For seedlings, start seed indoors 8–10 weeks before setting out in early spring. When seedlings' tops get leggy, cut them back to 2″ or so and by the time they're ready to be planted outdoors, their root systems will be quite vigorous. At transplanting time, soak the seed flats first to allow roots to untangle themselves with the least damage before planting. (Don't worry if they do break: many gardeners prune roots at this stage, especially if tops are quite tall.) To plant, dig shallow trenches about 2″ deep and 5″ apart in your bed, and set in transplants about 1″ deep, fanning out the roots as much as you can before covering with soil. Onions grow best when they are more than half out of the soil, so don't plant too deep.

For direct-seeding, plant seeds ¼″ deep and remember to thin plants to about 4″ apart when they attain some height.

- DEGREE OF DIFFICULTY: Fairly simple, with some attention
- TEMPERATURE TOLERANCE: Hardy; will tolerate hot weather, but at the cost of unusually fiery flavor
- WHEN TO SOW INDOORS: 8–10 weeks before setting out
- DAYS TO GERMINATION: 10
- WHEN TO SOW OUTDOORS OR SET TRANSPLANTS: As soon as soil can be worked
- DEPTH OF SEED: ¼″ for seed; 1″–1½″ for plants; full depth for sets
- DISTANCE BETWEEN PLANTS: 4″
- SOIL CONDITIONS: Rich, well-drained; pH 6.0–6.8

SOWING AND HARVESTING BY THE MOON

The moon moves into a new zodiac sign every few days. A major piece of gardening folklore is the notion that planting and harvesting crops in phase with the moon will have auspicious effects on the outcome. If you doubt this, try a little experiment. Plant a seed when the moon is in its most fruitful stage (Cancer, a water sign) and chart its growth for a few weeks. Then plant the same seed when the moon is in a barren stage (Leo) and compare. Consult the *Farmer's Almanac* for moon stages.

All harvesting of storage crops such as potatoes, onions, turnips, beets, carrots and other root crops should be done when the moon is in one of the dry signs: Aquarius, Aries, Gemini, Leo and Sagittarius. This will aid both in successful gathering and preservation of the crop.

If you pick apples and pears during the third and fourth quarters of the moon, folktales have it that bruised spots will heal over. In the third quarter, dig potatoes, onions and sweet potatoes for storing. The sweet potatoes especially will cure much better and last longer in storage if dug during this period.

- SUNLIGHT REQUIREMENTS: Full sun
- WATERING: Keep seedlings well-watered after transplanting; thereafter, a steady, heavy supply for large bulbs
- SIDEDRESSING: Topdress with compost every couple of weeks, and water with compost tea every week. Don't attempt to revive fallen tops with additional fertilizer, as this may create bulbs which do badly in storage
- DAYS TO FIRST HARVEST: 30–120
- HARVESTING TIPS: If winter storage is your goal, make certain you have chosen a variety well-suited to it. Harvest storage bulbs about a week after tops have fallen over and died—preferably on a warm and sunny day, so they can first dry in the sun. When the wiry rootlets snap off easily, the onions are ready for curing.

Spread them out in a dry, airy place, such as a screened-in porch and turn the bulbs every few days for uniform drying. Some gardeners claim that cutting off the tops and drying the bulbs upside down on a slightly elevated 1″ mesh chicken-wire screen will produce cured onions that never rot in storage. Whatever your method, after curing, bag the onions in mesh sacks, and hang them in a cool place for the winter

- VARIETIES: *Sweet onions:* Spanish Yellow Hybrid, Sweet Spanish, Bermuda; *Bunching onions:* Evergreen Long White Bunching, Long White Tokyo, White Lisbon Regular; *Storage onions:* Spartan Sleeper, Yellow Globe Hybrid, Elite, Autumn Spice; *Southern favorites:* Granex, Excel, Crystal Wax, Texas Early Grano
- PESTS AND DISEASES: Thrips, onion maggot; neck rot, pink root, mildew, bottom rot
- SPECIAL NOTES: Start onions as soon as you can get them into the garden, and in just a few short weeks you'll be rewarded with the first bounty from your vegetable patch

---

PARSNIPS

Annual

Parsnips get my vote as the most underrated vegetable in America. I hardly ever see them in home gardens. The problem, I think, is that seed germination takes 3–4 weeks, and beginning gardeners find that very threatening—as if they're doing something wrong when the seeds don't come up. As for other slow-germinators, cover parsnip seed with a soil-less medium rather than soil to help prevent suffocating crusting-over. Interplant with quick-sprouting radish seed to remember where the row is, and keep seedbed moist.

- DEGREE OF DIFFICULTY: After germination, easy
- TEMPERATURE TOLERANCE: Hardy
- WHEN TO SOW INDOORS: Not indoor starters
- DAYS TO GERMINATION: 21–28
- WHEN TO SOW OUTDOORS OR SET TRANSPLANTS: As soon as soil can be worked
- DEPTH OF SEED: ¼″
- DISTANCE BETWEEN PLANTS: 2″–3″
- SOIL CONDITIONS: Well-worked, well-drained; pH 6.0–6.8; try raised beds to effect good drainage, and don't add fresh manure to soil
- SUNLIGHT REQUIREMENTS: Full sun
- WATERING: Moderate supply
- SIDEDRESSING: Not necessary
- DAYS TO FIRST HARVEST: 105–120
- HARVESTING TIPS: Wait until after a solid frost, as parsnips are at their sweetest then. With heavy mulch, parsnips can be overwintered in the ground. Don't eat roots that have started to sprout again in the spring
- VARIETIES: Hollow Crown, All America, Harris' Model
- PESTS AND DISEASES: None

PEANUTS

Annual

Peanuts require almost 5 full months of frost-free growing season to produce a high quality crop, which is why they do so well in southern states. The Spanish variety can take cooler temperatures and is the choice for northern gardens. Order any peanuts only from dealers who will guarantee their quality.

Peanuts thrive in slightly acidic, sandy soil that contains lots of organic matter. A peanut "seed" consists of a hull filled with two kernels. Thin-hulled varieties can be planted unshelled, but thicker varieties should be shelled and the kernels planted individually. Plant seed 1″–2″ deep in the north, about 4″ down in hotter climates. For creeping varieties, make rows at least 3′ apart; erect cultivars demand less space overall.

Within several weeks, the young peanut plant will produce blossoms from whose centers long fruiting pegs soon form. This causes the flowers to arch toward the ground where the pegs take root. Then, beneath the soil surrounding the plant's roots, a shell containing several nuts forms from each peg. Remember that the looser the soil around the plant, the more easily the pegs can penetrate it and form a crop. As the plant approaches maturity, gather 2″–3″ of soil up around the stem to give growing peanuts more room. Creeping varieties do not have to be hilled. Be on guard for weeds and maintain a loose soil.

- DEGREE OF DIFFICULTY: Fairly easy, but can get tricky
- TEMPERATURE TOLERANCE: Tender

- WHEN TO SOW INDOORS: Not an indoor starter
- DAYS TO GERMINATION: 14
- WHEN TO SOW OUTDOORS OR SET TRANSPLANTS: After last frost
- DEPTH OF SEED: 1½″–2″
- DISTANCE BETWEEN PLANTS: 6″–8″
- SOIL CONDITIONS: Loose, well-drained; pH 5.0–6.0
- SUNLIGHT REQUIREMENTS: Full sun
- WATERING: Steady, moderate supply
- SIDEDRESSING: Unnecessary
- DAYS TO FIRST HARVEST: 110–150
- HARVESTING TIPS: Dig entire plants with a spading fork and hang to dry in a dry, airy place. Roast nuts in a 300 degree oven for 20 minutes
- VARIETIES: Spanish, Tennessee Red Valencia, Early Bunch Virginia, Jumbo Virginia
- PESTS AND DISEASES: None

PEAS

Annual

For me, peas are the sweetest vegetable in the garden: Sweet to watch grow, and sweet to eat. They were the very first vegetable I ever grew, and are the first seeds I plant in spring.

I still prefer the single-row method, but must admit that sowing wide rows is the most efficient way to get lots of peas without using up enormous garden space. And it's simple: prepare a block of ground, say 2′–3′ by 10′, broadcast the seeds, firm them in place with the back of a hoe, and then rake soil over them. To do it my way, make shallow drills across the narrow dimension of the seedbed, drop in seeds about 3″ apart, cover with soil or compost, and firm in place.

There are three types of peas available for the home gardener: English or garden peas; the edible-podded peas familiar in oriental cuisine; and the newer snap peas, whose crisp edible pods can be snapped open like green beans. Perhaps sweetest of all, snap peas also outproduce other types.

English peas are available in dwarf or bush types, which grow to 24″, and standard or telephone varieties which grow as tall as 6′. Telephone peas must be supported or they will fall onto themselves, blocking the sun and reducing production. Dwarf varieties planted in double, triple or wider rows will generally support themselves but I always set a few tree prunings or other stakes into my rows for support. It's not essential but can increase production.

Edible-podded peas are available in bush and climbing varieties, and snap peas are available in bush varieties.

SUPPORT FOR CLIMBING PEAS

When it comes to providing support for peas, you've got several choices. If you have access to brush or tree prunings, this is simplest—particularly birch or apple because they have so many side branches. After the lowest twigs have been snapped off, sink the branch's main stem 6″ into the ground among your newly planted peas. As the peas grow, they form tendrils which will grab hold of it and keep themselves erect.

You can also create a reusable support by positioning two 1″ by 2″ sticks to form an upside-down V over an entire row, and stretching chicken wire across them. These can be used season after season.

Finally, you can just run strings or wires between sticks at various intervals along the length of your row, and train the plants to the first level. Thereafter they'll climb fine by themselves.

For a continuous supply of peas, plant several varieties with different maturity dates. Although peas do best in cool weather, allowing for both a spring and fall crop, several varieties can also handle the heat of midsummer.

- DEGREE OF DIFFICULTY: Simple
- TEMPERATURE TOLERANCE: Hardy
- WHEN TO SOW INDOORS: Not an indoor starter
- DAYS TO GERMINATION: 10–14
- WHEN TO SOW OUTDOORS OR SET TRANSPLANTS: As soon as soil can be worked
- DEPTH OF SEED: 1″
- DISTANCE BETWEEN PLANTS: 2″–3″
- SOIL CONDITIONS: Well-worked; pH 6.0–7.5
- SUNLIGHT REQUIREMENTS: Full sun
- WATERING: Moderate steady supply
- SIDEDRESSING: Not necessary
- DAYS TO FIRST HARVEST: 60–75
- HARVESTING TIPS: English peas are ready for harvest when the pods become plump. Try a few as soon as they look ready; better to err on the side of earliness. Snap peas are also harvested when pods are plump, but they'll hold quality much longer. Edible-podded peas must be harvested before the seeds start to form, or pods will become too fibrous to enjoy. Once peas start coming in, they should be harvested every day
- VARIETIES: *English Peas:* Little Marvel, Frosty, Wando, Maestro, Novella, Alderman, Freezonian, Progress No. 9; *Edible-podded peas:* Snowbird, Oregon Sugar Pod, Dwarf Gray Sugar; *Snap peas:* Sugar Snap, Sugar Daddy, Sugar Bon, Sugar Mel
- PESTS AND DISEASES: Occasionally, red spider mites

Notes

_____ *Notes* _____

PEPPERS

Annual

Peppers are related to
tomatoes and eggplants,
but in certain ways are
more temperamental than
either of their nightshade
cousins, beginning right
at the germinating stage.
For one thing, if soil
temperature isn't at least 70°F, seeds can
remain ungerminated for so long that they'll
actually rot. So if you start seedlings
indoors, which is recommended, be sure to
start them in a warm place. Once up,
pepper seedlings require excellent air
circulation and balanced liquid feedings or
they will soon show signs of nutrient
deficiency. For best results, transplant
seedlings at least once to larger containers,
and harden them off when they reach 6″–7″.

Set plants out in the garden after all
danger of frost is past, and when evening
temperatures are consistently in the 60's:
peppers won't set blossoms below 60°F, and
will suffer if nighttime temperatures rise
above 70°F—a very narrow and often
unforgiving temperature range.

As blossoms begin to appear, sidedress
the plants with bone meal. Avoid a
nitrogen fertilizer at this time, or you may
wind up with a plant resplendent in foliage
but void of blossoms. Then, with a run of
cool, humid evenings in the 60's, and warm
humid days, you should get a wonderful
crop of peppers.

- DEGREE OF DIFFICULTY: Sometimes
  tricky to get a good crop
- TEMPERATURE TOLERANCE: Tender
- WHEN TO SOW INDOORS: 6–8 weeks
  before last frost

- DAYS TO GERMINATION: 14–21 at 70°F;
  fewer at 80°F; possibility of seed rotting
  at 60°F
- WHEN TO SOW OUTDOORS OR SET
  TRANSPLANTS: After danger of frost,
  about 2″ deeper than they were in their
  last container, and protected with a
  cutworm collar
- DEPTH OF SEED: ¼″
- DISTANCE BETWEEN PLANTS: 12″–18″.
  There is considerable controversy over
  this: some gardeners recommend 10–12″
  spacing and others 18″–24″. I've had luck
  both ways. Experiment
- SOIL CONDITIONS: Rich, well-drained;
  pH 5.5–6.8
- SUNLIGHT REQUIREMENTS: Full sun
- WATERING: Steady, moderate
- SIDEDRESSING: Just when plants start to
  blossom. Try a spritz of epsom salts
  directly on the foliage (1 tablespoon
  dissolved in a quart of warm water) to
  supply needed magnesium at blossom-
  time
- DAYS TO FIRST HARVEST: 65–75
- HARVESTING TIPS: Harvest sweet bell
  peppers when they are glossy-skinned and
  thick-walled. With the exception of
  certain yellow cultivars, all peppers will
  turn red if allowed to remain on the plant
  long enough. Then pick them
  immediately, or they'll get soft
- VARIETIES: *Sweet Peppers:* Cal Wonder,
  Big Bertha, Whopper, Yolo Wonder,
  Gedeon Hybrid, Tasty, Early Prolific,
  Gypsy, Purple Belle, Sweet Banana, Sweet
  Cherry; *Hot Peppers:* Hungarian Wax,
  Long Cayenne, Hot Cherry, Jalapeno,
  Anaheim
- PESTS AND DISEASES: Cutworms, slugs,
  flea beetles, aphids, corn borer, leaf
  hoppers; blossom-end rot, mosaic,
  anthracnose

POTATOES

Annual

The potato is native to the tropical highlands of Central and South America, where they grow in scores of varieties and colors.

The critical thing to remember about potatoes, which mature underground, is that they perform very poorly in a too-alkaline soil. Don't plant them where you've limed, thrown wood ashes, or spread fresh animal manures recently or they will develop an unsightly scabby surface that may also affect their food quality. Scab organisms can't survive in soil with a pH below 6.5. To reduce the alkalinity of your potato patch one unit of pH, add garden sulfur at the rate of ½ lb. per 100 sq. ft. of fairly light soil, or 2 lbs. for heavy soil. Other sulfur compounds are available at garden stores. Follow directions for application.

Most people start their crop from seed potatoes—grown especially for seeding and

GARDEN SULPHUR

It is said that if you sprinkle sulphur powder, available at garden stores, on pieces of potato seed, you'll never be bothered by potato beetles and other chewing insects. Sulphur will also reduce the soil pH if worked into the planting holes of acid-loving plants such as potatoes, peppers and eggplant.

GROWING POTATOES UNDER MULCH

Digging trenches for potato-planting, and then digging mature tubers at the end of the season can be hard work. Planting beneath a layer of straw mulch, popularized some years ago by Ruth Stout in *How To Have a Green Thumb Without a Broken Back,* offers an alternative.

Prepare a wide-row seedbed as you would for any other crop, and then space your seed pieces 12″ apart right on top of the soil. Cover with a thick layer of seed-free mulch such as oat straw. The tops will grow right up through the mulch, and the potatoes will form just beneath it. When you want to harvest, just lift the mulch.

certified to be disease-free. You can plant small seed potatoes whole; larger ones should be cut into sections containing at least two good buds or "eyes" each. Convention says cut pieces should "heal over" for a few days and form what is known as a "paraderm" before planting, but I've had excellent stands of potatoes without waiting for this. To plant, space seed-pieces 12″ apart in trenches 4″ deep; place a handful of compost between each, and fill in the trenches.

When the first leaves unfold above the surface, mound the plant over with soil. This process, called "hilling," gives the potatoes room to grow large and blocks out sunlight, which turns them green and poisonous (see page 108). As the plants develop, they will start to blossom (although some early varieties never do), signifying the presence of tubers beneath the soil. This is when you can actually start a limited harvest. See Harvesting Tips below.

One final note: Some years ago, a few catalogues began offering potato seed that could be started indoors and set out after danger of frost. I tried a variety called Explorer, with mixed results: the potatoes were strangely shaped and varied widely in size, but tasted quite good. Some catalogues have dropped them until uniformity is improved.

- DEGREE OF DIFFICULTY: Fairly easy
- TEMPERATURE TOLERANCE: Tender
- WHEN TO SOW INDOORS: Not an indoor starter, though you can pre-sprout seed potatoes by keeping them in a dark place for a couple of weeks before planting
- DAYS TO GERMINATION: 14
- WHEN TO SOW OUTDOORS OR SET TRANSPLANTS: Early to mid-spring
- DEPTH OF SEED: 4″
- DISTANCE BETWEEN PLANTS: 12″
- SOIL CONDITIONS: Light, well-worked, well-drained; pH 4.5–6.5
- SUNLIGHT REQUIREMENTS: Full sun
- WATERING TIPS: Moderate but steady supply, especially when tubers begin to form about 6 weeks after planting
- SIDEDRESSING: Unnecessary
- DAYS TO FIRST HARVEST: 60–100
- HARVESTING TIPS: You can harvest a few "new" potatoes during the growing period. Feel gently under the soil near the base of the plant and snap off the largest potato. Then, move to the next plant in the row until you have enough for a meal. For a late crop, wait until vines die back
- VARIETIES: *Early Potatoes:* Cherokee, Early Gem, Irish Cobbler, Red Lasoda, Norland; *Mid-season:* Chippewa, Superior, White Rose; *Late:* Kennebec, Red Pontiac, Russet Burbank, Sebago
- PESTS AND DISEASES: Colorado potato beetle, flea beetle, leafhopper, aphids; early and late blight, scab

PUMPKINS

Annual

If you have the space, I urge you to grow a hill of large-sized pumpkins. If you don't, try one of the newer bush varieties. There's no trick to growing pumpkins; they grow in almost the same way as winter squash and large pumpkins actually are just orange-colored winter

GROWING A HUNDRED-POUND PUMPKIN

If you want to grow a really huge pumpkin, something in the 70″-around range and weighing 100 pounds or more, you've got to supply lots of space, nutrients, water and attention. Here's the trick. Plant 3 seeds of a giant variety (e.g., *Big Max*) in a hill into which you've dug in several shovelfuls of compost or manure. When they sprout, keep only the best-looking plant of the three. When the young fruits reach softball size, leave the handsomest one on the vine and snip off all the others. Keep feeding the vine with compost and water every day. Derek Fell, in his book *Vegetables,* reports that you can even set up a sort of intravenous milk-supply through the vine stem to fatten pumpkins in their final weeks. Harvest when frost has killed vine.

STUFFED PUMPKIN RECIPE

Here's a unique Thanksgiving dish for vegetarians. Hollow out a pumpkin as if you were making a jack-o'-lantern, and stuff it with a savory whole grain and herb mixture. Replace the lid, and bake at medium heat until the pumpkin flesh is tender. Carve at the table as a festive main entree. A dessert alternative is to stuff the pumpkin with tart cored apples, raisins, nutmeg, cinnamon and allspice, and bake until tender.

squash. Give pumpkins a good shovelful of compost, a steady supply of moisture, and protection against insect attack, and they'll produce plenty.

- DEGREE OF DIFFICULTY: Requires rich soil and considerable tending
- TEMPERATURE TOLERANCE: Tender
- WHEN TO SOW INDOORS: Not an indoor starter, though you can pre-sprout seeds for a jump on the season (see page 38)
- DAYS TO GERMINATION: 10
- WHEN TO SOW OUTDOORS OR SET TRANSPLANTS: After all danger of frost
- DEPTH OF SEED: 1″–1 ½″
- DISTANCE BETWEEN PLANTS: Plant 3–4 seeds each in hills 6′–8′ apart, 10′ for larger varieties like *Big Max*
- SOIL CONDITIONS: Rich, moist, deep; pH 6.0–6.8
- SUNLIGHT REQUIREMENTS: Full sun
- WATERING: Pumpkins will enlarge with water intake and drink in as much as you can supply; if you want large pumpkins, water every day
- SIDEDRESSING: Frequent topdressings of manure or compost, followed by a deep watering
- DAYS TO FIRST HARVEST: 95–120
- HARVESTING TIPS: Harvest after frost has killed vines
- VARIETIES: Big Max, Howden Field, Jack-o-Lantern, Cinderella (bush variety), Triple Threat (hull-less seeds)
- PESTS AND DISEASES: Flea beetles, striped cucumber beetles, squash vine borers, corn earworms; powdery and downy mildews, bacterial wilt, mosaic

RADISH

Annual

Radishes are truly amazing. They come round, oblong and cylindrical; they're red, white, red and white, orange, and black. Small summer varieties mature in as little as 22 days  while others, known as winter radish, take 120 days, can weigh up to 5 pounds, and are best seeded in late spring for a fall crop.

Radishes are wonderful companion plants and can be seeded with literally every garden vegetable for mutual profitability. Make new plantings every 2 weeks for a steady supply throughout the season. Moist, fertile ground will spur them into quick growth without woodiness, but radishes will do fairly well anywhere in the garden.

- DEGREE OF DIFFICULTY: The easiest plant in the garden
- TEMPERATURE TOLERANCE: Hardy
- WHEN TO SOW INDOORS: Not an indoor starter
- DAYS TO GERMINATION: 5–10
- WHEN TO SOW OUTDOORS OR SET TRANSPLANTS: As soon as soil can be worked
- DEPTH OF SEED: ¼″
- DISTANCE BETWEEN PLANTS: 1″
- SOIL CONDITIONS: Best in light, well-drained soil, but will produce in average soil; pH 6.0–7.0
- SUNLIGHT REQUIREMENTS: Will tolerate some shade
- WATERING: Moderate
- SIDEDRESSING: Not necessary
- DAYS TO FIRST HARVEST: 25–35

- HARVESTING TIPS: Don't be afraid to take them at marble-size; bigness doesn't necessarily mean better and radishes get much tarter and woodier with age
- VARIETIES: Cherry Belle, Champion, Crystal White, Round Black, Icicle, Sukurajima
- PESTS AND DISEASES: Leaf hoppers, flea beetles

RHUBARB

Perennial

Rhubarb is a hardy perennial that will live for many years in even the coldest climates. Its chief appeal is its thick succulent stems which, when stewed and mixed with fresh strawberries, make the most wonderful pie. Rhubarb leaves are poisonous to livestock and humans alike, so put your little patch in a sunny spot outside the garden proper where even the most agile or mischievous child, chicken, or goat can't get to it. And remember, it's going to be there a long time, so choose carefully.

It is easiest to start rhubarb from root cuttings, which you can order through catalogues or get from a neighbor; but you can grow it almost as easily from seed. Just a few plants will provide more than enough for your family and friends.

In the spring, dig holes 8″ deep and about 3′ apart. Shovel in some compost or old manure, and then set in the root cutting or seed, and cover with 1″ of soil.

Sidedress during the first season, but don't harvest any stems. Make a limited harvest the following spring—no more than 1–2 weeks; but in the third year, you can pull stalks all season long.

- DEGREE OF DIFFICULTY: Very simple
- TEMPERATURE TOLERANCE: Hardy perennial
- WHEN TO SOW INDOORS: Not an indoor starter
- DAYS TO GERMINATION: 14–21
- WHEN TO SOW OUTDOORS OR SET TRANSPLANTS: Set cuttings or direct-seed in early spring
- DEPTH OF SEED: 1″
- DISTANCE BETWEEN PLANTS: 36″
- SOIL CONDITIONS: Rich, well-worked; pH 6.0–7.0
- SUNLIGHT REQUIREMENTS: Full sun
- WATERING: Keep young plants well-watered, particularly those started from seed
- SIDEDRESSING: Fertilize during initial planting; sidedress once or twice in first season; generally unnecessary thereafter in rich soil
- DAYS TO FIRST HARVEST: 2 years to limited harvest; full harvest following year
- HARVESTING TIPS: The more you harvest, the more the plant will produce. Grasp stems at base and pull off; don't cut stems or you will risk damaging the crown. Remove seed pods as they form, so roots will continue sending up tender new stalks all season long
- VARIETIES: Valentine is red-stalked; Victoria has green stalks with red tints
- PESTS AND DISEASES: Flea beetles, Japanese beetles, rhubarb curculio (snout beetle)
- SPECIAL NOTES: Remember to give rhubarb its own sunny spot somewhere outside, but near, the garden. Once plants are mature, you can dig up root sections and force them indoors during winter. They'll produce tight little rhubarb shoots with no leaves

Notes

_____ *Notes* _____

ROCKET

Annual

Rocket has many aliases: Roquette, Rucola, Rugula, Rocket Salad, Arrugula, and Garden Rocket are some of the names under which you will find this tangy-leaved cousin of mustard listed in seed catalogues.

Like most greens, rocket thrives in cool weather, so you will be able to grow both a spring and fall crop. If rocket isn't provided with conditions for speedy growth—rich soil, steady water supply, cool weather—the brilliant green leaves may become too tart for even the most ardent aficionado. Rocket is best eaten raw in salads, but can be steamed as you would spinach or escarole.

- DEGREE OF DIFFICULTY: Fairly simple
- TEMPERATURE TOLERANCE: Hardy
- WHEN TO SOW INDOORS: Not an indoor starter
- DAYS TO GERMINATION: 14
- WHEN TO SOW OUTDOORS OR SET TRANSPLANTS: As early in spring as possible, and again in late summer
- DEPTH OF SEED: ½″
- DISTANCE BETWEEN PLANTS: 6″–8″
- SOIL CONDITIONS: Loose, rich, moist; pH 6.0–7.0
- SUNLIGHT REQUIREMENTS: Full sun
- WATERING: Steady supply
- SIDEDRESSING: Not necessary
- DAYS TO FIRST HARVEST: 30–45
- HARVESTING TIPS: Begin harvest whenever there are enough leaves to eat. Pull up plants as summer approaches to prevent unwanted self-seeding
- VARIETIES: See above for aliases

- PESTS AND DISEASES: Aphids, flea beetles, cabbage loopers, cabbage worms; club root, black leg, yellows

RUTABAGAS

Biennial

Rutabagas have many aliases, including Swedish Turnip, Table Turnip, Mangel-Wurzel, Macomber, or Turnip-rooted cabbage. They are closely related to turnips, and, like turnips, are grown both for greens and round tangy-flavored roots. Turnip roots are white; rutabagas are orange.

Rutabagas don't do well in hot weather, so most gardeners direct-seed in mid-to-late summer for a fall crop. One of the nice things about these orange roots is that they do not become woody if left in the ground beyond maturity. This doesn't mean, however, you should wait until they are fully mature to eat them. In fact, you can start digging the roots when they're quite small—say, 2″ across.

- DEGREE OF DIFFICULTY: Simple
- TEMPERATURE TOLERANCE: Not good in hot weather
- WHEN TO SOW INDOORS: Not an indoor starter
- DAYS TO GERMINATION: 14
- WHEN TO SOW OUTDOORS OR SET TRANSPLANTS: Direct-seed in midsummer; good as crop to follow spinach

- DEPTH OF SEED: ½"
- DISTANCE BETWEEN PLANTS: 6"–8"
- SOIL CONDITIONS: Loose, well-drained; pH 5.5–7.0
- SUNLIGHT REQUIREMENTS: Full sun
- WATERING: Steady moderate supply
- SIDEDRESSING: Not necessary
- DAYS TO FIRST HARVEST: 45–90
- HARVESTING TIPS: Harvest greens whenever you prefer; dig roots starting when they reach 2" in diameter. Rutabagas can be waxed and stored in a cool location for many months
- VARIETIES: American Purple Top
- PESTS AND DISEASES: Aphids, flea beetles, cabbage loopers, cabbage worms; club root, black leg, yellows
- SPECIAL NOTES: As germination time varies with size of seed, try to find "sized" seed whenever possible

SALSIFY

Annual

Salsify, also known as oyster plant, grows like any other root crop, which is to say it needs well-worked deep soil to form even roots, and does quite nicely in wide rows. Salsify has a unique flavor (that some have clearly likened to oysters), and is delicious when sautéed in butter and garlic and sprinkled with fresh parsley.

- DEGREE OF DIFFICULTY: Sometimes tricky to get straight roots
- TEMPERATURE TOLERANCE: Hardy

- WHEN TO SOW INDOORS: Not an indoor starter
- DAYS TO GERMINATION: 14–21
- WHEN TO SOW OUTDOORS OR SET TRANSPLANTS: Early spring
- DEPTH OF SEED: ½"
- DISTANCE BETWEEN PLANTS: 4"
- SOIL CONDITIONS: Extremely loose, preferably sandy, free of stones, coarse material, and clumps; pH 7.0–7.5
- SUNLIGHT REQUIREMENTS: Full sun
- WATERING: Keep young seedlings well-watered
- SIDEDRESSING: Unnecessary
- DAYS TO FIRST HARVEST: 120–150
- HARVESTING TIPS: Wait until after a few frosts to harvest these delicate roots. Salsify can remain in the ground under heavy mulch and be harvested right through a severe winter. Some gardeners feel salsify is at its best when dug right after the ground thaws in spring. I like it best in late fall
- VARIETIES: Mammoth Sandwich Island
- PESTS AND DISEASES: Generally none

SHALLOTS

Annual

No really serious cook is ever without shallots, and no garden should be without them either. A pound of certified seed-shallots is fairly expensive, but because they deliver a seven-to-one return, enough to supply all your winter needs and seed for next year, it's really a one-time investment.

Shallots are cultivated much the way garlic is, and do best started very early in the season in nutrient-rich, well-worked soil. And like garlic, shallots also can be planted in wide rows for efficiency.

- DEGREE OF DIFFICULTY: Quite simple
- TEMPERATURE TOLERANCE: Hardy
- WHEN TO SOW INDOORS: Not an indoor starter
- DAYS TO GERMINATION: 7
- WHEN TO SOW OUTDOORS OR SET TRANSPLANTS: Plant cloves as soon as soil can be worked
- DEPTH OF SEED: Full depth of clove
- DISTANCE BETWEEN PLANTS: 4"–6"
- SOIL CONDITIONS: Loose, rich soil for largest bulbs; pH 5.8–6.8
- SUNLIGHT REQUIREMENTS: Full sun
- WATERING: Moderate
- SIDEDRESSING: Not necessary if soil is reasonably fertile
- DAYS TO FIRST HARVEST: 120
- HARVESTING TIPS: Shallot greens can be harvested during the season and used as you would chives or scallions, but be sure not to destroy the center shoot. When the tops die and fall over, pull up shallots and let them cure in a warm, dry place for a week or so. Then they can be stored in mesh bags for several months in a cool location where temperatures never drop below freezing
- VARIETIES: Usually listed merely as shallots; check Le Jardin du Gourmet catalogue for exceptional cultivars
- PESTS AND DISEASES: Rarely bothered by pests, but when they are, thrips and onion maggots are likely culprits

SHUNGIKU

Annual

The pungent flavor of this delicious green is hard to describe, but its aroma is unmistakably oriental. As a side-dish, these greens, known also as chop suey greens, or edible chrysanthemums, can be steamed as you would spinach. Like spinach, Shungiku thrives in cool weather, but unlike spinach, it manages lush growth even in average soil. Shungiku is also called Crown Daisy, and can be grown as a border flower.

- DEGREE OF DIFFICULTY: Extremely easy
- TEMPERATURE TOLERANCE: Hardy
- WHEN TO SOW INDOORS: Not an indoor starter
- DAYS TO GERMINATION: 10–14
- WHEN TO SOW OUTDOORS OR SET TRANSPLANTS: Direct-seed in early spring and then again in midsummer for a fall crop
- DEPTH OF SEED: ¼"
- DISTANCE BETWEEN PLANTS: 4"
- SOIL CONDITIONS: Average, well-drained soil
- SUNLIGHT REQUIREMENTS: Full sun
- WATERING: Moderate, steady supply
- SIDEDRESSING: Usually unnecessary unless soil very poor
- DAYS TO FIRST HARVEST: 45
- HARVESTING TIPS: Individual leaves can be plucked or entire plants can be cut just above ground level. It will sprout again if roots are undamaged
- VARIETIES: Generally available under its generic name
- PESTS AND DISEASES: Aphids, leaf miners; powdery mildew

SOYBEANS

Annual

Soybeans represent one of the largest cash crops in the United States, and yet only the rare home gardener attempts this highly nutritious vegetable, primarily because we don't know how to prepare it. They can be roasted and salted for snacks, and the seeds can be sprouted for salads or just munching. The pods are so tight they must be boiled 15 minutes before they'll release their contents, but then they can be eaten by holding the boiled pod between thumb and forefinger and shooting the beans right into your mouth.

Soybeans are easier to grow than other beans because they actually do well even in poor soil. They require a longer season than snap beans, but are certainly well within the frost-free range of most northern gardens. Soybeans are cultivated like shell beans, and harvested when pods are about 8" long (longer in some varieties).

- DEGREE OF DIFFICULTY: Simple
- TEMPERATURE TOLERANCE: Tender
- WHEN TO SOW INDOORS: Not an indoor starter
- DAYS TO GERMINATION: 7–10
- WHEN TO SOW OUTDOORS OR SET TRANSPLANTS: Sow after all danger of frost
- DEPTH OF SEED: 1"
- DISTANCE BETWEEN PLANTS: 4" in rows (single or double) 2' apart
- SOIL CONDITIONS: Average, even poor, soil will do, but enriched with organic matter is preferred; pH 6.0–7.0
- SUNLIGHT REQUIREMENTS: Full sun
- WATERING: Moderate, steady supply
- SIDEDRESSING: Unnecessary
- DAYS TO FIRST HARVEST: 75–90
- HARVESTING TIPS: Harvest as you would shell beans, when pods are nice and plump
- VARIETIES: Fiskby V, Prize, Frostbeater, Butterpea, Kanrich
- PESTS AND DISEASES: Bean leaf beetle, Mexican bean beetle, root-knot nematodes; anthracnose, bacterial wilt, mosaic, rust

SPINACH

Annual

Spinach is a fast-growing green that does best in rich soil and the cool temperatures of early spring. The main problem with growing spinach is that it reduces to such small amounts when cooked, you need to plant a sizable crop just to get more than a few meals' worth. This is offset by the speed with which spinach grows. Even if you've given over a big patch to spinach, when its season finishes in early summer is just the right time for a new planting of beans. So pull up the spinach, do a fast re-make of the

seedbed, and raise yourself a good batch of late-season beans. Then you can flip the coin when cool weather approaches in late summer and sow a new spinach crop in a spot vacated by something else.

Another advantage if space is a problem is that spinach is perfect for wide-row planting. You get more food per square foot of garden, and a lush-growing carpet of plants that keeps the soil cool and forestalls hot-weather bolting. Seed in drills along the narrow width of the wide row, and cover with only ¼″ of soil. Firm in place with the back of a hoe. When the seedlings emerge, thin them to stand 4″–6″ apart.

- DEGREE OF DIFFICULTY: Fairly simple with rich soil
- TEMPERATURE TOLERANCE: Hardy
- WHEN TO SOW INDOORS: Not an indoor starter
- DAYS TO GERMINATION: 10–14
- WHEN TO SOW OUTDOORS OR SET TRANSPLANTS: As soon as the soil can be worked in spring, and again in late summer for a fall crop; seed will not germinate well in soil temperatures much above 70°F, so keep seedbed moist and cool as possible

- DEPTH OF SEED: ¼″
- DISTANCE BETWEEN PLANTS: 3″–6″
- SOIL CONDITIONS: Rich loam; pH 6.0–7.5. The richer the soil the faster spinach will grow and the more tender it will be
- SUNLIGHT REQUIREMENTS: Full sun
- WATERING: Moderate, steady supply
- SIDEDRESSING: Generally unnecessary if soil is rich
- DAYS TO FIRST HARVEST: 30–50
- HARVESTING TIPS: Cut entire plant to within 2″ of the ground, as with leaf lettuce, and plants will grow back for a second cutting
- VARIETIES: Melody, Summer Savory, Bloomsdale Long Standing, Winter Bloomsdale
- PESTS AND DISEASES: Downy mildew sometimes

SUMMER SQUASH

Annual

There are several types of summer squash including green zucchini, crookneck, and yellow-colored versions. All are soft-skinned annuals native to Central and South America. Summer squash are among the easiest of all garden vegetables to grow, and perhaps the most prolific on a pound-for-pound basis. In fact, many beginning gardeners seriously overplant and are stuck with more zucchini and yellow squash than they know what to

SPINACH SUBSTITUTES WHEN THE WEATHER GETS HOT

Because spinach bolts when the weather gets warm, there's usually a gap in mid-to-late summer when this delicious green is not available. Three substitutes, however, whose flavor is mild and comparable to spinach, have found their way into the hearts of spinach-loving gardeners. They are New Zealand Spinach, which can be started indoors and then transferred to the garden after danger of frost; Tampala Spinach, a relative of amaranth, and another good candidate for an indoor start; and Malabar Spinach, a vining plant sensitive to frost, that produces delicious green leaves and grows well on fences or trellises.

Notes

do with. One or two hills of each type of summer squash is more than enough for a family of four.

- DEGREE OF DIFFICULTY: Extremely simple
- TEMPERATURE TOLERANCE: Tender
- WHEN TO SOW INDOORS: May be started indoors 6 weeks before last frost, 3 seeds to a pot, and thinned to the best plant. You may also just pre-sprout seeds for jump on the season
- DAYS TO GERMINATION: 7–10
- WHEN TO SOW OUTDOORS OR SET TRANSPLANTS: When ground is thoroughly warm
- DEPTH OF SEED: 1"–1½"
- DISTANCE BETWEEN PLANTS: Plant 3 seeds in hills spaced 3' apart, and thin later to one strong plant
- SOIL CONDITIONS: Soil with good supply of organic matter, well-drained; pH 6.0–7.5
- SUNLIGHT REQUIREMENTS: Full sun
- WATERING: Steady, moderate supply, especially after blossoms appear for high production
- SIDEDRESSING: Water with compost tea every 2 weeks and topdress with rotted manure or compost when plants start to blossom
- DAYS TO FIRST HARVEST: 55
- HARVESTING TIPS: Summer squash are best at about 6" when they are still extremely tender. Once they start coming in, harvest promptly—even daily isn't too often for a big patch
- VARIETIES: *Zucchini:* Zucchini Hybrid, Gold Rush, Elite, Black; *Crookneck and Straight Neck:* Multipik, Tara, Early Prolific Straightneck, Golden Summer Crookneck; *Scallop squash:* Peter Pan, Early White Bush
- PESTS AND DISEASES: Striped and spotted cucumber beetle, cutworms, squash vine borer, aphids, squash bugs; bacterial and fusarium wilt, mosaic, downy and powdery mildew

WINTER SQUASH

Annual

Many varieties of winter squash grow on long, crawling vines that take up a great deal of garden space, but plant breeders are now offering bush types producing fruit of equal quality in considerably less space. Like summer squash, winter squash are easy to grow, but you must wait almost 3 months to harvest even the earliest varieties. The exception is Jersey Golden Acorn which can be harvested when 2" in diameter and eaten raw or steamed.

Plant 3–4 seeds each in hills 6' apart (4' for bush types), and then thin plants to the best two for best results.

- DEGREE OF DIFFICULTY: Extremely simple
- TEMPERATURE TOLERANCE: Tender
- WHEN TO SOW INDOORS: Can be started indoors about 6 weeks before last frost, or seeds can be pre-sprouted for about a 10-day jump on growing time
- DAYS TO GERMINATION: 7–10
- WHEN TO SOW OUTDOORS OR SET TRANSPLANTS: When ground is thoroughly warm
- DEPTH OF SEED: 1"
- DISTANCE BETWEEN PLANTS: 6' for sprawling varieties; 4' for bush types
- SOIL CONDITIONS: Soil fortified with organic matter, well-drained; pH 5.5–7.0
- SUNLIGHT REQUIREMENTS: Full sun
- WATERING: Need steady supply after blossom set

- SIDEDRESSING: Topdress with rotted manure or compost just before vines start to crawl; water with manure or compost tea every 2 weeks after blossom set
- DAYS TO FIRST HARVEST: 80–110
- HARVESTING TIPS: Most winter squash should be fully mature when harvested— meaning their skins must be hard. Acorn squash is ripe when the yellow spot where it touches the ground turns a light orange; butternut squash changes from light to darker tan when ripe; buttercup types should be picked when they're 5"– 6" across; later varieties such as Blue Hubbard are ripe when the vines die back. Winter squash will last a long time in storage, but must be cured for a week or more under dry, hot conditions first
- VARIETIES: *Acorn type:* Table Ace, Jersey Golden Acorn; *Butternut type:* Waltham Butternut, Butter Bush, Butter Boy; *Buttercup types:* Sweet Mama, Buttercup; *Other winter squash of merit:* Blue Hubbard, Spaghetti Squash, Golden Nugget, Boston Marrow
- PESTS AND DISEASES: Striped and spotted cucumber beetle, cutworms, squash vine borer, aphids, squash bugs; bacterial and fusarium wilt, mosaic, downy and powdery mildew
- SPECIAL NOTES: Where space is at a premium, you can grow winter squash vertically, using special towers available in garden stores, or by erecting your own trellis. Try a simple frame out of plastic water pipe, a couple of elbows, and a draping length of stock fence

SUNFLOWER SNOW FENCE

If winter snow always piles up too close to your house, and the prospect of erecting snow fence every year is not a pleasant one, sow a wide, thick band of mammoth Sunflowers at the back of your garden. Grown closely together, the plants will become a solid mass of three-foot stalks that will resist snow passage. For western gardens, where lack of moisture is often a problem, this trick keeps snow in the vegetable plot where it melts during spring and adds to the water table.

SUNFLOWERS

Annual

After Marigolds, Sunflowers may be the most popular flowers in American gardens. They should be planted at the north end of the garden to avoid shading smaller plants: these golden giants can attain heights of 12' or more.

As seedheads begin to mature they must be protected from marauding birds, especially bluejays, if you want to harvest the seeds as a crop. Wrap the heads in mesh bags until the seeds are completely ripe, then follow Harvesting Tips below.

- DEGREE OF DIFFICULTY: Very simple
- TEMPERATURE TOLERANCE: Tender
- WHEN TO SOW INDOORS: Can be started indoors, but do just as well when direct-seeded after frost
- DAYS TO GERMINATION: 10–14
- WHEN TO SOW OUTDOORS OR SET TRANSPLANTS: After last frost
- DEPTH OF SEED: ½"–1"
- DISTANCE BETWEEN PLANTS: 18"
- SOIL CONDITIONS: Best in rich, loamy soil; pH 6.0–8.0
- SUNLIGHT REQUIREMENTS: Full sun
- WATERING TIPS: Steady moderate-to-heavy supply
- SIDEDRESSING: Usually unnecessary, but if you feel they need a boost, topdress with compost or apply compost tea
- DAYS TO FIRST HARVEST: 80–90
- HARVESTING TIPS: Cut seedheads leaving about 2' of stem attached, and hang them in any airy place protected from birds, like a well-ventilated attic. Once the heads are completely dry, rub out the seeds and store them in air-tight jars or plastic bags

- VARIETIES: Mammoth, Russian Giant
- PESTS AND DISEASES: Aphids, flea beetles, corn earworm, Sunflower maggot
- SPECIAL NOTES: Giant Sunflowers can be grown in blocks to act as a snow fence in northern climates

SWEET POTATOES

Annual

I love the way a row of sweet potatoes looks in the garden—the broad spade-shaped leaves are full and lush and teeming with life. Although they are more commonly grown in the South, it's a myth that these sweet roots can't be grown successfully north of the Mason-Dixon. Like potatoes, sweet potatoes are not grown from seed. You can either purchase plants from a seed catalogue or propagate your own from a mature sweet potato—one from the supermarket is fine—about 8–10 weeks before the last frost. Harden off the seedlings for a week or so when they are about 6–7 weeks old, and then plant them outdoors up to the top leaves in a ridge about 12" across raised about 10" higher than the soil surface.

- DEGREE OF DIFFICULTY: Can be tricky up north; quite easy in the South
- TEMPERATURE TOLERANCE: Tender
- WHEN TO SOW INDOORS: 8 weeks before last frost

PROPAGATING FROM A STOREBOUGHT SWEET POTATO

One full-sized sweet potato can generate 25–50 shoots—more than enough for a decent-sized harvest. Poke 3 or 4 toothpicks into the sweet potato for support and suspend it halfway in a jar of water, or lay it on its side and plant half-depth in vermiculite or other artificial planting medium. Soon shoots will appear. When they are 2 weeks old, snap them off and transplant them to flats. Feed them with liquid fertilizer and keep them either under lights or in a sunny window until time to harden off.

- DAYS TO GERMINATION:
- WHEN TO SOW OUTDOORS OR SET TRANSPLANTS: After last expected frost
- DEPTH OF SEED: Set transplants 3″ deep
- DISTANCE BETWEEN PLANTS: 18″
- SOIL CONDITIONS: Light, loose, well-drained; pH 5.0–7.0
- SUNLIGHT REQUIREMENTS: Full sun
- WATERING: Moderate
- SIDEDRESSING: Not necessary in reasonably rich soil
- DAYS TO FIRST HARVEST: 120–150
- HARVESTING TIPS: Dig roots before frost kills vines. Cure between 70–80°F for a week or so. Separate wounded roots from perfect ones and eat those first
- VARIETIES: Centennial, Nemagold, Bush Porto Rico
- PESTS AND DISEASES: Rarely bothered
- SPECIAL NOTES: According to some old-timers, once sweet potatoes are in storage they should not be turned for fear of encouraging rot. If you have a liberal harvest, experiment by turning a few to see what happens

TOMATILLO

Annual

Tomatillos (pronounced, TOE-MA-TEE-YOS) are a favorite vegetable from the Southwest. They are the main ingredient in green taco sauce, or *salsa verde*.

Tomatillos grow 3′–4′ tall and produce small yellow flowers that eventually give way to a sticky green fruit a little larger than a cherry tomato, half-hidden in a brownish husk. Each plant should yield about 1 lb. of these. Space the young plants about 18″ apart and, after watering, apply a light mulch to help conserve moisture.

- DEGREE OF DIFFICULTY: Very easy
- TEMPERATURE TOLERANCE: Tender
- WHEN TO SOW INDOORS: 4 weeks before last frost
- DAYS TO GERMINATION: 10
- WHEN TO SOW OUTDOORS OR SET TRANSPLANTS: When soil is thoroughly warm
- DEPTH OF SEED: ¼″
- DISTANCE BETWEEN PLANTS: 18″
- SOIL CONDITIONS: Average, well-drained; pH 5.5–6.5
- SUNLIGHT REQUIREMENTS: Full sun
- WATERING: Will tolerate dry conditions if it must, but prefers a moderate water supply; mulch to conserve moisture
- SIDEDRESSING: Unnecessary
- DAYS TO FIRST HARVEST: 110–120
- HARVESTING TIPS: Harvest the tomatillos at the end of the summer when the berries are green. Left on the vine much past maturity, they'll turn yellow or blue and lose their distinctive flavor.

Unbruised fruit will keep for weeks in a well-ventilated area
- VARIETIES: Available from only a few catalogues; check Bauman's Pickle Room and Horticultural Enterprises, Spring Valley, California
- PESTS AND DISEASES: Unaffected by diseases, rarely attacked by insects

TOMATOES

Annual

Considering the vast popularity tomatoes enjoy in home gardens throughout the world, it is surprising that, until relatively recently, they were actually thought to be poisonous—no doubt, because of their membership in the Solanaceae or nightshade family.

In America alone tomatoes are now grown by nearly 40 million families. Appealing to the inquisitive tastes and climatic concerns of that broad market, breeders have developed cultivars that will produce fruit in sizes ranging from marbles to softballs and colors from red to yellow, pink and orange, along with guarantees of success in every conceivable growing environment.

- DEGREE OF DIFFICULTY: Moderately easy
- TEMPERATURE TOLERANCE: Tender
- WHEN TO SOW INDOORS: 6–8 weeks before last expected frost

Two Transplanting Techniques

There are two ways of setting tomato seedlings in the ground: either standing straight up, or on their sides. The most popular is to set the seedling upright in the soil. Dig a 6"–8" hole; lay in a couple of trowels' worth of compost or aged stable manure, a couple more of soil, and mix together at the bottom of the hole. Strip off all but the top leaves of the seedling, and set the plant into the hole—right up to the bottom of the topmost leaves. Fill the hole with soil, or a soil-and-compost mixture, firm well around the stem to eliminate air pockets, and water deeply.

The second method also involves stripping all but the top leaves from the seedling, but instead of standing the plant upright, lay it on its side in a shallow fertilized trench, 3"–4" deep. With the plant in place, bury everything but the top. Soon it will begin to grow upwards at right angles to its main stem buried in the trench. This system has two advantages: (1) it allows for the creation of a massive root system all along the length of the underground stem, and (2) the plant will probably deliver ripe fruit earlier because the roots are closer to the warm soil surface. On the other hand, plants will require extra water due to rapid surface evaporation, and are more susceptible to damage from the surface.

- DAYS TO GERMINATION: 7–10
- WHEN TO SOW OUTDOORS OR SET TRANSPLANTS: When ground is thoroughly warm
- DEPTH OF SEED: ¼" and see above for depth of transplants
- DISTANCE BETWEEN PLANTS: Staked: 12"–18" in rows 3' apart; unstaked: 18"–

PRUNING TOMATOES

Many gardeners prune staked or caged tomato plants regularly, to keep them manageable and insure that water and nutrients make their way to the main producing stems. To prune, pinch off the shoots or "suckers" that grow in what the oldtimers refer to as "the forks of the branch" as soon as they appear. When a plant has become as tall as its support, you can pinch off the bud at the top of each main stem to check the plant's upward growth.

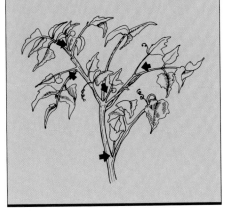

24" in rows 4' apart; caged: 24"–36" in rows 4' apart
- SOIL CONDITIONS: Rich, well-worked; pH 5.5–7.5
- SUNLIGHT REQUIREMENTS: Full sun
- WATERING: Steady, moderate supply
- SIDEDRESSING: Topdress every week with compost or aged manure after plants start to blossom, and water in well; water with compost or manure tea at will
- DAYS TO FIRST HARVEST: 55–90
- HARVESTING TIPS: Allow fruit to ripen fully if temperatures are moderate (75°F or under); if it gets above 85°F, pick fruit when pink and allow to ripen indoors. Green tomatoes can be wrapped individually in newspaper, and when stored at 50–60°F will hold quality for up to several months
- VARIETIES: See "Tomato varieties"
- PESTS AND DISEASES: Flea beetles, Colorado potato beetles, tomato hornworms, tomato fruitworms; wilt,

_____ *Notes* _____

HILLING TOMATOES

Tomatoes and potatoes are kissing cousins and have certain growth patterns in common. For instance, wherever their stems are covered with soil, they will send out new roots. When potato vines begin to appear, the common practice is to rake soil right up to their shoulders, virtually burying the new leaves (see Potatoes, page 97). This traditional technique is known as hilling. It is much less common to hill tomato plants, but many gardeners report that several repeated hillings of young plants insulates the primary root systems from drying wind, reduces evaporation, and allows for a more consistent supply of moisture for much of the growing season—all conditions that can improve productivity.

Supporting or Sprawling Your Tomatoes

Should tomato plants be supported, or should they be allowed to sprawl unchecked along a mulched-over ground? Both methods have their advantages and drawbacks. You must decide in advance, because the method chosen determines spacing when you set out the seedlings.

There are three popular ways to support tomato plants: staking, caging, and trellising.

STAKING. The greatest advantage of staking is the space it saves in the garden. Plants can be as close as 12"–18" in rows 3' apart, so long as the suckers—side shoots that grow between the main stem and leaf stem—are diligently removed and the main stem systematically tied to the support as it grows. The disadvantage is that staking reduces production by restricting growth to a single stem. As a compromise, you can space plants 24" apart and let 3 or 4 large stems develop on each one. This allows heavier blossoming (and therefore more fruit) and generates more foliage, which protects the fruit from sun-scalding. For further protection of the succulent and

vulnerable young fruit, use only soft material such as strips of old bedsheets to tie the plants to stakes, and whenever possible, tie them to the downwind side of the stake. This will prevent damage by insuring the plant is pulled *away* from the stake when the prevailing wind blows rather than pushed *into* it.

CAGING. Cylindrical wire cages offer excellent protection and support and may be the perfect solution if you have only a dozen or so plants to set out. Caging more than that will require a large capital outlay, whether you buy the cages ready-made at a garden store or make them yourself with sturdy galvanized mesh from building suppliers. Either way it is a one-time expense since the cages will last for years, and they take no time to construct. For each plant, get a 6-ft. length of 5-ft-high mesh (to accommodate tall-growing varieties) and roll it into a cylinder about 2' in diameter. Twist the wire ends together to close the cage. Next, set the cage firmly in the soil and, to keep it from overturning in a strong wind, secure with twine to a short stake driven in the ground on either side.

TRELLISING. Trellising tomatoes does save space, and it does keep tomatoes safe from some insects and disease organisms on the ground—notably during wet seasons. But it takes time and energy some gardeners just don't have. Building a trellis for just a few plants can be fun, however, and the plants look gorgeous when the fruit begins to ripen.

SPRAWLING TOMATOES. For many gardeners, letting tomatoes sprawl on their own beats all for labor-saving and production both. But it does take a lot of room, and, if the season is wet, a great deal of mulch around plants—which can be an expense. Even then, pests and disease can be greater-than-normal threats, and production will be curtailed somewhat as a result.

tobacco mosaic, early and late blight, anthracnose
• SPECIAL NOTES: Smokers must either wash their hands or wear gloves when

examining tomatoes or other nightshades to avoid transmitting tobacco mosaic disease

FIVE TYPES OF TOMATOES YOU CAN GROW

All the hundreds of varieties of tomatoes for the home garden fall into only five categories:

MAIN CROP. Most varieties are main crop types. They produce medium to large-sized fruit, and are the most versatile, being equally suitable for cooking and for eating fresh in salads or on sandwiches.

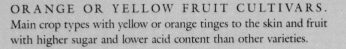

ORANGE OR YELLOW FRUIT CULTIVARS. Main crop types with yellow or orange tinges to the skin and fruit with higher sugar and lower acid content than other varieties.

SALAD TOMATOES. Often called cherry tomatoes, these are the familiar yellow or red miniatures whose flesh has a sweet taste and is firm even when ripe.

PASTE CULTIVARS. Also known as plum tomatoes, the egg-shaped fruits contain fewer seeds, less water, and more flesh than main crop types. They are therefore used frequently for tomato paste and ketchup, but can—and should—be eaten fresh.

CONTAINER CULTIVARS. Although any tomato can be put into a container and supported on a stake, these are special dwarf varieties designed for container growing. They produce small—but not miniature—fruit on short bushy vines.

POPULAR TOMATO VARIETIES

Early Season (50-65 days from transplanting)

Variety	Comments
Burpee's Big Early	Early-ripening; rugged hybrid
Early Girl	4-6 oz. tomatoes; stake or cage
Fireball	4 oz. fruits; sets in cool weather
New Yorker	Widely recommended; 6 oz. fruits
Pixie	Very early; sets fruit in cool weather
Spring Giant	High yields; large fruits
Springset	Widely adapted; short harvest
Starfire	6 oz. fruits
Sweet 100	Stake or cage; many 1 oz. fruits

Midseason (65-75 days)

Variety	Comments
Avalanche	Very crack resistant
Better Boy	Widely recommended and adapted, but susceptible to blossom end rot
Bonny Best	Old-time favorite in South
Burpee's Big Boy	Very popular; large 12 oz. fruits. Long producer
Burpee's Big Girl	Like Big Boy, but has resistance
Burpee's VF	Widely recommended; resistant to cracking and catfacing
Campbell 1327	Sets fruit in adverse conditions
Floradel	Stake or cage. Crack resistant
Floramerica	Compact growth. Tolerant to many diseases
Heinz 1350	Productive canning tomato
Jet Star	Widely recommended; 8 oz. fruits
Manapal	Bred for humid conditions. Good Southern variety
Marglobe	Old favorite. Smooth, firm 6 oz. fruits
Moreton Hybrid	6-8 oz. fruits; Northeast favorite
Rutgers	Large, 6-8 oz. fruits
Super Sioux	Widely adapted; sets fruit in high temp
Supersonic	Widely recommended

Late Season (80-90 days)

Variety	Comments
Manalucie	Grows well in adverse conditions. Widely recommended in South

Late Season (80-90 days)

Variety	Comments
Oxheart	Heart-shaped tomatoes up to 2 lbs.
Ramapo	Sets well in adverse conditions. Resistant to cracking, blossom end rot
Wonder Boy	Heavy producer of 8 oz. tomatoes

Beefsteak Varieties (large tomatoes; 80-90 days)

Beefmaster	Hefty fruits; up to 2 lbs.
Pink Ponderosa	Meaty, firm tomatoes. Cage plants to protect from sunscald

Yellow Orange Varieties (80-85 days)

Golden Boy	Somewhat lower acid tomato
Jubilee	
Sunray	

Paste Varieties

Roma	Widely recommended
San Marzano	Quite popular canner

Cherry and Container Varieties

Burgess Early Salad	Plant grows only 8 inches tall, but good producer
Patio Hybrid	2-inch tomatoes
Pixie Hybrid	Great early variety for garden or sunny window. Fruits larger than cherry types
Small Fry	Heavy producer of small fruits. Plant in garden or 5-gallon container
Tiny Tim	¾-inch fruits. Great for pots, windowsills

List Courtesy of *Gardens For All*, Burlington, VT.

TURNIPS

Biennial

Like rutabagas, turnips are a double-value crop: they are grown both for their tops and their roots. They also prefer cool weather. Several varieties with different maturity dates can be planted at  the same time for a steady supply. Turnips also make an excellent succession crop, so be sure to plant more in midsummer for a fall harvest. Germination time varies with size of seed, so try and find uniform "sized" seed for both turnip and rutabaga.

- DEGREE OF DIFFICULTY: Simple
- TEMPERATURE TOLERANCE: Hardy; does best in cool weather
- WHEN TO SOW INDOORS: Not an indoor starter
- DAYS TO GERMINATION: 14–21, depending on seed size
- WHEN TO SOW OUTDOORS OR SET TRANSPLANTS: As soon as soil can be worked in spring, and again in mid-summer for fall crop
- DEPTH OF SEED: ¼″
- DISTANCE BETWEEN PLANTS: 4″–6″
- SOIL CONDITIONS: Loose, moderately fertile; pH 5.5–7.0
- SUNLIGHT REQUIREMENTS: Full sun
- WATERING: Moderate supply
- SIDEDRESSING: Unnecessary, unless soil is poor
- DAYS TO FIRST HARVEST: 30–55
- HARVESTING TIPS: Harvest greens as early as you like; roots are delicious when quite small
- VARIETIES: Tokyo Cross, Purple Top White Globe, Early Purple Top Milan

- PESTS AND DISEASES: Aphids, flea beetles, cabbage loopers, cabbage worms; club root, black leg, yellows

WATERCRESS

Annual

Watercress is the most popular of three cresses planted in home gardens—the other two being garden cress, a snappy, peppery-tasting green, and winter or upland cress, fairly similar in looks and taste to watercress. Contrary to what many beginning gardeners assume, you do not need a stream or pond to grow watercress. You must, however, have either a spot in the garden that stays moist much of the time and even offers a bit of late afternoon shade, or be prepared to keep the area well-watered all season long. There's one other option: after starting seeds indoors, transfer seedlings to clay pots, and keep them in pans constantly filled with water. In any case, you can transfer seedlings outdoors a few weeks before the last expected frost

- DEGREE OF DIFFICULTY: Finicky about its water supply, which must be both abundant and constant
- TEMPERATURE TOLERANCE: Semi-hardy
- WHEN TO SOW INDOORS: 6 weeks before last hard frost

_____ *Notes* _____

- DAYS TO GERMINATION: 14
- WHEN TO SOW OUTDOORS OR SET TRANSPLANTS: One month before last expected frost
- DEPTH OF SEED: ¼″
- DISTANCE BETWEEN PLANTS: 2″
- SOIL CONDITIONS: Well-limed, but otherwise average soil; pH 6.5–7.5
- SUNLIGHT REQUIREMENTS: Half-sun
- WATERING: Steady abundant supply. Try keeping watercress in clay pots resting in pans of water
- SIDEDRESSING: Not necessary
- DAYS TO FIRST HARVEST: 30–40
- HARVESTING TIPS: Cut top 3″–4″ of plant
- VARIETIES: Watercress is sold under its generic name by most seed catalogues
- PESTS AND DISEASES: None

WATERMELON

Annual

I gardened for some years in Kentucky and experienced the fun and pleasure of growing watermelons there as easily as I grow lettuce here in western Massachusetts. My soil was light and sandy, the season long and humid—perfect conditions for sweet, juicy watermelons. Up north, conditions are rarely so agreeable—late frosts, cool and windy spells in early summer, and what often feels like endless rain—and so cultivating watermelons in the north can be tricky.

Start seedlings indoors about 6 weeks before the last expected frost, and, after gradually hardening them for a week or so, place them out in the garden in hills—2 plants per hill—under hot caps or some other heat-enhancer. If your soil is only average, you must fortify each hill beforehand with a few shovelfulls of compost or rotted manure; if it leans to the heavy side, mix in a bucket or two of clean builder's sand available at any construction supply house.

After fruit set, keep an eye out for shrivelled melons; pick them off and destroy them, as they will spread disease like wildfire. Also, be sure to stay out of the melon patch when it is wet, for water is a great conductor of disease organisms. Some gardeners recommend snipping the terminal vine buds to halt outward growth, but I fear that that sort of open wound may be asking for trouble.

Many varieties of watermelons are available. The old standby vining types, in my experience, produce the best melons. The miniature or ice-box melons which grow on truncated vines are good, and improving all the time, but when it comes to texture and sweetness, they can't compare with the large ones. Nevertheless, the smaller types are far easier to bring in than the old standards, and are worth growing.

- DEGREE OF DIFFICULTY: Can be tricky up north; easy in warmer climates
- TEMPERATURE TOLERANCE: Tender
- WHEN TO SOW INDOORS: 6 weeks before last frost, in individual containers, thinned to a single healthy plant each
- DAYS TO GERMINATION: 7–10
- WHEN TO SOW OUTDOORS OR SET TRANSPLANTS: Set transplants under cover until daytime temperatures are consistently in the upper 70's or higher
- DEPTH OF SEED: ½″; 4–5 seeds each in hills 6′–8′ apart for vining types, 4′–6′ apart for bush types
- DISTANCE BETWEEN PLANTS: Thin down to two healthy plants per hill
- SOIL CONDITIONS: Sandy, well-drained, highly enriched soil; pH 5.5–6.5
- SUNLIGHT REQUIREMENTS: Full sun
- WATERING: Steady, moderate supply after blossom and fruit set

- SIDEDRESSING: Topdress with compost when vines start to crawl; water weekly with compost or manure tea
- DAYS TO FIRST HARVEST: 75–85
- HARVESTING TIPS: Watermelons are ripe when the light green spot formed where the melon rests on the ground turns yellow. The thump-test is also effective: rap the melon with your knuckles, and if you get a hollow report, the melon is ripe
- VARIETIES: Choose varieties immune to anthracnose and wilt. *Vining types:* Sweet Favorite, Charleston Gray, Crimson Sweet; *Ice-box types:* Sweet Treat, Sugar Baby, New Hampshire Midget
- PESTS AND DISEASES: Striped and spotted cucumber beetle, cutworms, squash vine borer, aphids, squash bugs; bacterial and fusarium wilt, mosaic, downy and powdery mildew. Pay special attention to the striped cucumber beetle which also brings with it wilt disease

❦ 7 ❦
HERBS

Herbs are pure pleasure. Even weeding them can be pleasant: merely brush against an herb plant and its aroma is released as though from long imprisonment.

I planted my first patch of herbs without knowing much more about them than that I loved the way they smelled and delighted in the flavor they added to many of my favorite dishes.

WHERE TO PLANT HERBS

If you've never planted herbs before, I recommend starting with the simplest annuals, and perhaps a few perennials in a separate bed so they can spread—as some are wont to do—without taking over your vegetables. Annual herbs can be interplanted among your vegetables, given their own section in the vegetable garden, or grown in separate beds or containers handy to the kitchen.

If you grow herbs for non-culinary purposes, such as dyes, medicines and cosmetics, you might choose to organize your herb beds according to function. Feel free to experiment with various designs. Just learn how each variety grows so you can accord each its proper sun and space.

GENERAL CULTURE

Almost all annual herbs along with some perennials may be started from seed, but French tarragon produces no seed and must therefore be started from plant cuttings. Many other herbs are extremely small-seeded, and many are also extremely slow to germinate—difficult conditions to cope with.

For herbs in these groups, consider buying a few nursery plants or getting cuttings or root clumps from a neighbor's garden (see Propagation, below). You can always start additional plants from seed while these are producing.

Soil, Watering, Fertilizer, Care

The only time you will want to consider sidedressing herb plants is after a particularly large harvest—after removing say ⅓–½ of the plant. Topdress with compost and water heavily with a concentrated manure or compost tea. This will help the plant revive, and, if there is time enough, produce another flush of foliage for you before frost.

Thinning Perennial Herbs

Once you've established a few perennial herbs in your garden, it won't be long before you'll need to perform routine maintenance on them, generally called thinning out or renewal, to keep them from growing unchecked and leggy, or impinging on other plants. This is done annually with some plants, less frequently with others. In many cases, the thinnings can be planted elsewhere (see below).

PROPAGATION

The practice of starting new plant life from existing plants, as opposed to seed, is called propagation. It is accomplished in various ways, and is very common for starting perennial herbs.

Root Division

Root division is used for thinning and propagating herbs that grow in spreading clumps, such as oregano, lavender, chives and tarragon. With a sharp spade or strong hand trowel, cut a 6″ square of soil and roots from the plant. Prune off any dead wood or roots. The clump can now be planted elsewhere in the garden, or perhaps given as a gift to a friend.

Stem Cuttings

This method involves cutting a 5″ piece of stem from a mature plant just below a leaf node. Remove flowers and leaves from the lower portion of the stem. Place it in water or in moist soil in a shaded section of the garden until it takes root. New growth should appear in 2–4 weeks. Spring cuttings can be transplanted, but fall cuttings should be left in place over winter. You can also grow cuttings indoors in containers for winter use. Herbs which propagate readily from stem cuttings include bay, lavender, marjoram, mint, pineapple sage, rosemary, sorrel, tarragon and winter savory.

Layering

This process works best for plants whose stems will root if they touch the ground. You just help the process by selecting particularly droopy stems, tipping them over to the ground, and burying them in soil. In a matter of days roots will form and a new plant will be anchored in the spot. You can then gingerly cut well around it and dig it out (snipping the connection to the original plant first) and plant it where you like—or give it away. Herbs which can be propagated by layering include lemon balm, marjoram, sage, thyme, and winter savory.

PESTS AND DISEASES

Few herbs are bothered by insects, doubtless because many pests tend to avoid strong fragrances, and most herbs are strongly aromatic. From time to time, however, you may see some Japanese beetles in the borage, or aphids in the basil. Handpick the larger pests, and spray the small ones off with a

COMPANION PLANTING

Herb	Companions and Effects	Herb	Companions and Effects
Basil	Companion to tomatoes; improves growth and flavor. Repels flies and mosquitoes.	Marjoram	Plant here and there in garden; improves flavors.
Bee balm	Companion to tomatoes; improves growth and flavor.	Mint	Companion to cabbage and tomatoes; improves health and flavor; deters white cabbage moth.
Borage	Companion to tomatoes and squash; deters tomato worm; improves growth and flavor.	Nasturtium (flower)	Companion to radishes, cabbage, and cucurbits; plant under fruit trees. Deters aphids, squash bugs, striped pumpkin beetles. Improves growth and flavor.
Caraway	Plant here and there in garden; loosens soil.		
Catnip	Plant in borders; deters flea beetle.	Pot Marigold (flower)	Companion to tomatoes, but plant elsewhere in garden, too. Deters asparagus beetle, tomato worm, and general garden pests.
Chervil	Companion to radishes; improves growth and flavor.		
Chives	Companion to carrots; improves growth and flavor.		
Dead Nettle	Companion to potatoes; deters potato bug; improves growth and flavor.	Rosemary	Companion to cabbage, beans, carrots, and sage; deters cabbage moth, bean beetles, and carrot fly.
Dill	Companion to cabbage; dislikes carrots; improves growth and health of cabbage.	Sage	Plant with rosemary, cabbage, and carrots; keep away from cucumbers. Deters cabbage moth, carrot fly.
Fennel	Plant away from gardens. Most plants dislike it.	Summer Savory	Plant with beans and onions; improves growth and flavor. Deters bean beetles.
Garlic (vegetable)	Deters Japanese beetle.		
		Tarragon	Good throughout garden.
Horseradish	Plant at corners of potato patch to deter potato bug.	Thyme	Plant here and there in garden; deters cabbage worm.
Lovage	Improves flavor and health of plants if planted here and there.	Yarrow (flower)	Plant along borders, paths, near aromatic herbs; enhances essential oil production.
Marigold (flower)	The workhorse of the pest deterrents. Plant throughout garden; it discourages Mexican bean beetles, nematodes, and other insects.		

This information was collected from many sources, most notably the Bio-Dynamic Association and the Herb Society of America.

hose. If you must use a repellant, use a nontoxic one, such as a garlic-onion-hot pepper conconction filtered and sprayed from a windex bottle type sprayer.

USING HERBS IN COOKING

Fresh herbs are generally mild and can be used rather liberally (within reason) but dried herbs are much more intense and should be added sparingly. Herbs are meant to add a hint of subtle flavor to foods, not overpower them with their own strong taste and aroma. Always use sharp scissors or a sharp knife when harvesting herbs or preparing them for fresh use; otherwise you will needlessly crush their delicate leaves. Information on drying your herbs for winter use or gifts—a big reason for growing them as a crop—is given below.

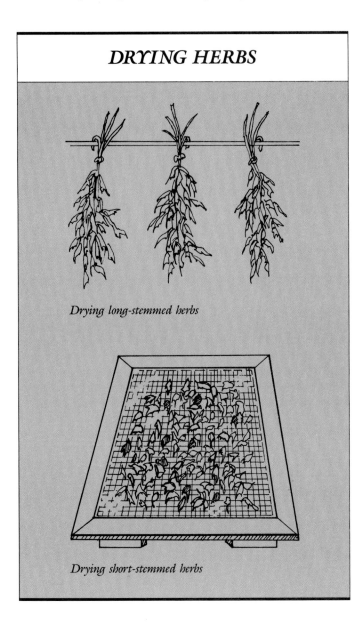

DRYING HERBS

Drying long-stemmed herbs

Drying short-stemmed herbs

HARVESTING AND STORING

Tips for individual herbs are in each listing, but generally speaking, harvest should occur just before the plant begins to flower, when its essential oils are at their peak. Once flowers form, the plant begins to devote attention and energy to seed production and the quality of the foliage deteriorates. Herbs are best harvested (using sharp scissors or knife) in the morning after the dew has dried, instead of at the end of a long day of hot sun when their oils are depleted.

Once you've picked your herbs, get them out of the sun and wash them under cold water. Then shake them off and lay them out on a comfortable work surface where you can examine them closely. Since you want to store only prime leaves, pick off anything dead—brown leaves, dead flowers, and the like.

Drying Herbs

Herbs with long stems can be tied tightly together with string in small bunches. Suspend a line in a warm, airy place out of the sun, and tie the bunches to this line. Be sure to label each bunch.

Herbs with short stems, such as thyme and marjoram, or large leaves, such as bay and basil, dry nicely when the leaves are separated from their stems and spread out individually (not touching) on window screens that are raised for good air circulation. Don't worry if a few leaves are touching; just don't pile them up on one another and expect good results.

Herbs are dry when they are brittle and crumble readily between your thumb and fingers. During spells of high humidity herbs can refuse to dry thoroughly. Some gardeners will spread leaves on a cookie sheet, preheat an oven to 150°F, and put the leaves in with door ajar for 2 or 3 minutes to complete the drying process.

Herb seeds from dill, coriander and caraway should be threshed (that is, separated from the chaff of the seedhead) when they've turned brown, then dried on screens or in paper bags poked with holes before being stored.

Storing Dried Herbs

Many herb gardeners store dried herbs in airtight glass jars. They make attractive containers and allow for easy inspection for water droplets that indicate the drying process is still incomplete. If this happens to you, dump out the contents onto a screen or try the oven trick suggested earlier. Store glass jars away from sunlight, and away from the direct heat of the cooking area.

Freezing Herbs

Many herbs, including chives, parsley, basil, dill and fennel, can be successfully frozen for future use, but must first be blanched in boiling water. Harvest and wash herbs exactly as you would in preparation for drying, except leave the foliage on the stems. Plunge the herbs into boiling water for 45 seconds, and remove them instantly to an ice-cold water bath to cool them. Once they are completely cooled, allow them to drain in a colander. Pack convenient amounts of the blanched herbs in carefully labeled freezer bags and place in a freezer that can hold temperature at a maximum of 0°F.

The landscaping of this herb knot at the
Brooklyn Botanic Garden was inspired by
similar gardens at Hampton Court, England.

An herb cluster lies in a peaceful setting.

Garden Sage is a beautiful and tasty
addition to any herb garden.

ANISE

Annual

Best known for its flavoring of the alcoholic beverage anisette, this sweetest-smelling of herbs is grown both for its seeds, which are used in baking and confections, and its leaves,  unmistakable ingredients in soups, stews, salads and sauces. The flowers are white and resemble Queen Anne's Lace, except they are more delicate.

- DEGREE OF DIFFICULTY: Easy
- TEMPERATURE TOLERANCE: Tender
- WHEN TO SOW INDOORS: About 6 weeks before last frost; does just as well direct-seeded outdoors
- DAYS TO GERMINATION: 14
- WHEN TO SOW OUTDOORS OR SET TRANSPLANTS: When ground is warm
- DEPTH OF SEED: ¼″
- DISTANCE BETWEEN PLANTS: 6″–8″ in rows 2′ apart
- SOIL CONDITIONS: Rich, well-drained
- SUNLIGHT REQUIREMENTS: Full sun
- WATERING: Keep well-watered
- SIDEDRESSING: Unnecessary
- DAYS TO FIRST HARVEST: Leaves can be harvested starting when plants are about 10″ tall. Harvest seeds beginning in mid- to late summer when seedheads turn brownish-gray
- HARVESTING TIPS: Cut stalks and tie in bunches of several each. Then hang bunches upside down in a warm but airy location out of the sun, and thresh seeds when they are completely dry

- VARIETIES: Generally found under its own name
- PESTS AND DISEASES: Usually none

BALM

Annual

Also known as Lemon Balm and Sweet Balm, the flowers of this cousin-of-mint herb are not particularly showy, but they are a definite attraction for bees. In fact, the *Melissa* of its Latin name *Melissa officinalis* actually means bee in Greek. Excellent as a tea, punch, in fruit desserts and as a garnish for fish dishes, Balm oil is used also as perfume and even a furniture polish.

- DEGREE OF DIFFICULTY: Quite simple if propagated by root cuttings. Seed germination is slow
- TEMPERATURE TOLERANCE: Hardy
- PROPAGATION: Seed (very slow), root division, cuttings
- WHEN TO SOW INDOORS: Early winter
- DAYS TO GERMINATION: 6 weeks
- WHEN TO SOW OUTDOORS OR SET TRANSPLANTS: Set transplants in mid-spring
- DEPTH OF SEED: ¼″
- DISTANCE BETWEEN PLANTS: 12″–18″
- SOIL CONDITIONS: Will grow freely in well-drained location
- SUNLIGHT REQUIREMENTS: Will accept partial shade

- WATERING TIPS: Moderate supply; don't waterlog soil
- SIDEDRESSING: Unnecessary
- DAYS TO FIRST HARVEST: start modest harvest in 6 weeks
- VARIETIES: Sold as Balm, Lemon Balm or Sweet Balm

BASIL

Annual

Basil has become so popular in the past several years that new varieties and colors have begun to appear on a regular basis. Basil is excellent in soups and stews, is a must in tomato  sauce, and makes an excellent vinegar. It grows to a height of 18″.

- DEGREE OF DIFFICULTY: Simple
- TEMPERATURE TOLERANCE: Tender
- WHEN TO SOW INDOORS: 6–8 weeks before last expected frost
- DAYS TO GERMINATION: 7–10
- WHEN TO SOW OUTDOORS OR SET TRANSPLANTS: After danger of frost
- DEPTH OF SEED: ¼″
- DISTANCE BETWEEN PLANTS: 10″–12″
- SOIL CONDITIONS: Reasonably rich, well-drained
- SUNLIGHT REQUIREMENTS: Full sun
- WATERING: Keep soil moist
- SIDEDRESSING: Unnecessary
- DAYS TO FIRST HARVEST: 30

- HARVESTING TIPS: Make first harvest when plants are 5″–6″ tall, by pinching back the tops. This will also promote bushier growth. Foliage is best and essential oil strongest just before plants flower. If you intend to dry leaves for winter use, harvest them before flowers open
- VARIETIES: Sweet Basil, Green Ruffles, Lemon, Dark Opal
- PESTS AND DISEASES: Slugs, Japanese beetles
- SPECIAL NOTES: Basil leaves are best dried individually on screens, and then stored in airtight containers. They can be dried in bunches, but have a tendency to blacken in the process; taste is not affected however

BORAGE

Annual

If you want honeybees around, plant borage. Known as the "herb of gladness," chopped borage adds a cool light flavor to salads, while sprays of its delightful star-shaped blue flowers  add a special zest to cold drinks. Iced borage tea is especially pleasing on a sweltering summer day, sweetened as you like and spritzed with the juice of fresh lemon. Borage takes up quite a bit of room, so give it the space it needs—about 2′–3′ up and out.

- DEGREE OF DIFFICULTY: Simple
- TEMPERATURE TOLERANCE: Tender

- WHEN TO SOW INDOORS: Not a good indoor starter
- DAYS TO GERMINATION: 7–10
- WHEN TO SOW OUTDOORS OR SET TRANSPLANTS: After all danger of frost
- DEPTH OF SEED: 1¼″
- DISTANCE BETWEEN PLANTS: 24″; borage is a large, spreading plant
- SOIL CONDITIONS: Well-worked loamy soil that is not continually moist
- SUNLIGHT REQUIREMENTS: Full sun
- WATERING: Not successful in wet soil; water only in dry spells
- SIDEDRESSING: Unnecessary
- DAYS TO FIRST HARVEST: 40–50
- HARVESTING TIPS: Harvest leaves when they are still young and tender. Harvest blossoms just before they open
- VARIETIES: Sold under its own name
- PESTS AND DISEASES: Japanese beetles

BURNET

Perennial

Also known as Salad Burnet, this cucumber-flavored herb forms interesting mounds of foliage in the perennial garden. It's a tough plant to start indoors because it will not transplant very  well. Burnet leaves are chopped and added to salads and soups, or made into an herb vinegar, as I do with chive flowers. Saxifrage burnet, known as lesser burnet, is grown for its root which is used medicinally—particularly for stomach upset.

_____ *Notes* _____

- DEGREE OF DIFFICULTY: Moderately simple
- TEMPERATURE TOLERANCE: Half-hardy
- WHEN TO SOW INDOORS: Not a good indoor starter
- DAYS TO GERMINATION: 7–10
- WHEN TO SOW OUTDOORS OR SET TRANSPLANTS: Sow seed or root divisions in place in mid-spring
- DEPTH OF SEED: ¼″
- DISTANCE BETWEEN PLANTS: 12″
- SOIL CONDITIONS: Sandy and well-drained, but will do well in poor soil if not wet
- SUNLIGHT REQUIREMENTS: Full sun
- WATERING: Don't overwater
- SIDEDRESSING: Annual application of manure or compost
- DAYS TO FIRST HARVEST: 40–50 after sprouting—as soon as leaves large enough to use
- HARVESTING TIPS: Harvest leaves when they're about ¾″ long
- VARIETIES: Sold under its own name
- PESTS AND DISEASES: Generally none
- SPECIAL NOTES: Freezing is the storage method of choice, as dried burnet leaves are hardly flavorful. Propagate new plants by root division in the spring

CARAWAY

Biennial

Caraway's aromatic and somewhat pungent seeds are traditionally used in rye bread, in stews and casseroles, and steeped in a tea for relief from stomach gas. Being a biennial, caraway will not

bear seeds until its second season, unless it is sown the previous fall before a killing frost.

- DEGREE OF DIFFICULTY: Simple
- TEMPERATURE TOLERANCE: Tender
- WHEN TO SOW INDOORS: Not a good indoor starter
- DAYS TO GERMINATION: 10–14
- WHEN TO SOW OUTDOORS OR SET TRANSPLANTS: 3–4 weeks before last expected frost or in fall for spring harvest
- DEPTH OF SEED: ½″
- DISTANCE BETWEEN PLANTS: 12″ in rows 3′ apart
- SOIL CONDITIONS: Light, well-drained soil
- SUNLIGHT REQUIREMENTS: Full sun
- WATERING: Only when soil becomes dry
- SIDEDRESSING: Unnecessary
- DAYS TO FIRST HARVEST: If sown in late summer or fall, the following spring; if sown in spring, the following spring
- HARVESTING TIPS: Harvest a month after flowering, when seedheads turn a brownish-gray
- VARIETIES: Sold under its own name
- PESTS AND DISEASES: Usually none

CATNIP

Perennial

Even if you don't have cats, and even if you don't value catnip tea as a soporific or cold remedy, you should still find a place for catnip at some point in your gardening life. Because if nothing else, catnip makes a beautiful ornamental border or background planting, growing nearly 4' tall and spreading out about 2'. Its flowers, which are usually white or blue, remain in blossom over an extended period. You can start catnip from seeds or root divisions.

- DEGREE OF DIFFICULTY: Relatively simple
- TEMPERATURE TOLERANCE: Hardy
- WHEN TO SOW INDOORS: Not an indoor starter
- DAYS TO GERMINATION: 7–10
- WHEN TO SOW OUTDOORS OR SET TRANSPLANTS: Sow seeds or root divisions directly in place as soon as soil can be worked
- DEPTH OF SEED: ¼"
- DISTANCE BETWEEN PLANTS: 18"–24"
- SOIL CONDITIONS: Light, sandy, well-drained
- SUNLIGHT REQUIREMENTS: Full sun
- WATERING: Water only when soil becomes dry
- SIDEDRESSING: Unnecessary
- DAYS TO FIRST HARVEST: 50–60 after seeding
- HARVESTING TIPS: Once plant is mature, cut leaves and stems at any time
- VARIETIES: Sold under its own name, also as "Catmint"
- PESTS AND DISEASES: To protect plants from cats at early stages, lay chicken wire over planting
- SPECIAL NOTES: Cut back foliage to the stem to encourage new flowering

CHERVIL

Biennial

Chervil's delicate, refined parsley-like flavor is great in soups, omelets, salads and sauces. The only real difficulty connected with growing chervil is its unwillingness to be successfully transplanted.  That problem is solved by a careful direct-seeding in mid-spring. And because chervil self-sows quite readily, you'll never have to buy seeds again.

- DEGREE OF DIFFICULTY: Moderately simple
- TEMPERATURE TOLERANCE: Hardy
- WHEN TO SOW INDOORS: Not an indoor starter
- DAYS TO GERMINATION: 7–14
- WHEN TO SOW OUTDOORS OR SET TRANSPLANTS: 3 weeks before last frost, and again in late summer where winters are mild
- DEPTH OF SEED: ¼"
- DISTANCE BETWEEN PLANTS: 8"
- SOIL CONDITIONS: Rich, well-drained soil
- SUNLIGHT REQUIREMENTS: Partial shade
- WATERING: Keep soil evenly moist
- SIDEDRESSING: Unnecessary
- DAYS TO FIRST HARVEST: 40–60
- HARVESTING TIPS: Pick leaves just before flower buds open
- VARIETIES: Sold under its own name
- PESTS AND DISEASES: Free of pests and diseases
- SPECIAL NOTES: If you like denser foliage, cut flower stems before they bloom

CHIVES

Perennial

Chives are almost as versatile in the kitchen as dill. They are excellent as an onion substitute in omeletes and salads, and are wonderful chopped and sprinkled on cold soups, sandwiches, and of course, with baked potatoes and sour cream. To make vinegar, place a dozen or so of the gorgeous pink chive flowers in a quart of pure distilled vinegar; in a week, the mixture turns bright pink and you'll have a supply of chive vinegar for the best vinaigrette dressings you ever made. You can start chives from seeds or use root divisions.

- DEGREE OF DIFFICULTY: Extremely simple
- TEMPERATURE TOLERANCE: Hardy
- WHEN TO SOW INDOORS: Early in spring
- DAYS TO GERMINATION: 7–14
- WHEN TO SOW OUTDOORS OR SET TRANSPLANTS: Plant seeds, seedlings, or root divisions; set small clumps of seedlings in early to mid-spring; direct-seed 3 weeks before last frost
- DEPTH OF SEED: ¼"
- DISTANCE BETWEEN PLANTS: 12" between seeds or clumps
- SOIL CONDITIONS: Thrives in rich, well-worked and moist soil, but will tolerate almost any conditions
- SUNLIGHT REQUIREMENTS: Full sun
- WATERING: Water only in periods of drought
- SIDEDRESSING: Annual application of manure or compost when dividing roots
- DAYS TO FIRST HARVEST: 15 after setting transplants; 40–45 after seeding

- HARVESTING TIPS: Snip anytime after plant is mature to within 2″ of the ground; avoid flower stems
- VARIETIES: Sold under its own name
- PESTS AND DISEASES: Almost none
- SPECIAL NOTES: Divide root clumps regularly

CORIANDER

Annual

Coriander is also known as cilantro and chinese parsley. Coriander seeds are essential to oriental cooking, being used whole or crushed in curries and mixed with chopped vegetables for stuffing tomato and zucchini. I think a sprig of leaves adds a pleasant and unexpected flavor to chicken soup.

- DEGREE OF DIFFICULTY: Simple
- TEMPERATURE TOLERANCE: Tender
- WHEN TO SOW INDOORS: Not a good indoor starter
- DAYS TO GERMINATION: 7–14
- WHEN TO SOW OUTDOORS OR SET TRANSPLANTS: About 3 weeks before last frost
- DEPTH OF SEED: ¼″
- DISTANCE BETWEEN PLANTS: 8″
- SOIL CONDITIONS: Well-drained, but otherwise average
- SUNLIGHT REQUIREMENTS: Full sun
- WATERING: Steady, moderate supply
- SIDEDRESSING: Unnecessary
- DAYS TO FIRST HARVEST: 35–40

- HARVESTING TIPS: Harvest seeds in midsummer when they turn brown. Cut seed stems, tie together, and hang upside-down in a paper bag to catch the seeds. Poorly dried seeds have a bitter taste, so be sure drying is complete before using in any recipes
- VARIETIES: Sold under its own name
- PESTS AND DISEASES: None
- SPECIAL NOTES: Coriander seeds coated with sugar can be used in preserves and cakes, or even eaten as snacks

DILL

Annual

Dill is without question my favorite herb. In season, I use it with literally everything I eat: salads, dips, pickles, chicken soup, and in a sauce for grilled or poached salmon. There is nothing on the dill plant that is not edible, including its stems and seeds, and it exudes a fragrance in the garden which I find irresistible. It is quite easy to grow, although its principal difficulty lies in its unwillingness to germinate quickly—taking between 3–4 weeks. Still, the results are well worth the wait.

- DEGREE OF DIFFICULTY: Easy
- TEMPERATURE TOLERANCE: Tender
- WHEN TO SOW INDOORS: 6 weeks before last frost in peat pots; seeds need light to germinate, so don't cover completely
- DAYS TO GERMINATION: 21–28

- WHEN TO SOW OUTDOORS OR SET TRANSPLANTS: Direct-sow about 3 weeks before last frost; set transplants carefully when threat of frost is past
- DEPTH OF SEED: Barely cover, as seeds need light for germination
- DISTANCE BETWEEN PLANTS: 8″–12″
- SOIL CONDITIONS: Rich, moist soil
- SUNLIGHT REQUIREMENTS: Full sun
- WATERING: Steady, moderate supply
- SIDEDRESSING: Unnecessary
- DAYS TO FIRST HARVEST: 25–30 after germination or setting transplants
- HARVESTING TIPS: You can cut leaves anytime, but they are best just as flowers open
- VARIETIES: Generally sold under its own name, there is one extremely popular variety: Bouquet
- PESTS AND DISEASES: None to speak of
- SPECIAL NOTES: Dill will self-sow quite readily if you allow the seedhead to mature and cast its seeds to the ground. Be alert next season

FENNEL

Perennial grown as Annual

Fennel comes in two basic types: sweet (or wild) fennel, which is grown for its spidery leaves, and Florence fennel, grown mainly for its stems and thickened plant base; both add a licorice flavor to salads. The leaves of sweet fennel, which bear a great resemblance to dill, are excellent with oily fish, as they are

reputed to improve digestion. Fennel leaf tea is traditionally given to babies with colic. The seeds mature in late summer and make for excellent chewing.

- DEGREE OF DIFFICULTY: Moderately simple
- TEMPERATURE TOLERANCE: Tender
- WHEN TO SOW INDOORS: Not a good indoor starter
- DAYS TO GERMINATION: 10–14
- WHEN TO SOW OUTDOORS OR SET TRANSPLANTS: 3 weeks before last frost
- DEPTH OF SEED: ¼"
- DISTANCE BETWEEN PLANTS: 12"
- SOIL CONDITIONS: Well-drained, rich soil
- SUNLIGHT REQUIREMENTS: Full sun
- WATERING: Water only after soil becomes dry
- SIDEDRESSING: Unnecessary
- DAYS TO FIRST HARVEST: 35 days from germination for leaves; stems a few weeks later, just before seeds open
- HARVESTING TIPS: Blanch stems, if you prefer, a week before harvesting. (See page 78 for techniques.) Seeds are harvested when they turn brown, but before they fall
- VARIETIES: Sweet fennel for leaves, Florence fennel for stems
- PESTS AND DISEASES: Wireworms and greenfly

HORSERADISH

Perennial

Horseradish is grown for its roots which, when peeled, ground, and mixed with a little vinegar, make a fiery sauce for beef, smoked fish, and the traditional Yiddish *Gefilte Fish.* Never planted from seed, horseradish is propagated primarily by root division. Like mint, horseradish has a tendency to spread rapidly. Outward growth can be checked by planting roots within a ceramic pot or short length of drainage tile. Otherwise, you'll have a digging job on your hand year after year.

- DEGREE OF DIFFICULTY: Easy
- TEMPERATURE TOLERANCE: Hardy
- PROPAGATION: Root division
- WHEN TO SOW INDOORS: Never started from seed
- WHEN TO SOW OUTDOORS OR SET TRANSPLANTS: Plant 3" pieces of root horizontally in holes 2" deep
- DEPTH OF SEED: 2"
- DISTANCE BETWEEN PLANTS: 6"
- SOIL CONDITIONS: Rich, well-worked and moist soil
- SUNLIGHT REQUIREMENTS: Full sun
- WATERING: Keep evenly moist
- SIDEDRESSING: Unnecessary if soil is suitably rich to begin with
- DAYS TO FIRST HARVEST: 60 days
- HARVESTING TIPS: Dig horseradish roots as you would any other root crop. Store roots indoors in a box filled with moist sand
- VARIETIES: Sold as horseradish
- PESTS AND DISEASES: None

Notes

Notes

• SPECIAL NOTES: Although even misshapen roots are quite edible, horseradish is much easier to prepare when the roots are straight. So prepare your soil to a depth of 12″ before planting

LAVENDER

Perennial

Lavender comes in several different forms, but the two most popular are the French and English, or so-called True Lavender. The English has the more notable fragrance, though the French is by no means to be considered inferior. Foliage is blue to gray-green, and the blue-violet flowers are a lovely addition to any garden. Prune lavender to keep its growth compact. Good drainage is essential to prevent winterkill. You can propagate new plants by taking cuttings in the early spring and rooting them directly. Roots may be divided each spring to increase your stock.

• DEGREE OF DIFFICULTY: Slow to germinate from seed, but otherwise quite easy
• TEMPERATURE TOLERANCE: Hardy
• PROPAGATION: Seed, cuttings, root division
• WHEN TO SOW INDOORS: Seeds are best started outdoors
• DAYS TO GERMINATION: 21–28
• WHEN TO SOW OUTDOORS OR SET TRANSPLANTS: Early spring
• DEPTH OF SEED: ¼″

• DISTANCE BETWEEN PLANTS: 12″
• SOIL CONDITIONS: Light, well-limed, rich and well-drained soil, although plants grown in poorer soil will produce greater fragrance
• SUNLIGHT REQUIREMENTS: Full sun
• WATERING: Keep evenly moist, but not wet
• SIDEDRESSING: Unnecessary
• DAYS TO FIRST HARVEST: When leaves are sufficiently fragrant, perhaps 90 days from planting
• HARVESTING TIPS: Cut spikes just before flowers begin to open
• VARIETIES: French, English or True
• PESTS AND DISEASES: None
• SPECIAL NOTES: Keep plants from coming to blossom the first year to create bushiness

LOVAGE

Perennial

Known of old both as Smallage and Smellage, this tall-growing perennial herb reaches heights of 6′–7′ if given partial shade, and deep, fertile, evenly moist soil. All parts of lovage, save

its roots, can be used: the stems, blanched and eaten like celery; the leaves, also celery-like in flavor, are an excellent soup flavoring; the seeds, coated with sugar and eaten as confection.

• DEGREE OF DIFFICULTY: Easy
• TEMPERATURE TOLERANCE: Hardy
• PROPAGATION: Seed, root division

- WHEN TO SOW INDOORS: Not an indoor starter
- DAYS TO GERMINATION: 7–14 days
- WHEN TO SOW OUTDOORS OR SET TRANSPLANTS: Sow seeds in midsummer, and transplant seedlings to permanent bed in autumn or the following spring
- DEPTH OF SEED: ½"–1"
- DISTANCE BETWEEN PLANTS: 3'
- SOIL CONDITIONS: Rich, deeply worked, and well-drained
- SUNLIGHT REQUIREMENTS: Partial shade
- WATERING: Keep soil evenly moist
- SIDEDRESSING: Fertilize after first major harvest
- DAYS TO FIRST HARVEST: About 9 months
- HARVESTING TIPS: For good quality leaf harvest, do not let plants flower and seed
- VARIETIES: Sold under its own name
- PESTS AND DISEASES: None
- SPECIAL NOTES: One lovage plant should be enough for a family of four

MARJORAM, SWEET

Annual

Sweet Marjoram is an annual, but there are also perennial marjorams available. Even they, however, do best in colder climates when treated as annuals—that is, started fresh each year. Extremely aromatic, sweet marjoram goes very well with poultry. As a tea, it is said to provide relief from diarrhea, headache,

nausea and cough. Marjoram will grow to about 18" tall and spread about 25". Its beautiful purple and pink flowers attract honeybees.

- DEGREE OF DIFFICULTY: Easy
- TEMPERATURE TOLERANCE: Half-hardy
- WHEN TO SOW INDOORS: 6–8 weeks before last frost
- DAYS TO GERMINATION: 8–14
- WHEN TO SOW OUTDOORS OR SET TRANSPLANTS: Direct-seed as soon as soil can be worked; set transplants 3 weeks before last frost
- DEPTH OF SEED: ¼"
- DISTANCE BETWEEN PLANTS: 12"
- SOIL CONDITIONS: Light, rich, well-drained
- SUNLIGHT REQUIREMENTS: Full sun
- WATERING: Water only when soil becomes dry
- SIDEDRESSING: Unnecessary
- DAYS TO FIRST HARVEST: 40–45 after seeding; 21 from transplants
- HARVESTING TIPS: Cut leaves and stems at any time for fresh use; harvest just before flowering if your intention is to dry and store leaves
- VARIETIES: Usually sold under its own name
- PESTS AND DISEASES: None

MINT

Perennial

There are many different kinds of mint belonging to the *menthe* group, and, judging from the catalogues, more varieties are making their appearances with each season. Most mint likes  wet soil; in fact, some species grow right in the middle of shallow, fast-flowing streams.

Give mint a place of its own, for it will soon take over. Despite what you read about mint as a companion plant for cabbage family crops, don't succumb to the temptation. It will repel the cabbage moth from laying eggs on your broccoli, but at the cost of endless pulling up of excess mint later on. As a perennial, mint doesn't go away at the end of the year.

In addition to the standard peppermint and spearmint, try the various fruit flavors too. You can start mint from seeds, stem or runner cuttings.

- DEGREE OF DIFFICULTY: Easy
- TEMPERATURE TOLERANCE: Hardy
- WHEN TO SOW INDOORS: Early spring
- DAYS TO GERMINATION: 14–21
- WHEN TO SOW OUTDOORS OR SET TRANSPLANTS: Plant seeds, seedlings, stem or runner cuttings 3 weeks before last frost
- DEPTH OF SEED: ¼"
- DISTANCE BETWEEN PLANTS: 12"
- SOIL CONDITIONS: Rich, moist soil
- SUNLIGHT REQUIREMENTS: Full sun or partial shade
- WATERING: Keep well watered
- SIDEDRESSING: Unnecessary
- DAYS TO FIRST HARVEST: 35 after seeding

- HARVESTING TIPS: Harvest leaves as soon as they can be handled by cutting stems at the base of the plant. Leaves for drying should be gathered as plant begins to flower
- VARIETIES: There are many kinds of mint: peppermint, spearmint, curled mint, apple and orange mint. Look for interesting flavor combinations
- PESTS AND DISEASES: Mint leaves are too aromatic for most insects, but rust disease occasionally attacks

OREGANO

Perennial

This easy-to-establish herb will spread considerably, so give it a special place in your perennial garden, and keep it well groomed or it will run wild. Used often in Italian sauces, leaves are also good in salads, soups, casseroles and teas. You can start oregano from seed or root divisions.

- DEGREE OF DIFFICULTY: Easy
- TEMPERATURE TOLERANCE: Hardy
- WHEN TO SOW INDOORS: Not a good indoor starter
- DAYS TO GERMINATION: 10–14
- WHEN TO SOW OUTDOORS OR SET TRANSPLANTS: Plant seeds or root divisions 3 weeks before last frost
- DEPTH OF SEED: ¼"
- DISTANCE BETWEEN PLANTS: 12"

- SOIL CONDITIONS: Light, well-drained soil, but will do well even under adverse conditions
- SUNLIGHT REQUIREMENTS: Full sun
- WATERING: Water only in periods of drought
- SIDEDRESSING: Annual application of manure or compost
- DAYS TO FIRST HARVEST: 35 after seeding
- HARVESTING TIPS: Cut back flowers to increase bushiness
- VARIETIES: Generally sold under its own name
- PESTS AND DISEASES: None

PARSLEY

Biennial

Parsley is the indispensable kitchen herb. Chicken soup without parsley is not chicken soup; ditto for Italian marinara sauce. The only difficulty with parsley is that it is a slow germinator. The process can be hastened in two ways: soak the seeds in warm water overnight before outdoor planting; get the soil temperature up to 75 degrees when planting indoors (keep the seed pots well-covered on top of the refrigerator). As parsley is not tolerant of transplanting, be sure to start several seeds in individual pots and transplant without attempting to separate them. Parsley does well in crowded conditions, particularly if the soil is rich; so don't hesitate to plant clumps closely, and you'll wind up with a lush row.

- DEGREE OF DIFFICULTY: Easy
- TEMPERATURE TOLERANCE: Hardy
- WHEN TO SOW INDOORS: 6–8 weeks before last frost
- DAYS TO GERMINATION: 14–21
- WHEN TO SOW SEEDS OUTDOORS OR SET TRANSPLANTS: Seeds can be sown outdoors about 2 weeks before last frost; or, in areas where winters are mild, in October. Transplants begun indoors may be set out in early spring
- DEPTH OF SEED: ¼"
- DISTANCE BETWEEN PLANTS: 6"–10" apart
- SOIL CONDITIONS: Rich, well-drained soil
- SUNLIGHT REQUIREMENTS: Full sun or partial shade
- WATERING: Keep well-watered
- SIDEDRESSING: When plants are 6" tall
- DAYS TO FIRST HARVEST: As soon as there are leaves to pick
- HARVESTING TIPS: You can pinch leaves as needed, but it is best to cut "hunks" of parsley to within a couple inches of the soil surface. In second year, harvest before the plant begins to flower
- VARIETIES: There are two basic types: plain or curled. I like them both
- PESTS AND DISEASES: Not much to speak of, though woodchucks and rabbits can be a nuisance
- SPECIAL NOTES: Parsley can be potted and brought indoors, where it will grow throughout the winter in a sunny window

ROSEMARY

Perennial grown as Annual

This woody shrub originally comes from the south of France; though technically a perennial, it does best in colder climates when treated as an annual. It can get as tall as 5' so give it a spot where it won't shade smaller plants.

Rosemary, to quote *Richter's Herb Catalogue,* is "one of the most fragrant herbs with many unexpected uses. A little freshly chopped rosemary is interesting with orange sections, appealing in dumplings, biscuits, preserves, and has few equals for poultry stuffings." It is also a major ingredient in homemade shampoos as well as hair and skin treatments.

You can start rosemary with stem cuttings or root divisions as well as seeds.

- DEGREE OF DIFFICULTY: Moderately simple
- TEMPERATURE TOLERANCE: Tender
- WHEN TO SOW INDOORS: 8 weeks before last frost
- DAYS TO GERMINATION: 21
- WHEN TO SOW OUTDOORS OR SET TRANSPLANTS: Sow seeds 3 weeks before last frost; set transplants, cuttings, or root divisions after threat of frost
- DEPTH OF SEED: 1/4"
- DISTANCE BETWEEN PLANTS: 12"; closer for evergreen shrub effect
- SOIL CONDITIONS: Well-limed, light and well-drained
- SUNLIGHT REQUIREMENTS: Full sun
- WATERING: Keep soil evenly moist
- SIDEDRESSING: Unnecessary
- DAYS TO FIRST HARVEST: 35 from germination; 21 from transplant

- HARVESTING TIPS: Pinch tops at first harvests, to encourage bushiness
- VARIETIES: There are many varieties available, with flowers in colors ranging from pink to dark blue. Some grow low, like Prostrate, others grow quite tall, like Tuscan Blue
- PESTS AND DISEASES: Spider mites occasionally
- SPECIAL NOTES: If your winters get below 10°F, bring rosemary plants indoors for use all year long. In areas of mild winters, cut stems and leaves as flowers begin to open

SAGE

Perennial

This sprawling herb is a must if you make your own sausage, and with its fuzzy, whitish-green leaves and violet-blue flower spikes makes a lovely plant to have growing in the garden  besides. Sage is excellent in omeletes, soups and stews, and sage tea is an effective gargle for sore throats.

Sage comes in a wide range of aromas and varieties, including pineapple sage, purple sage and more. Check herb specialty catalogues (pages 229–236) for what's available.

Notes

In addition to seed, sage can be propagated using root divisions, stem cuttings, or layering methods.

- DEGREE OF DIFFICULTY: Fairly difficult to get going; but easy to maintain once established
- TEMPERATURE TOLERANCE: Hardy
- WHEN TO SOW INDOORS: 8 weeks before setting out
- DAYS TO GERMINATION: 14–21
- WHEN TO SOW OUTDOORS OR SET TRANSPLANTS: Plant seed, seedlings, or propagating stock 3 weeks before last frost
- DEPTH OF SEED: ¼"
- DISTANCE BETWEEN PLANTS: 24"
- SOIL CONDITIONS: Light, well-limed, well-drained soil
- SUNLIGHT REQUIREMENTS: Full sun
- WATERING: Water only when soil becomes dry
- SIDEDRESSING: Unnecessary
- DAYS TO FIRST HARVEST: 35 after germination, 21 from transplants; or until following year
- HARVESTING TIPS: Many gardeners wait until the second year to get leaves richer in essential oil. You might try a little from both seasons, to compare. Harvest leaves when young, and again just before flowers bloom for drying. Cut leaves and stems together when stems are 6" long. Prune flower stems after blooming to encourage new and bushy growth
- VARIETIES: Garden sage, Pineapple sage, Painted sage, Golden sage, Purple sage. Check herb specialty catalogues for other varieties available
- PESTS AND DISEASES: Rarely a problem, especially if planted near marigolds or other richly aromatic plants
- SPECIAL NOTES: Sage tends to become scruffy over time, so it is wise to renew your planting every 3–4 years by root division, layering, or stem cuttings

SAVORY, _Summer_

Annual

SAVORY, _Winter_

Perennial

Though both forms of this popular herb produce flavorful leaves, I find that Summer savory has a more refined taste. Both forms produce lovely low shrub-like plants with weak stems that, when mature and covered with white and lavender flowers, fall over to form what appears to be a mound of freshly fallen light snow. Winter savory, in fact, is occasionally used as an edging. Summer savory is used in salad, sauce, meats of all kinds, in poultry stuffing, in soups, and even in scrambled eggs.

- DEGREE OF DIFFICULTY: easy
- TEMPERATURE TOLERANCE: tender
- PROPAGATION: Summer: Seed. Winter: seed (slow), cuttings from sideshoots, and by layering
- WHEN TO SOW INDOORS: Not an indoor starter
- DAYS TO GERMINATION: 10–14 (summer); 21–28 (winter)
- WHEN TO SOW OUTDOORS OR SET TRANSPLANTS: Sow seeds in late spring for both types
- DEPTH OF SEED: Just barely cover summer type; leave winter seeds exposed, as they require light to germinate
- DISTANCE BETWEEN PLANTS: 6" (summer); 12"–15" for perennial; or 2' apart if started from cuttings
- SOIL CONDITIONS: Summer savory prefers rich, well-worked soil; winter

savory will do well in poorer ground. Both require well-drained conditions

- SUNLIGHT REQUIREMENTS: Full sun
- WATERING: Both Summer and Winter savory prefer slightly dry conditions
- SIDEDRESSING: Unnecessary
- DAYS TO FIRST HARVEST: About 6 weeks for Summer; somewhat longer for Winter
- HARVESTING TIPS: Cut shoots just before flowers open. Winter savory does not dry well, so use fresh and plant cuttings for indoor pot plants for use all year through
- VARIETIES: Sold as Summer and Winter savory
- PESTS AND DISEASES: None
- SPECIAL NOTES: To ease pain of insect stings, crush fresh savory leaves and apply in a poultice. Dried, savory is an ingredient for aromatic baths

SORREL

Perennial

This delightful, lemony herb, reputed to be a prevention against scurvy, resembles the weed Dock. It is a lovely surprise in salads, and adds a pleasant acid flavor when cooked with greens, eggs, veal and fish.

- DEGREE OF DIFFICULTY: Easy
- TEMPERATURE TOLERANCE: Hardy
- PROPAGATION: Seed, root division

- WHEN TO SOW INDOORS: Best started outdoors
- DAYS TO GERMINATION: 14
- WHEN TO SOW OUTDOORS OR SET TRANSPLANTS: Early spring
- DEPTH OF SEED: ¼"
- DISTANCE BETWEEN PLANTS: 6"
- SOIL CONDITIONS: Rich, well-drained soil
- SUNLIGHT REQUIREMENTS: Full sun, but will do well in partial shade
- WATERING: Keep soil evenly moist
- SIDEDRESSING: Unnecessary
- DAYS TO FIRST HARVEST: 90 days from first seeding; thereafter whenever suitably tangy
- HARVESTING TIPS: Early in the season, the leaves are quite bland; therefore, wait until they become tangy before harvesting
- VARIETIES: French Sorrel, Garden Sorrel
- PESTS AND DISEASES: None

TARRAGON

Perennial

Beginning herb gardeners should learn quickly the difference between Russian and French tarragons. Russian is the taller, tougher, and less flavorful of the two. The culinary delight is the French, and, since this type is not known to ever set seed, it must be started either by cuttings or root division. Young plant cuttings are available from just about every

herb catalogue (see page 229–236), or from garden stores. Tarragon is used as a seasoning for fish, chicken and beef; in soups and casseroles, and the wonderful tarragon vinegar for salads.

- DEGREE OF DIFFICULTY: Easy
- TEMPERATURE TOLERANCE: Tender
- PROPAGATION: Cuttings, root division
- WHEN TO SOW INDOORS: French tarragon has no seed
- DAYS TO GERMINATION: Does not apply
- WHEN TO SOW OUTDOORS OR SET TRANSPLANTS: Set plants in late spring
- DISTANCE BETWEEN PLANTS: 18"
- SOIL CONDITIONS: Rich, well-drained soil
- SUNLIGHT REQUIREMENTS: Will tolerate partial shade
- WATERING: Do not waterlog soil
- SIDEDRESSING: Fertilize after dividing roots every fourth year
- DAYS TO FIRST HARVEST: 45 days
- HARVESTING TIPS: The more tarragon leaves you pick, the more you will have. For drying, cut plants to within two inches of the ground. The plants will restore themselves in just a couple of weeks
- VARIETIES: Only French tarragon is worth growing
- PESTS AND DISEASES: None

THYME

Perennial

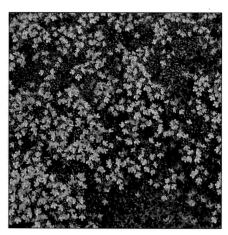

Legend has it that this heady herb enables one "to see the fairies," and if you've ever stumbled unsuspecting onto a hillside of wild mountain thyme, you'll understand why. There are more than

100 varieties of thyme for the home garden, each a special complement to a favorite dish. Thyme is delicious as a seasoning for chicken, pork, meatloaf, most soups, zucchini, and a delightful garnish for any plate. Fresh lemon thyme is nice when chopped and added to salads, and thyme tea and honey are reputed to make an excellent cough syrup.

Besides seed, you can start thyme with layering and root division.

- DEGREE OF DIFFICULTY: Moderately easy
- TEMPERATURE TOLERANCE: Hardy
- WHEN TO SOW INDOORS: 8 weeks before last frost
- DAYS TO GERMINATION: 21–30
- WHEN TO SOW OUTDOORS OR SET TRANSPLANTS: 3 weeks before last frost
- DEPTH OF SEED: ¼″
- DISTANCE BETWEEN PLANTS: 10″
- SOIL CONDITIONS: Light, well-drained
- SUNLIGHT REQUIREMENTS: Full sun
- WATERING: Keep soil on the dry side
- SIDEDRESSING: Unnecessary

- DAYS TO FIRST HARVEST: As soon as there are enough leaves to season a dish
- HARVESTING TIPS: Clip plants regularly to keep them bushy
- VARIETIES: See herb specialty catalogues, page 229–236, for the dozens of interesting thyme varieties available
- PESTS AND DISEASES: None
- SPECIAL NOTES: Renew plantings every 3–4 years to avoid woody, scruffy appearance

❦ 8 ❦
FLOWERS

ANNUALS, BIENNIALS AND PERENNIALS

Technically speaking, annual flowers live for a single season, during which they grow from seeds, flower, fruit, produce seeds, and die off. Biennials live for two seasons, storing food the first year and producing flowers and seeds the second. Perennials are defined as plants that can survive in the garden three years or more, producing flowers and seeds each season. All trees are perennials.

In practice, these differences become less sharp as the realities of climate and growing habits come into play. Some annuals, for instance, self-sow so freely that, despite their botanical classification, they reappear in the garden like biennials or perennials. Conversely, many perennials and biennials not hardy enough to withstand severe winters behave—and are grown—like annuals in cold-climate gardens.

Most of the flowers presented here are annuals, as they are most readily grown from seed. But there are a good number of biennials and perennials in the listings which have been included because they are either easy to grow or can easily be grown as if they were annuals.

REGIONAL CONSIDERATIONS

Where you live has a real bearing on when to plant certain flowers so you'll get maximum blooming periods. For example, some early-blooming perennials and biennials grown as annuals (Pot Marigold and Sweet William, for example) can be planted outdoors in colder climates in very early spring to bloom with late spring sun; in milder climates they could be planted in late fall for winter blooming. Flowers like Pansies and Violas, which do not tolerate heat well enjoy a longer planting season and will bloom comfortably over a longer period in climates with cool summers, but must be started very early in areas where summers are hot in order to enjoy a

good flowering period before midsummer's heat brings it to a close. In areas with cool summers succession plantings of these flowers will extend their blooming period, while in hotter climates, only a single early planting will produce abundant blooms.

Check with your local extension service or nursery for details on the growth habits of certain varieties in your region.

CHOOSING CULTIVARS AND VARIETIES

Part of the fun of flower gardening·is experimenting with your own choices—picking the height, colors or forms that are most appealing to you from the vast and colorful options in the seed catalogues. As you flip through their pages, you will notice that some flowers like Marigolds, Geraniums, Impatiens and Pansies (to name only a few) are offered in dozens of cultivars—cultivated varieties—while there are only a few choices for other flowers, like Ageratum and Alyssum.

Even when the choice is large, I rarely recommend specific varieties because our responses to flowers are so entirely subjective: what appeals to me as the quintessential Daisy or Marigold might leave you unimpressed.

As explained above, be on the lookout for cultivars that may be particularly suited to your garden and climate—plants, for instance, with inbred resistance to heat, drought and disease. Be aware, however, that sometimes in the course of breeding *in* certain strengths and resistances, plant biologists can breed out a characteristic like fragrance (as in some newer hybrids of Mignonette), in which case you might want to select the old standard version.

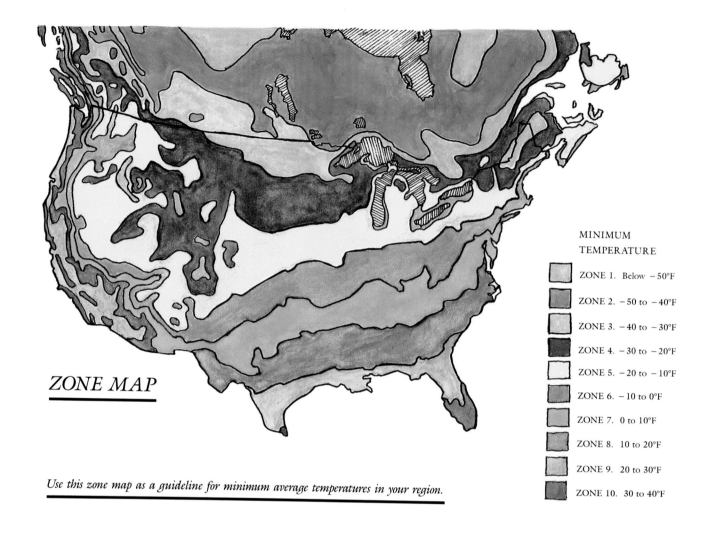

ZONE MAP

MINIMUM TEMPERATURE

ZONE 1. Below −50°F

ZONE 2. −50 to −40°F

ZONE 3. −40 to −30°F

ZONE 4. −30 to −20°F

ZONE 5. −20 to −10°F

ZONE 6. −10 to 0°F

ZONE 7. 0 to 10°F

ZONE 8. 10 to 20°F

ZONE 9. 20 to 30°F

ZONE 10. 30 to 40°F

Use this zone map as a guideline for minimum average temperatures in your region.

FROST TOLERANCE

Hardiness refers to a plant's ability to withstand cold temperatures, not its general vigor. In a classification set up by English gardeners long ago, the term "hardy" originally described plants that could survive a winter in England. A "tender" plant would not. Throughout the world we still use these terms to describe a plant's capacity to survive freezes in a given climate — far beyond the shores of England.

An additional term, "half-hardy," has been added to describe certain annuals that are in between. So the current range works like this:

Tender plants like melons, squash, basil, Cosmos and Zinnias will be killed by even the lightest kiss of frost, and so must not be set out before the soil is warm, and even then, protected should temperatures be expected below 32°F.

Half-hardy plants, such as irish potatoes, Gloriosa Daisy and Mexican Sunflower, can survive a touch of frost and even tolerate some degree of extended cold weather without sustaining serious damage. They can be seeded or set out a few weeks earlier than tender plants.

Hardy annuals like dill, leek, Larkspur and Sweet Alyssum will survive all but the hardest killing frosts and can therefore be planted as soon as the ground can be worked in spring without threat of damage. Some hardy annuals, such as Sweet Pea and spinach, are so durable their seeds can be planted in the fall, will survive in the soil over a cold winter and bloom the following spring.

Perennials, which come back year after year, are another story. *Tender perennials,* such as Hibiscus and Blue Marguerite, will succumb like tender annuals to the least bit of frost. If grown in very cold climates, they won't live over the winter and therefore must be grown as annuals. *Hardy perennials,* such as rhubarb and Columbine, can winter over successfully for renewed spring blooming every year.

Check the Zone Map for your location, and be guided by seed catalogues and the individual listings for specific information on hardiness.

HYBRID FLOWERS

Like hybrid vegetables, hybrid flowers are not true to seed, which means that plants grown from seed produced in hybrid flowers will not bear the same characteristics as the original plants. Frequently hybrids produce sterile, non-viable seeds that will never germinate; some, like the Triploid Marigold, produce no seed at all. The allure of these annual hybrids is that they are spectacular performers in their lone season; but to repeat the show you must purchase fresh seed each year.

GERMINATION TEMPERATURES

Occasionally, books on flower-growing will list different soil temperature ranges for germination of given flower seeds. This refined information may be useful to commercial growers who can cordon off one temperature-controlled section from another, but it isn't much help to the home gardener, who will be starting all his or her seeds in the same room. The truth is, most flower seeds will germinate readily if soil is between 60°–70°F (usually closer to 60°F)—which fortunately coincides with typical home temperatures. Remember that even outdoors, where we sow seeds directly yet have no such control, plenty of seeds still manage to germinate. In the listings which follow, finicky germinators are noted; in such cases, it may be wise to sow a little extra seed to compensate.

My advice about germinating temperatures is to relax. Let nature work her magic.

CLEAN SEEDS

Some flowers—Gazania (Treasure Flower) is a prime example—naturally encase their seeds in a mass of fuzz or fiber. Before these seeds can be planted, they must be separated from the fluff. In many cases, this job is done by the seed house, which will advertise its offering as "clean." In some cases it is not, and should you open a packet to find a lot of extraneous fuzzy stuff, remember to remove it from each seed before planting.

BREAKING DORMANCY

Some seeds require special treatment to break dormancy and thereby hasten the germination process. *Soaking* seed for 12–24 hours is one such method. *Scarification*—nicking or scratching the seedcoat to more readily allow it to take up moisture—is another. A metal nail file is the safest tool for this tricky job. *Stratification*, pre-chilling seeds for some days or even weeks before planting is a third method of breaking dormancy. (Germination occurs when the seeds warm up, because the artificial chill you've given them mimics winter; thawing means spring and time to start growth.) Seeds requiring such treatments will be identified under SPECIAL NOTES.

CUTTING FLOWERS

Flowers should be cut in the morning or in the evening, when they have the most water, and not during the heat of the day. You should always use a sharp knife or scissors, and cut the stems at an angle, which gives both the new stem ends as much surface area as possible to absorb water. Bring a pail of warm water with you into the garden, and plunge each cut flower into it immediately. When you get inside strip off the leaves that would be under water anyway, make a new diagonal cut in each stem, then stand the flowers in cool water. Leave the flowers in a cool spot for several hours. To keep them beautiful as long as possible, change the water and give the stems a new diagonal cut every day.

DRIED FLOWERS

A good number of plants in the listings (Strawflower, Starflower and Statice, to name a few) are grown for the beauty of their dried flowers. Drying instructions for each are usually sent by the seed house along with your order. For the most commonly dried flowers, I've included instructions under SPECIAL NOTES.

A bed of Rose Moss catches the morning sun.

Irises and Wallflowers grow freely
in this fragrance garden.

A patchwork of color unfolds before this rustic garden seat.

AFRICAN DAISY

ARCTOTIS STOECHADIFOLIA
**Also called Blue-Eyed African Daisy,
African Lilac Daisy**
Annual

African Daisy is easy to grow, tolerates drought, and prefers cool climates, or at least cool nights. Cactus-type flowers have shimmering petals that close at night and during cloudy weather and the blooms, up to 4″ across, are excellent for fresh arrangements.

Several other, mostly Daisy-like, flowers like the Cape Marigold (also known as Star-of-the-veldt), the perennial Transvaal Daisy, Gazania and even Golden Ageratum, are also frequently called African Daisy. So if this is the flower you like, order it by its Latin name.

- DEGREE OF DIFFICULTY: Easy
- USES: Borders, beds, cutting
- HEIGHT: 10″–12″
- COLORS: White, yellow, violet and orange, pink and bronze; dark centers
- SIZE OF BLOOM: 3″–4″
- FROST TOLERANCE: Tender
- PREFERS: Cool weather
- WHEN TO SOW INDOORS: 6–8 weeks before last frost
- DAYS TO GERMINATION: 21–30
- WHEN TO SOW OUTDOORS OR SET TRANSPLANTS: In spring when weather has warmed; set transplants when night temperatures reach 50°F and ground has warmed
- SOIL CONDITIONS: Sandy, light, average or even poor soil, with good drainage
- DISTANCE BETWEEN PLANTS: 6″–12″
- SUNLIGHT REQUIREMENTS: Full sun

DEADHEADING FLOWERS

Deadheading is the process of removing unsightly dead or dying flowers from a plant. The best tool for the job is a pair of sharp scissors, but I have certainly done my share of manual pinching-back while on my evening garden inspection tour.

Aesthetics aside, deadheading is important for another reason. To insure its own reproduction, a plant expends much of its energy on producing flower and setting seed. If you remove the dead blossoms before they have a chance to set mature seed, the plant flowers again and again in an effort to conclude the interrupted cycle. Thus the more you deadhead, the more flowers the plant produces, and because none of the plant's energy will have been put into seed production, you will be rewarded with strong, continuous blossoming over much of the season.

- WATERING: Allow to dry out between waterings, avoid standing water
- DAYS TO BLOOM/BLOOMING PERIOD: 8–10 weeks from seed; summer until fall
- SPECIAL NOTES: Deadhead spent blossoms

AGERATUM

AGERATUM HOUSTONIANUM
Also called Floss Flower
Annual

While the dainty Ageratum is best known for having the "truest blues" in the garden, and is often planted especially to get this stripe of color along the low front edge of a tiered border grouping, pink and white hybrids are now also quite common. The dwarf types are most commonly grown, but one or two tall cultivars do appear in seed catalogues. Ageratum can be planted directly in the garden, but because it is tender and has to go in the ground late, and because it takes many weeks from seed to flower, it is advisable to start it indoors in cold climates.

- DEGREE OF DIFFICULTY: Easy
- USES: Bedding, borders, rock gardens, excellent edging for plant; tall varieties good for cutting
- HEIGHT: 5″–9″; tall varieties grow to 2′
- COLORS: Blue, pink, white
- SIZE OF BLOOM: ¼″–½″ in fluffy clusters
- FROST TOLERANCE: Tender
- PREFERS: Warm weather
- WHEN TO SOW INDOORS: 6–8 weeks before last frost; do not cover seeds, need light to germinate
- DAYS TO GERMINATION: 7–10
- WHEN TO SOW OUTDOORS OR SET TRANSPLANTS: After danger of frost
- SOIL CONDITIONS: Average, well-drained, but will grow in almost any soil
- DISTANCE BETWEEN PLANTS: 8″–12″
- SUNLIGHT REQUIREMENTS: Sun or light shade
- WATERING: Water moderately

- DAYS TO BLOOM/BLOOMING PERIOD: 9–10 weeks from seed; early summer to fall
- SPECIAL NOTES: Fertilize monthly. Cut off faded flowers. Most popular varieties: Blue Danube, Blue Blazer, Blue Tango

ALYSSUM

LOBULARIA MARITIMA
Also called Sweet Alyssum
Annual

Alyssum's low height makes it popular for edgings, borders and as a ground cover. It is very easy to grow, can be started in early spring, and adapts to many soil conditions. One of the best cool-weather performers, Alyssum flowers from spring until frost. It quickly produces many small sweetly-scented white or brightly colored flowers on compact, low-spreading plants. Alyssum grows easily when sown outdoors from seed.

- DEGREE OF DIFFICULTY: Easy
- USES: Beds, borders, edging, ground cover
- HEIGHT: 2″–4″
- COLORS: White, lavender, pink, purple
- SIZE OF BLOOM: 1″–2″ clusters on many-branched mounds spreading 6″–12″
- FROST TOLERANCE: Hardy
- PREFERS: Cool weather
- WHEN TO SOW INDOORS: 6 weeks before last frost
- DAYS TO GERMINATION: 8–15; do not cover—seeds need light to germinate

- WHEN TO SOW OUTDOORS OR SET TRANSPLANTS: Early spring, several weeks before last frost
- SOIL CONDITIONS: Average, well-drained soil, but tolerates diverse conditions
- DISTANCE BETWEEN PLANTS: 5″–8″
- SUNLIGHT REQUIREMENTS: Prefers full sun, tolerates partial shade
- WATERING: Keep moist but well-drained
- DAYS TO BLOOM/BLOOMING PERIOD: Spring until frost
- SPECIAL NOTES: Trim to remove spent blossoms. Occasional shearing will encourage flowering. Most popular varieties: Carpet of Snow, Rosie O'Day, Royal Carpet

AMARANTHUS

AMARANTHACEAE
Annual

This family of mostly warm-climate plants counts among its members some irksome weeds like Pigweed and Tumbleweed, detracting, perhaps, from the popularity of the extremely lovely ornamental varieties. (The so-called Globe Amaranth, on page 172, is a different genus.) All varieties are easy to grow, both from seeds and propagated from cuttings, provided they're given an open, sunny spot.

Three of the more popular types are listed here: Love-lies-bleeding (caudatus); Prince's Feather (hybridus), and Joseph's Coat (tricolor). Harlequin bugs are sometimes a problem for all Amaranthus varieties, as are carrot beetles. Handpick and spray often with garlic-hot-pepper concoction. See page 47 for how to prepare. Amaranth does not transplant well once it is in flower.

Notes

JOSEPH'S COAT
AMARANTHUS TRICOLOR
Also called Joseph's Coat, Chinese Spinach

The most commonly found and most popular of the Amaranth family, this plant is grown primarily for the beauty of its leaves which can be scarlet, bronze, yellow, orange, green or a mixture of all of these colors. Tricolor is easy to grow, and thrives better, producing even more colorful foliage, if the soil is somewhat poor. The leaves of this plant are eaten in some parts of the world as the herb Tampala.

- DEGREE OF DIFFICULTY: Easy
- USES: Beds, borders
- HEIGHT: 1"–4"
- COLORS: Deep red flowers; scarlet, bronze, yellow, orange, green or multi-colored leaves
- SIZE OF BLOOM: Tiny
- FROST TOLERANCE: Tender
- PREFERS: Warm season
- WHEN TO SOW INDOORS: 3–4 weeks before last frost
- DAYS TO GERMINATION: 10–15
- WHEN TO SOW OUTDOORS OR SET TRANSPLANTS: After all danger of frost
- SOIL CONDITIONS: Average
- DISTANCE BETWEEN PLANTS: 12"–24"
- SUNLIGHT REQUIREMENTS: Full sun
- WATERING: Keep evenly moist
- DAYS TO BLOOM/BLOOMING PERIOD: Midsummer until frost
- SPECIAL NOTES: Amaranthus does not transplant well once it is in flower

LOVE-LIES-BLEEDING
AMARANTHUS CAUDATUS
Also called Kiss-Me-Over-the-Garden-Gate, Tassel-Flower

Love-lies-bleeding is grown for the beauty of its leaves as well as its long, drooping ropes of blood-red flowers borne in clusters. It prefers sunny and warm conditions, is easy to grow and quite showy.

- DEGREE OF DIFFICULTY: Easy
- USES: Beds, borders, cutting
- HEIGHT: 2'–5'
- COLORS: Always red, but some foliage also reddish-colored
- SIZE OF BLOOM: Long, slender drooping spikes in clusters
- FROST TOLERANCE: Tender
- PREFERS: Warm weather
- WHEN TO SOW INDOORS: 3–4 weeks before setting out
- DAYS TO GERMINATION: 10–15
- WHEN TO SOW OUTDOORS OR SET TRANSPLANTS: After all danger of frost, when soil warms
- SOIL CONDITIONS: Average, even poor
- DISTANCE BETWEEN PLANTS: 12"–24"
- SUNLIGHT REQUIREMENTS: Full sun
- WATERING: Keep evenly moist
- DAYS TO BLOOM/BLOOMING PERIOD: Midsummer until frost
- SPECIAL NOTES: Amaranthus does not transplant well once it is in flower

PRINCE'S FEATHER
AMARANTHUS HYBRIDUS

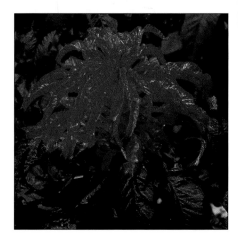

Similar to Love-lies-bleeding, this variety of Amaranthus is showy, with foliage that is sometimes red and red or brown flowers which grow upright in clusters, rather than drooping over like *Amaranthus caudatus.* It thrives in warm and sunny conditions, average soil, and blooms from midsummer until frost.

- DEGREE OF DIFFICULTY: Easy
- USES: Beds, borders
- HEIGHT: 3'–4'
- COLORS: Red, brownish red
- SIZE OF BLOOM: Tiny flowers in dense, multi-branched clusters
- FROST TOLERANCE: Tender
- PREFERS: Warm weather
- WHEN TO SOW INDOORS: 3–4 weeks before last frost
- DAYS TO GERMINATION: 10–15
- WHEN TO SOW OUTDOORS OR SET TRANSPLANTS: After all danger of frost
- SOIL CONDITIONS: Average
- DISTANCE BETWEEN PLANTS: 12"–24"
- SUNLIGHT REQUIREMENTS: Full sun
- WATERING: Water moderately
- DAYS TO BLOOM/BLOOMING PERIOD: Midsummer until frost
- SPECIAL NOTES: Amaranthus does not transplant well once it is in flower

BABY BLUE EYES
NEMOPHILA MENZIESII
Annual

This plant, as commonly called *Nemophila* as by its "common" name, is hard to find in catalogues. This is unfortunate, since its easy growing requirements, pleasant fragrance and multiple uses make it a wonderful addition to any garden. *Nemophila* can grow in most soils and produces masses of pretty sky blue flowers from early summer until frost. The mounded plants are neat and compact.

- DEGREE OF DIFFICULTY: Easy
- USES: Edging, ground cover, rock gardens, beds, borders, containers
- HEIGHT: 6"–12"
- COLORS: Blue
- SIZE OF BLOOM: 1½"
- FROST TOLERANCE: Hardy
- PREFERS: Cool weather
- WHEN TO SOW INDOORS: Not an indoor starter
- DAYS TO GERMINATION: 7–12
- WHEN TO SOW OUTDOORS OR SET TRANSPLANTS: Early spring, as soon as ground can be worked
- SOIL CONDITIONS: Light, sandy, average soil with good drainage
- DISTANCE BETWEEN PLANTS: 6"–9"
- SUNLIGHT REQUIREMENTS: Full sun to partial shade
- WATERING: Moderate watering; will tolerate dry soil
- DAYS TO BLOOM/BLOOMING PERIOD: Early summer until frost

- SPECIAL NOTES: Self-sows readily. If planted in full sun, keep well watered

BABY'S BREATH
GYPSOPHILA ELEGANS
Annual

Found under "Gypsophila" in most catalogues, Baby's Breath is an easy-to-grow annual that blooms quickly and produces myriad airy clouds of white or pink flowers on delicate twig-like sprays. It thrives in poor soil, preferably alkaline, and tolerates drought. The flowers are great for fresh bouquets and long-lasting when dried. Since Baby's Breath only blooms for about a month, make successive sowings every 2 weeks except for the hottest part of the summer for continuous display.

- DEGREE OF DIFFICULTY: Easy
- USES: Bedding, borders, rock gardens, ground cover, cutting, dried
- HEIGHT: 8"–18"
- COLORS: White (most common), pinks, red
- SIZE OF BLOOM: ¼"–1"
- FROST TOLERANCE: Hardy
- PREFERS: Cool weather
- WHEN TO SOW INDOORS: 4–5 weeks before setting out; easily direct-seeded
- DAYS TO GERMINATION: 10–18
- WHEN TO SOW OUTDOORS OR SET TRANSPLANTS: Early spring, every 2 weeks thereafter except in hottest summer

- SOIL CONDITIONS: Well-drained, nutrient-poor and alkaline
- DISTANCE BETWEEN PLANTS: 18″–24″
- SUNLIGHT REQUIREMENTS: Full sun
- WATERING: Do not overwater
- DAYS TO BLOOM/BLOOMING PERIOD: Blooms quickly, lasts about a month; can bloom from early spring to frost
- SPECIAL NOTES: Taller plants may require staking. Shear dead flowers. Do not overfertilize. Addition of some lime is good to keep the soil alkaline

BACHELOR'S BUTTONS

CENTAUREA CYANUS
Also called Cornflower
Annual

This flower appears in most catalogues, but under a variety of names, so remember both listed here to prevent confusion. These flowers make excellent bouquets, and provide a profusion of blooms in early summer. The seed heads also attract birds. Very easy to grow, Bachelor's Buttons do best if direct-seeded outside. Originally known for their blue color, they are now available in other shades as well.

- DEGREE OF DIFFICULTY: Easy
- USES: Beds, borders, good for cutting
- HEIGHT: 12″–30″
- COLORS: Best-known for cornflower blue color; also comes in pinks, reds, white
- SIZE OF BLOOM: 1″–2½″
- FROST TOLERANCE: Hardy

- PREFERS: Cool weather
- WHEN TO SOW INDOORS: Not a good indoor starter, but can try starting 4 weeks before setting outside in individual peat pots or pellets
- DAYS TO GERMINATION: 7–14; need darkness to germinate
- WHEN TO SOW OUTDOORS OR SET TRANSPLANTS: Early spring
- SOIL CONDITIONS: Prefer rich, moist soil, but will tolerate both drought and poor soil
- DISTANCE BETWEEN PLANTS: 6″–12″
- SUNLIGHT REQUIREMENTS: Full sun
- WATERING: Moderate watering; do not overwater
- DAYS TO BLOOM/BLOOMING PERIOD: Can bloom from early summer until frost; less profuse after midsummer—sow successive plantings for continuous show
- SPECIAL NOTES: Taller types may need staking. Flowers are good for drying as they retain their color. Cornflowers often reseed

BASKET OF GOLD

AURINIA SAXATILIS
Also called Goldentuft, Madwort
Perennial

Basket of Gold has masses of tiny, vivid yellow flowers over grey-green foliage. It is present in most catalogues, but can be truly challenging to find. For 200 years it bore the name *Alyssum*

saxatile and was only recently reclassified; one fragrant variety, which flowers a little later than *saxatilis,* is still called *Alyssum montanum.* This is even more confusing because the flower we know commonly as Alyssum (see page 147) isn't related at all to this group, but comes from the Lobelia family! Basket of Gold is thus frequently found under *Saxatile,* or combinations of the names already mentioned. This flower tolerates, even appreciates, poor and dry soil, but not hot and humid weather. Showy, hardy and long-lived, it is a favorite spring-blooming perennial.

- DEGREE OF DIFFICULTY: Easy
- USES: Edging, rock gardens
- HEIGHT: 6″–12″
- COLORS: Yellow and gold
- SIZE OF BLOOM: ⅛″ flowers in dense 2″–3″-across clusters
- FROST TOLERANCE: Zones 3–8
- PREFERS: Cooler weather
- WHEN TO SOW INDOORS: Spring or summer; easy to sow directly outdoors
- DAYS TO GERMINATION: 7–14; needs light to germinate
- WHEN TO SOW OUTDOORS OR SET TRANSPLANTS: Early spring; can also set transplants in fall—should be good-sized in either case
- SOIL CONDITIONS: Sandy, dry, well-drained
- DISTANCE BETWEEN PLANTS: 6″–10″
- SUNLIGHT REQUIREMENTS: Full sun
- WATERING: Moderate watering when needed; do not overwater, plants prefer dry soil

A CURIOUS PARADOX

Though most garden flowers do best in rich, evenly moist soil, some desert natives, such as Basket of Gold, Lupine, Joseph's Coat and various Daisies, actually do better in extremely dry, nutrient-poor ground. The reason is that many of our most common garden flowers have been adapted for domestic cultivation from a variety of climates and environments. And to get them to perform at their best requires that we duplicate their native conditions as closely as possible.

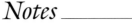
- DAYS TO BLOOM/BLOOMING PERIOD: Seeds sown in spring bloom early the following spring
- SPECIAL NOTES: Do not fertilize; this plant does not like rich soil. After flowering, shear back about half the length of the stems to encourage new growth and lengthen the life of the plant

BEGONIA

TUBEROUS BEGONIA
Perennial

Tuberous Begonias are usually grown from tender bulbs, or tubers, rather than seed, and as such are technically perennials. They can, however, be grown from seed, and at the end of the season either treated as annuals— allowed to die—or the tubers they've grown  dug up, stored, and replanted the following spring. I include them here despite the difficulty of growing them successfully from seed because they are spectacular and should have a place in the garden, whether you buy tubers or seed. Unsurpassed as a source of rich color for shady areas, they have huge lush blooms in a wide range of colors including picotee and bicolors, in single, double and multilayer forms resembling Roses, Carnations and Camellias.

- DEGREE OF DIFFICULTY: Moderately difficult
- USES: Beds, containers
- HEIGHT: 10″–12″

- COLORS: Scarlet, red, yellow, orange, rose, white, pink, copper
- SIZE OF BLOOM: Up to 5″–6″ across
- FROST TOLERANCE: Half-hardy
- PREFERS: Cool weather
- WHEN TO SOW INDOORS: In February, 12–16 weeks before last frost date
- DAYS TO GERMINATION: 15–40
- WHEN TO SOW OUTDOORS OR SET TRANSPLANTS: Cannot be sown directly outdoors. Plant tubers or set seedlings after all danger of frost is past
- SOIL CONDITIONS: Light, rich, both moist and well-drained
- DISTANCE BETWEEN PLANTS: 8″–10″
- SUNLIGHT REQUIREMENTS: Partial shade
- WATERING: Soil should be allowed to dry out between waterings
- DAYS TO BLOOM/BLOOMING PERIOD: Ten weeks from transplanting; from then to frost
- SPECIAL NOTES: Tuberous Begonias also do well as house plants set outside in the summer. They should be fertilized every two weeks with compost topdressing

BELLS OF IRELAND

MOLUCCELLA LAEVIS
Also called Molucca Balm, Shell-Flower
Annual

Because the pale green bell-shaped bracts of this plant look like flowers, it is often said to have green  flowers. It doesn't, but the shape and color of the bracts is so uncommon that it is in great demand

_____ *Notes* _____

Notes

for arrangements, both fresh and dried. It also does well at the back of borders. The plant is very slow to germinate, but once up grows quickly, producing tiny fragrant white flowers. It dries very well, and can be stored and used as an everlasting in the winter.

- DEGREE OF DIFFICULTY: Moderately easy
- USES: Cutting, dried, borders
- HEIGHT: 24"–36"
- COLORS: Tiny white blooms set deep inside bell-shaped green bracts
- SIZE OF BLOOM: 1"
- FROST TOLERANCE: Half-hardy
- PREFERS: Cool weather
- WHEN TO SOW INDOORS: 6–8 weeks before planting outside
- DAYS TO GERMINATION: 25; needs light to germinate
- WHEN TO SOW OUTDOORS OR SET TRANSPLANTS: Early spring
- SOIL CONDITIONS: Average, with good drainage
- DISTANCE BETWEEN PLANTS: 12"–15"
- SUNLIGHT REQUIREMENTS: Full sun or light shade
- WATERING: Keep regularly watered
- DAYS TO BLOOM/BLOOMING PERIOD: Midsummer until frost
- SPECIAL NOTES: Frequent cutting encourages flower production. May require staking. Fertilize monthly. Self-sows readily

BLACK-EYED SUSAN VINE

THUNBERGIA ALATA
Also called Clock Vine
Perennial, also grown as Annual

In mild climates the Black-eyed Susan Vine is a perennial, but in northern gardens it is grown as an annual. This plant is a delightful fast-growing climber that blooms all summer. And  it will bloom all winter inside. Some varieties have flowers with black centers (the eyes); some newer ones produce blooms without them.

- DEGREE OF DIFFICULTY: Easy
- USES: Ground cover, on trellises and fences, hanging baskets, planters, screens
- HEIGHT: 6′
- COLORS: Orange, yellow and white
- SIZE OF BLOOM: 1"–2"
- FROST TOLERANCE: Half-hardy
- PREFERS: Cool weather
- WHEN TO SOW INDOORS: 6–8 weeks before last frost
- DAYS TO GERMINATION: 10–20
- WHEN TO SOW OUTDOORS OR SET TRANSPLANTS: After last frost
- SOIL CONDITIONS: Rich, light, moist, well-drained
- DISTANCE BETWEEN PLANTS: 12"–15"
- SUNLIGHT REQUIREMENTS: Full sun to light shade
- WATERING: Water frequently
- DAYS TO BLOOM/BLOOMING PERIOD: Early summer until frost
- SPECIAL NOTES: Fertilize moderately. Do not prune this plant. May flower less during periods of intense heat, but will

rejuvenate as the weather gets cooler again

BLANKET-FLOWER

GAILLARDIA PULCHELLA
Also called Indian Blanket
Annual and Perennial

Very often known by its Latin name, Blanketflower is not fussy and tolerates drought, heat and poor soil, but not wet conditions. Some varieties have double flowers that may be bicolored, while others are fringed. The perennial Gaillardias produce large Daisy-like blooms from early summer through frost if started early enough. Annuals and perennials alike make excellent cutting flowers.

- DEGREE OF DIFFICULTY: Easy
- USES: Borders, bedding, cutting
- HEIGHT: 10″–18″
- COLORS: Yellow, red, red tipped with yellow
- SIZE OF BLOOM: 2″–3″
- FROST TOLERANCE: Half-hardy
- PREFERS: Warm weather
- WHEN TO SOW INDOORS: 4–6 weeks before setting out
- DAYS TO GERMINATION: 15–20
- WHEN TO SOW OUTDOORS OR SET TRANSPLANTS: After all danger of frost

- SOIL CONDITIONS: Light, sandy, well-drained
- DISTANCE BETWEEN PLANTS: 8″–15″
- SUNLIGHT REQUIREMENTS: Full sun
- WATERING: Do not overwater
- DAYS TO BLOOM/BLOOMING PERIOD: All summer until frost
- SPECIAL NOTES: Remove faded flowers to prolong bloom

BLUE DAISY

FELICIA AMELLOIDES
Also called Blue Marguerite
Perennial

Also sold as *Agathaea coelestis* when it can be found at all in seed catalogues, this wonderful plant produces beautiful, showy and numerous sky blue Daisy-like flowers. The slender stems sport interestingly hairy green leaves. It does best in cool climates. Lift plants from garden before a killing frost and bring these old greenhouse favorites inside for the winter.

- DEGREE OF DIFFICULTY: Moderate
- USES: Bedding, borders, rock gardens
- HEIGHT: 1′–3′
- COLORS: Sky blue
- SIZE OF BLOOM: 1″
- FROST TOLERANCE: Half-hardy
- PREFERS: Cool weather
- WHEN TO SOW INDOORS: Early spring
- DAYS TO GERMINATION: 20–30

- WHEN TO SOW OUTDOORS OR SET TRANSPLANTS: Early spring when ground can be worked; set transplants after danger of frost is past
- SOIL CONDITIONS: Slightly rich and somewhat dry
- DISTANCE BETWEEN PLANTS: 2′–3′
- SUNLIGHT REQUIREMENTS: Full sun
- WATERING: Moderate watering during dry periods
- DAYS TO BLOOM/BLOOMING PERIOD: Midsummer until frost
- SPECIAL NOTES: Blue Daisy needs cool weather and dry soil to thrive, and grows best in northern areas or on the West Coast

BLUE LACE-FLOWER

TRACHYMENE COERULEA
Annual

When found at all in seed catalogues, Blue Lace-flower is usually listed under its common and not its Latin name. It is easy to grow, thrives in cool summers, but does not do well in ponderous heat. The flowers are a lovely blue; they resemble Queen Anne's Lace, and are long-lasting as cut flowers.

- DEGREE OF DIFFICULTY: Easy
- USES: Bedding, borders, cutting
- HEIGHT: 24″–30″
- COLORS: Blue or lavender

- SIZE OF BLOOM: 2″–3″
- FROST TOLERANCE: Half-hardy
- PREFERS: Cool weather
- WHEN TO SOW INDOORS: Resents transplanting; best started outdoors, but can be started 6–8 weeks before last frost in individual peat pellets
- DAYS TO GERMINATION: 15–20; needs darkness to germinate
- WHEN TO SOW OUTDOORS OR SET TRANSPLANTS: After last frost
- SOIL CONDITIONS: Sandy, light, rich, very well-drained
- DISTANCE BETWEEN PLANTS: 12″
- SUNLIGHT REQUIREMENTS: Full sun
- WATERING: Moderate watering
- DAYS TO BLOOM/BLOOMING PERIOD: Summer
- SPECIAL NOTES: May require staking

BLUE SAGE

SALVIA FARINACEA
Also called: Mealy-Cup Sage
Perennial

Found under "Salvia" in most seed catalogues— along with its cousin *Salvia splendens* (Scarlet Sage)—this half-hardy perennial frequently grown as an annual will bloom the first year from seed if sown early enough. The plant has beautiful vivid blue flowers on upright spikes, and a white-flowered variety is now also available. Excellent for cutting and as a dried flower, it blooms from early summer until frost.

- DEGREE OF DIFFICULTY: Easy
- USES: Borders, bedding, planters, dried, cutting
- HEIGHT: 18″–36″
- COLORS: Blue, violet
- SIZE OF BLOOM: ½″
- FROST TOLERANCE: Half-hardy
- PREFERS: Warm weather
- WHEN TO SOW INDOORS: 12 weeks before last frost
- DAYS TO GERMINATION: 12–15
- WHEN TO SOW OUTDOORS OR SET TRANSPLANTS: Can be sown outdoors from spring until 2 months before first fall frost; set plants in garden when soil is warm
- SOIL CONDITIONS: Well-drained, moist, rich
- DISTANCE BETWEEN PLANTS: 6″–18″
- SUNLIGHT REQUIREMENTS: Full sun or light shade
- WATERING: Keep well-watered
- DAYS TO BLOOM/BLOOMING PERIOD: Early summer until frost
- SPECIAL NOTES: Fertilize monthly

BUTTERFLY FLOWER

SCHIZANTHUS × WISETONINSIS
Also called Poor Man's Orchid
Annual

The Butterfly Flower is a bushy plant with large, Orchidlike blooms. It thrives well in containers, and only in regions with long cool summers, such as the Pacific Northwest. But wherever you are, if

you can give it some cooling shade, this flower still might do well in your garden. It's an unusual plant, as you can see from the photograph, and perhaps worth trying for that reason alone.

- DEGREE OF DIFFICULTY: Moderately easy
- USES: Bedding, borders, planters, cutting
- HEIGHT: 12″–24″; some very dwarf varieties also available
- COLORS: Pinks, reds, lilac, violet, purples, yellows, and combined colors
- SIZE OF BLOOM: 1½″
- FROST TOLERANCE: Half-hardy
- PREFERS: Cool weather
- WHEN TO SOW INDOORS: 12 weeks before last frost date
- DAYS TO GERMINATION: 20–30; the fine seeds should not be covered, but darkness is helpful in germination, so cover flat with black plastic or put in a dark place
- WHEN TO SOW OUTDOORS OR SET TRANSPLANTS: As soon as danger of frost is past
- SOIL CONDITIONS: Moist and rich with excellent drainage
- DISTANCE BETWEEN PLANTS: 12″
- SUNLIGHT REQUIREMENTS: Full sun to partial shade
- WATERING: Keep evenly watered
- DAYS TO BLOOM/BLOOMING PERIOD: In later summer
- SPECIAL NOTES: Pinch tops to encourage bushiness. Although it flowers best when potbound and is thus a great choice for container planting, Butterfly Flower may not be the ideal indoor plant as it really thrives best in greenhouse conditions, with cool nights and high humidity

CALIFORNIA POPPY

ESCHSCHOLZIA CALIFORNICA
Annual

Found under its common
name in almost all seed
catalogues, the California
Poppy is early-blooming,
easy to grow, and
produces an abundance of
silky, bright flowers with
almost no effort. It
should be started in place outdoors, and
tolerates drought after the seedlings have
emerged; in fact, it likes dry, hot areas and
poor soil.

- DEGREE OF DIFFICULTY: Very easy
- USES: Bedding, borders, edging, rock gardens
- HEIGHT: 12″–15″
- COLORS: Oranges, yellows, golds, scarlet, crimson, white
- SIZE OF BLOOM: 3″–4″
- FROST TOLERANCE: Hardy
- PREFERS: Cool weather
- WHEN TO SOW INDOORS: Not an indoor starter
- DAYS TO GERMINATION: 10–20
- WHEN TO SOW OUTDOORS OR SET TRANSPLANTS: Early spring; in areas with mild winters, sow outdoors in fall for early spring bloom
- SOIL CONDITIONS: Light, sandy, well-drained, moderately dry
- DISTANCE BETWEEN PLANTS: 6″–8″
- SUNLIGHT REQUIREMENTS: Full sun is best, but will tolerate partial shade
- WATERING: Keep well-watered until seedlings are up; then avoid overwatering
- DAYS TO BLOOM/BLOOMING PERIOD: Late spring until frost

- SPECIAL NOTES: Pick faded flowers to prolong blooming. It may reseed, but the results will probably be smaller, mostly orange flowers

CANDYTUFT

IBERIS AMARA
Also called Rocket Candytuft
Annual

This flower comes in
colors and has a different
shape than its cousin
Iberis umbellata, and
slightly different habits.
The seeds are also less
widely available. In areas
with mild winters, it is
frequently sown in winter for early spring
bloom. Dwarf forms are said to be
available, although I could find none in the
many catalogues I looked through. Rocket
Candytuft is fragrant.

- DEGREE OF DIFFICULTY: Moderately easy
- USES: Bedding, borders, edging, cutting
- HEIGHT: 10″–15″
- COLORS: White
- SIZE OF BLOOM: ½″–1″
- FROST TOLERANCE: Hardy
- PREFERS: Cool weather
- WHEN TO SOW INDOORS: 6–8 weeks prior to frost; easy to direct-seed
- DAYS TO GERMINATION: 10–15
- WHEN TO SOW OUTDOORS OR SET TRANSPLANTS: After danger of frost; in mild climates, can be sown outdoors in late summer for early spring bloom
- SOIL CONDITIONS: Well-drained, average soil

Notes

_____ *Notes* _____

- DISTANCE BETWEEN PLANTS: 9″–15″
- SUNLIGHT REQUIREMENTS: Full sun
- WATERING: Water when dry
- DAYS TO BLOOM/BLOOMING PERIOD: About 6 weeks from germination; early summer until frost
- SPECIAL NOTES: Remove faded flowers to prolong bloom

- SOIL CONDITIONS: Well-drained, moist soil, but will tolerate average soil and occasional drought
- DISTANCE BETWEEN PLANTS: 8″–15″
- SUNLIGHT REQUIREMENTS: Full sun
- WATERING: Let soil dry out between waterings
- DAYS TO BLOOM/BLOOMING PERIOD: 6 weeks after germination; all summer long
- SPECIAL NOTES: Cut faded flowers to prolong bloom

CANDYTUFT

IBERIS UMBELLATA
Also called Globe Candytuft
Annual

This Candytuft has tiny flowers clustered in a 2″ umbrella shape, forming a uniform dense blanket of color on compact, bushy plants. It is easy to grow and does best in areas with cool summers. Start seeds directly outdoors in early spring in cold climates, and in late winter in milder areas.

- DEGREE OF DIFFICULTY: Moderately easy
- USES: Beds, borders, edging, rock gardens, cutting
- HEIGHT: 8″–18″
- COLORS: Red, pink, lavender, rose, white
- SIZE OF BLOOM: 2″
- FROST TOLERANCE: Hardy
- PREFERS: Cool weather
- WHEN TO SOW INDOORS: 6–8 weeks prior to last frost; easy to start outdoors
- DAYS TO GERMINATION: 10–15
- WHEN TO SOW OUTDOORS OR SET TRANSPLANTS: After all danger of frost

CANTERBURY BELLS

CAMPANULA MEDIUM
Biennial grown as Annual

Canterbury Bells, listed as "Campanula" in most seed catalogues, are easy-to-grow biennials, which are frequently grown as annuals. The bell-shaped flowers are long-lived and bloom over a period of several weeks. The plants will thrive in sun or partial shade, and are not terribly particular about soil conditions.

- DEGREE OF DIFFICULTY: Easy
- USES: Beds, borders, edgings, ground cover
- HEIGHT: 2′–4′
- COLORS: White, blue, pink
- SIZE OF BLOOM: 1″–2″
- FROST TOLERANCE: Biennial; can be grown as a hardy annual
- PREFERS: Cool weather

- WHEN TO SOW INDOORS: As annual, sow indoors 6–8 weeks before setting out; as biennial, sow outdoors
- DAYS TO GERMINATION: 10–21
- WHEN TO SOW OUTDOORS OR SET TRANSPLANTS: Late spring to early summer
- SOIL CONDITIONS: Average, moist soil
- DISTANCE BETWEEN PLANTS: 4"–18"
- SUNLIGHT REQUIREMENTS: Sun or partial shade
- WATERING: Keep well-watered
- DAYS TO BLOOM/BLOOMING PERIOD: If started indoors, blooms same summer; sown outdoors, blooms second summer

CAPE DAISY

VENIDIUM FASTUOSUM
Also called Monarch of the Veldt
Annual

Listed under "Venidium" in the seed catalogues that have it at all, this is a rather hard seed to find under any of its names. As long as it is kept well-drained and in full sun, Cape Daisy, with its  young leaves that look as if they are covered with cobwebs, is easy to grow even in difficult soil, and will produce an abundance of blooms from summer until late fall that last well when cut.

- DEGREE OF DIFFICULTY: Moderately easy
- USES: Borders, cutting
- HEIGHT: 1½'–3'
- COLORS: Yellow and orange with purple-black zone around a dark center

- SIZE OF BLOOM: 4"–5"
- FROST TOLERANCE: Half-hardy
- PREFERS: Cool weather, but can tolerate heat
- WHEN TO SOW INDOORS: 6–8 weeks before last frost
- DAYS TO GERMINATION: 6–15; seeds need light to germinate
- WHEN TO SOW OUTDOORS OR SET TRANSPLANTS: After danger of frost
- SOIL CONDITIONS: Sandy, light, well-drained
- DISTANCE BETWEEN PLANTS: 12"
- SUNLIGHT REQUIREMENTS: Full sun
- WATERING: Do not overwater; needs to be kept well-drained
- DAYS TO BLOOM/BLOOMING PERIOD: Summer to late fall
- SPECIAL NOTES: May require staking. Even as cut flowers, blooms will continue to open in the morning and close at night

CARNATION

DIANTHUS CARYOPHYLLUS
Perennial grown as Annual

The Carnation, sometimes listed as Dianthus, is a member of the Dianthus family, along with Sweet William and China Pinks (sometimes just called Pinks see page 159). With its spicy fragrance and long-lasting blooms of rich color (especially its brilliant reds), the Carnation is perhaps the most popular cutting flower. Dwarf varieties are common, as are those which produce fringed and fully double flowers. Carnations thrive in cool climates, but newer heat-resistant hybrids bred for extremely warm climates will produce abundant blooms in even the hottest summer weather. But be prepared to keep the soil good and moist. The Carnation is technically a perennial, but is best grown as an annual. (Some varieties may even be grown as biennials). To winter-over, cut Carnations back in the fall and apply a heavy mulch after the ground has frozen.

- DEGREE OF DIFFICULTY: Easy
- USES: Bedding, borders, containers, rock gardens, cutting
- HEIGHT: 1'–3'
- COLORS: Red, pink, white, rose, crimson, lavender, scarlet, yellow
- SIZE OF BLOOM: 2"–3"
- FROST TOLERANCE: Half-hardy
- PREFERS: Cool weather
- WHEN TO SOW INDOORS: 8–10 weeks before last frost date
- DAYS TO GERMINATION: 10–20
- WHEN TO SOW OUTDOORS OR SET TRANSPLANTS: If started indoors or sown direct, when soil is warm; for biennial, plant in midsummer to bloom following year
- SOIL CONDITIONS: Sandy, loose, well-drained
- DISTANCE BETWEEN PLANTS: 8"–12"
- SUNLIGHT REQUIREMENTS: Full sun
- WATERING: Prefers damp and cool conditions; keep soil moist, especially in hotter climates
- DAYS TO BLOOM/BLOOMING PERIOD: 5 months from seed; started very early, will flower from late spring to frost, can be brought inside for further bloom
- SPECIAL NOTES: Fertilize moderately. Tall varieties, excellent for cutting, may require staking. Remove secondary buds to promote finer flowers

CELOSIA

CELOSIA CRISTATA
Also called Cockscomb
Annual

This is an unusual-looking flower in both shape and texture. *Celosia cristata*, or Cockscomb, is the extraordinary crested form whose bloom resembles a wavy mass of rooster combs. Flowers are brightly colored and long-lasting when fresh cut and make excellent dried bouquets. The plant is easy to grow, starts blooming early and continues until frost. In addition, it will tolerate poor soil and dry conditions.

- DEGREE OF DIFFICULTY: Easy
- USES: Bedding, borders, cutting, dried
- HEIGHT: 1'–2'
- COLORS: Red, orange, purple, pink
- SIZE OF BLOOM: 6"–12"
- FROST TOLERANCE: Tender
- PREFERS: Warm weather
- WHEN TO SOW INDOORS: 4 weeks before last frost date
- DAYS TO GERMINATION: 10–15
- WHEN TO SOW OUTDOORS OR SET TRANSPLANTS: When soil is warm, after all danger of frost
- SOIL CONDITIONS: Rich, well-drained soil
- DISTANCE BETWEEN PLANTS: 9"–12"
- SUNLIGHT REQUIREMENTS: Full sun
- WATERING: Water moderately
- DAYS TO BLOOM/BLOOMING PERIOD: A few weeks after sowing, continues until frost
- SPECIAL NOTES: Sowing or setting out transplants too early can ruin the performance of Celosia, nor do they transplant well once they are in flower. Use spent blooms as dried flowers

CELOSIA

CELOSIA PLUMOSA
Annual

Celosia plumosa is entirely different from its cousin *C. cristata*. The plants have plumes rather than crests, they are generally a little taller than *cristata*, and the color range is greater. Growing habits, however, are similar, and *plumosa* is an equally extraordinary-looking plant.

- DEGREE OF DIFFICULTY: Easy
- USES: Borders, beds, cutting, dried
- HEIGHT: 7"–36"
- COLORS: Red, cream, rose, yellow, orange
- SIZE OF BLOOM: 5"–12"
- FROST TOLERANCE: Tender
- PREFERS: Warm weather
- WHEN TO SOW INDOORS: 4 weeks before last frost
- DAYS TO GERMINATION: 10–15
- WHEN TO SOW OUTDOORS OR SET TRANSPLANTS: When ground is warm, after danger of frost
- SOIL CONDITIONS: Rich, well-drained
- DISTANCE BETWEEN PLANTS: 9"–12"
- SUNLIGHT REQUIREMENTS: Full sun
- WATERING: Keep evenly moist
- DAYS TO BLOOM/BLOOMING PERIOD: Several weeks after sowing, continues until frost

- SPECIAL NOTES: Apply compost monthly. Celosia does not transplant well once it is in full flower. Use spent blooms for dried flowers

CHINA ASTER

CALLISTEPHUS CHINENSIS
Also called Aster
Annual

There is a large family of perennial Asters, but this is a long-stemmed, long-lasting annual—one of the most popular flowers for cutting. China Asters are available in a broad range of colors, sizes and flower forms. They are easy to grow, and can be started inside or sown directly outside. However, the plants are susceptible to wilt. Though most are now sold in wilt-resistant or wilt-tolerant varieties, to reduce the chance of wilt disease never plant them in the same spot two seasons running.

- DEGREE OF DIFFICULTY: Moderately difficult
- USES: Bedding, borders, cutting
- HEIGHT: Dwarf varieties 6"–12"; medium varieties, 15"–18"; tall varieties, 20"–36"
- COLORS: Blues, purple, pinks, white, red, yellow
- SIZE OF BLOOM: Single-petalled to fully double flowers 3"–5" across
- FROST TOLERANCE: Tender
- PREFERS: Warm weather

- WHEN TO SOW INDOORS: 5–7 weeks before last frost date; cover seeds only lightly
- DAYS TO GERMINATION: 8–14
- WHEN TO SOW OUTDOORS OR SET TRANSPLANTS: After all danger of frost
- SOIL CONDITIONS: Fertile, well-drained and sandy. Asters thrive in dry, hot locations, and their color may be more brilliant when grown in poor soil
- DISTANCE BETWEEN PLANTS: 10″–18″
- SUNLIGHT REQUIREMENTS: Full sun
- WATERING: Keep moist but well-drained; mulch to conserve moisture
- DAYS TO BLOOM/BLOOMING PERIOD: Midsummer until frost
- SPECIAL NOTES: Plant both early- and late-flowering varieties, and make successive plantings, both for a longer blooming season and because Asters stop blooming after they are cut. Powderpuff Bouquet Asters make perfect whole-plant bouquets

CHINA PINK

DIANTHUS CHINENSIS
Also called Indian Pink
Annual

China Pinks are often listed as *Dianthus* or just Pinks, but this can be misleading as there are also perennial varieties of *Dianthus* called Pinks. To further confuse the situation, Pinks are

sometimes grouped with Sweet William and Carnations, which are yet other types of *Dianthus*. In these listings, the three—China Pinks, Sweet William and Carnations—are considered separately. China Pinks are an old-fashioned favorite, good for container growing as well as for bedding and borders, but readily overwhelmed by heat. Otherwise, they are easily started outdoors and flower profusely and continuously over a long season. Some of the newer hybrids are much more heat-tolerant, so look for these varieties in the catalogues. Some varieties are also slightly fragrant.

- DEGREE OF DIFFICULTY: Easy
- USES: Bedding, borders, edgings, rock gardens, containers
- HEIGHT: 4″–18″
- COLORS: White, red, pinks, purple, lilac
- SIZE OF BLOOM: ½″–2″
- FROST TOLERANCE: Half-hardy
- PREFERS: Cool weather
- WHEN TO SOW INDOORS: 6–8 weeks before last frost
- DAYS TO GERMINATION: 5–10
- WHEN TO SOW OUTDOORS OR SET TRANSPLANTS: After danger of frost
- SOIL CONDITIONS: Well-drained, alkaline, light, sandy
- DISTANCE BETWEEN PLANTS: 6″–12″
- SUNLIGHT REQUIREMENTS: Full sun
- WATERING: Water moderately; tolerates drought
- DAYS TO BLOOM/BLOOMING PERIOD: Starts blooming in late spring, and, unless too hot, continues until frost
- SPECIAL NOTES: Keep moderately fertilized, and well limed. Remove spent blossoms frequently to encourage continuous bloom

Notes

_____ *Notes* _____

CHINESE FORGET-ME-NOT

CYNOGLOSSUM AMABILE
Also called Hound's Tongue
Biennial grown as Annual

Breathtaking pure sky-blue flowers, grey-green foliage, and leaves shaped like a dog's tongue are the trademarks of Chinese Forget-me-not. Though not a good cutting flower, it is very easy to grow,  tolerates wet or dry soil, cold temperatures or the heat of midsummer and produces an abundance of densely covering flowers on a tough plant. Despite all this, it is not common in gardens or in seed catalogues. Chinese Forget-me-not is a biennial, usually grown as a hardy annual, which blooms the first season from seed, and then flowers again the second year.

- DEGREE OF DIFFICULTY: Easy
- USES: Bedding, borders, rock gardens
- HEIGHT: 18″–24″
- COLORS: Usually blue, but also pink, white
- SIZE OF BLOOM: ¼″–⅓″
- FROST TOLERANCE: Hardy
- PREFERS: Cool weather, but enjoys warm or cool
- WHEN TO SOW INDOORS: 5–7 weeks before setting out
- DAYS TO GERMINATION: 5–10; cover—seeds need darkness to germinate
- WHEN TO SOW OUTDOORS OR SET TRANSPLANTS: Early spring, as soon as ground can be worked
- SOIL CONDITIONS: Well-drained, moderately dry

- DISTANCE BETWEEN PLANTS: 9″–12″
- SUNLIGHT REQUIREMENTS: Full sun
- WATERING: Water moderately
- DAYS TO BLOOM/BLOOMING PERIOD: Early spring until frost

CHRYSANTHEMUM

CHRYSANTHEMUM ×
MORIFOLIUM
Perennial

Several popular flowers are part of the genus *Chrysanthemum;* the one described here is the Garden Chrysanthemum, commonly called "mum." It is a perennial which can be grown as an  annual to flower the first year from seed, but will continue to produce flowers for years to come. The blooms come in many forms and sizes. Mums are easy to grow and flower long after most plants have given up for the winter.

- DEGREE OF DIFFICULTY: Moderately easy
- USES: Beds, borders, containers, cutting
- HEIGHT: 9″–4′
- COLORS: Every color but blue
- SIZE OF BLOOM: ½″–10″
- FROST TOLERANCE: Hardy
- PREFERS: Cool weather
- WHEN TO SOW INDOORS: 8–12 weeks before last frost
- DAYS TO GERMINATION: 8–15

- WHEN TO SOW OUTDOORS OR SET TRANSPLANTS: Can be sown outside in spring or summer up to 2 months before frost (for bloom the following summer); set transplants after danger of frost
- SOIL CONDITIONS: Well drained and rich
- DISTANCE BETWEEN PLANTS: 10″–20″
- SUNLIGHT REQUIREMENTS: Full sun
- WATERING: Keep well-watered
- DAYS TO BLOOM/BLOOMING PERIOD: Late summer through fall
- SPECIAL NOTES: Deadhead spent blossoms. Mums should be pinched at the tips to encourage flowering. May require staking. A layer of mulch in the winter is beneficial, but must be placed after frost as mums will rot if they sit in soggy soil

CLARKIA

CLARKIA UNGUICULATA
Also called Rocky Mountain Garland Flower, Farewell-to-Spring
Annual

Clarkia offers myriad feathery blooms on bushy plants in both semi-double and double forms and a wide range of colors. It belongs to the same family as Godetia, but is generally listed separately in seed catalogues, even though both are now considered hybrids of the same genus. Clarkia is available mainly in catalogues from Great Britain—notably Thompson & Morgan—and is

unfortunately a rarity in American gardens. It should be sown directly outside, and thrives in marginal soil with excellent drainage. Cool nights and cool, dry summers are best for Clarkia, but it will be productive—for a shorter time—in hotter climates. Look for varieties that may bloom throughout the summer if you are in a warmer climate. Clarkia is a great cutting flower.

- DEGREE OF DIFFICULTY: Easy
- USES: Bedding, containers, cutting
- HEIGHT: 18″–36″
- COLORS: White, red, pinks, orange, purples
- SIZE OF BLOOM: 2″
- FROST TOLERANCE: Hardy
- PREFERS: Cool weather
- WHEN TO SOW INDOORS: Not an indoor starter
- DAYS TO GERMINATION: 5–10
- WHEN TO SOW OUTDOORS OR SET TRANSPLANTS: Early spring—barely cover the fine seeds; in frost-free areas sow in fall for early bloom the following spring
- SOIL CONDITIONS: Sandy, light, not rich, excellent drainage
- DISTANCE BETWEEN PLANTS: 8″–10″
- SUNLIGHT REQUIREMENTS: Full sun or light shade; in hotter climates, partial shade may extend flowering
- WATERING: Allow to dry out between waterings; do not overwater, but keep soil moist if weather very hot and dry
- DAYS TO BLOOM/BLOOMING PERIOD: Where the summers are cool and dry from summer until frost; in hotter and more humid areas, only for several early-summer weeks
- SPECIAL NOTES: Crowding encourages blooming, so plant in clumps, or thin sparingly

COLUMBINE

AQUILEGIA
Perennial grown as Annual

Found in seed catalogues both under its common and Latin names, this plant can flower the first year from seed if started early inside. Even though it self-sows readily, it is not very long-lived and requires frequent resowings. If the foliage is not attacked by leaf miners or borers, it will remain beautiful through most of the summer.

- DEGREE OF DIFFICULTY: Moderately difficult
- USES: Beds, borders, rock gardens, cutting
- HEIGHT: 1′–3′
- COLORS: Red, yellow, pink, blue, lavender, white, bicolors
- SIZE OF BLOOM: 1½″–4″
- FROST TOLERANCE: Hardy
- PREFERS: Cool weather
- WHEN TO SOW INDOORS: 10–14 weeks before setting out; seeds need light to germinate; after sowing, refrigerate the seed flat for 3 weeks, then allow seeds to germinate at room temperature
- DAYS TO GERMINATION: 18–25
- WHEN TO SOW OUTDOORS OR SET TRANSPLANTS: Early spring, as soon as the ground can be worked. Sow in late summer for flowers early the following spring, but may need to protect under mulch
- SOIL CONDITIONS: High in organic material, cool, moist, excellent drainage
- DISTANCE BETWEEN PLANTS: 12″–24″

- SUNLIGHT REQUIREMENTS: Partial shade preferable; full sun tolerable in climates with cooler summers
- WATERING: Keep very well watered
- DAYS TO BLOOM/BLOOMING PERIOD: Spring and early summer
- SPECIAL NOTES: Keep the soil enriched. See page 44 for control of leaf miners

COREOPSIS

COREOPSIS TINCTORIA
Also called Calliopsis, Golden Coreopsis
Annual

Coreopsis are very showy, vividly colored single or double Daisy-like flowers. Originally available as long-stalked cultivars with thin, wiry stems, Coreopsis now also comes in dwarf varieties.  Strangely enough, all forms of Coreopsis are difficult to find in seed catalogues. Exactly why, I'm not sure: it is not prone to disease, tolerates poor soil, and even likes to be crowded, making it an excellent choice for a naturalized wildflower planting. Look for Coreopsis; it's worth planting.

- DEGREE OF DIFFICULTY: Moderate
- USES: Bedding, borders, edging, cutting
- HEIGHT: 8″–36″
- COLORS: Yellow, maroon, crimson, pinks, bicolors
- SIZE OF BLOOM: 1¼″
- FROST TOLERANCE: Hardy
- PREFERS: Warm weather; generally heat-resistant

- WHEN TO SOW INDOORS: 6–8 weeks before last frost
- DAYS TO GERMINATION: 7–10
- WHEN TO SOW OUTDOORS OR SET TRANSPLANTS: After all danger of frost has passed
- SOIL CONDITIONS: Light, sandy soil, excellent drainage; tolerates poor soil well
- DISTANCE BETWEEN PLANTS: 8″–12″
- SUNLIGHT REQUIREMENTS: Full sun
- WATERING: Moderate; dislikes wet soil
- DAYS TO BLOOM/BLOOMING PERIOD: All summer long
- SPECIAL NOTES: Do not thin—Coreopsis blooms better when crowded. The tall varieties may need staking for support, as the stems are slender. Remove spent blossoms frequently to prolong blooming

COSMOS

COSMOS BIPINNATUS
Also called Garden Cosmos, Mexican Aster
Annual

Both this Cosmos, which comes in the pink-crimson range, and the Yellow Cosmos in the orange-yellow-red spectrum are beautiful, very easy-to-grow annuals that thrive in average soil and tolerate poor conditions and even occasional neglect. They are easy to sow directly outside, and are lovely in the garden or as a cutting flower for arrangements, where their radiant color and lacy foliage will enliven any room. Many varieties are available.

- DEGREE OF DIFFICULTY: Easy
- USES: Beds, borders, edgings; taller varieties for cutting
- HEIGHT: 3′–6′
- COLORS: White, pink, crimson
- SIZE OF BLOOM: 1″–5″
- FROST TOLERANCE: Tender
- PREFERS: Warm weather
- WHEN TO SOW INDOORS: Direct-seeds well, but to get an early start, sow 5–7 weeks before setting out
- DAYS TO GERMINATION: 5–10 days
- WHEN TO SOW OUTDOORS OR SET TRANSPLANTS: After all danger of frost
- SOIL CONDITIONS: Does well even in dry and poor soil, but should be well-drained
- DISTANCE BETWEEN PLANTS: 12″–24″
- SUNLIGHT REQUIREMENTS: Full sun
- WATERING: Tolerates infrequent waterings
- DAYS TO BLOOM/BLOOMING PERIOD: Summer until frost
- SPECIAL NOTES: Stake tall plants. Deadhead spent blooms

COSMOS

COSMOS SULPHUREUS
Also called Yellow Cosmos
Annual

This Cosmos is also a very easy to grow, easy to start annual that thrives on neglect and tolerates poor conditions well. The flowers of *C. sulphureus* are very brilliantly colored and a little 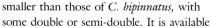 smaller than those of *C. bipinnatus,* with some double or semi-double. It is available in a more dwarf variety but also comes in a tall type, and is somewhat earlier to flower. Sulphureus is free-flowering, even in hot weather.

- DEGREE OF DIFFICULTY: Easy
- USES: Borders, beds, edgings; taller varieties for cutting and background
- HEIGHT: 2'–6'
- COLORS: Orange, yellow and reds
- SIZE OF BLOOM: Up to 3"; some semi-double
- FROST TOLERANCE: Tender
- PREFERS: Warm weather
- WHEN TO SOW INDOORS: 5–7 weeks before setting out
- DAYS TO GERMINATION: 5–10
- WHEN TO SOW OUTDOORS OR SET TRANSPLANTS: After all danger of frost
- SOIL CONDITIONS: Average, dry or poor soil
- DISTANCE BETWEEN PLANTS: 1'–2'
- SUNLIGHT REQUIREMENTS: Full sun
- WATERING: Don't let it stand in water
- DAYS TO BLOOM/BLOOMING PERIOD: Summer until frost
- SPECIAL NOTES: Deadhead spent blossoms. Recommeded variety: Bright Lights Mixed

CREEPING ZINNIA

SANVITALIA PROCUMBENS
Annual

Creeping Zinnia produces masses of Zinnia-type flowers on delightful plants. Very easy to grow, it will tolerate various adverse conditions, such as heat and drought, alkaline or poor soil, and partial shade. Once up and going, it takes little care. It is free-flowering, and looks especially nice in hanging baskets.

- DEGREE OF DIFFICULTY: Easy
- USES: Bedding, edging, rock gardens, ground cover, hanging baskets
- HEIGHT: 6"
- COLORS: Golden yellow with purple centers
- SIZE OF BLOOM: ¾"–1"
- FROST TOLERANCE: Tender
- PREFERS: Warm weather
- WHEN TO SOW INDOORS: Not a good indoor starter
- DAYS TO GERMINATION: 6–12
- WHEN TO SOW OUTDOORS OR SET TRANSPLANTS: After all danger of frost; do not cover, seeds need light to germinate
- SOIL CONDITIONS: Well-drained, light, open
- DISTANCE BETWEEN PLANTS: 5"–6"
- SUNLIGHT REQUIREMENTS: Full sun
- WATERING: Do not overwater
- DAYS TO BLOOM/BLOOMING PERIOD: Summer through frost

Notes

_____ *Notes* _____

CUPFLOWER

NIEREMBERGIA HIPPOMANICA
Perennial grown as Annual

The Cupflower is a tender perennial grown as an annual except where winters are mild. Few catalogues offer it, and those which do usually list only one type—Purple Robe—but the Cupflower deserves to be more popular. Easy to grow and dependable to flower the first year from seed if started early indoors, the plants are smothered with continuous masses of small blue-violet flowers all summer long.

- DEGREE OF DIFFICULTY: Easy
- USES: Bedding, edging, borders, rock gardens, containers, hanging baskets
- HEIGHT: 6″–12″
- COLORS: Blue-violet
- SIZE OF BLOOM: 1″
- FROST TOLERANCE: Half-hardy
- PREFERS: Warm weather
- WHEN TO SOW INDOORS: 10–12 weeks before setting out
- DAYS TO GERMINATION: 10–21
- WHEN TO SOW OUTDOORS OR SET TRANSPLANTS: After last frost
- SOIL CONDITIONS: Sandy, light, moist, well-drained
- DISTANCE BETWEEN PLANTS: 6″–12″
- SUNLIGHT REQUIREMENTS: Full sun to partial shade
- WATERING: Keep moist
- DAYS TO BLOOM/BLOOMING PERIOD: All summer

DAHLBERG DAISY

DYSSODIA TENUILOBA
Also called Golden Fleece
Annual

Rarely offered in seed catalogues, the Dahlberg Daisy is extremely easy to grow, generally disease-free, tolerant of drought and heat and thrives in poor soil. It produces an abundance of small, long-lasting brilliant yellow flowers atop dense mossy foliage. Considering its minimal requirements and long blooming period, this Daisy should be better-known.

- DEGREE OF DIFFICULTY: Easy
- USES: Edgings, borders, rock gardens, ground cover
- HEIGHT: 4″–12″
- COLORS: Yellow or yellow-orange
- SIZE OF BLOOM: 1″
- FROST TOLERANCE: Hardy
- PREFERS: Cool weather but tolerates heat
- WHEN TO SOW INDOORS: 6–8 weeks before setting out
- DAYS TO GERMINATION: About 10
- WHEN TO SOW OUTDOORS OR SET TRANSPLANTS: After danger of frost
- SOIL CONDITIONS: Dry or with good drainage
- DISTANCE BETWEEN PLANTS: 6″–10″
- SUNLIGHT REQUIREMENTS: Full sun
- WATERING: Water only when soil dry; do not overwater
- DAYS TO BLOOM/BLOOMING PERIOD: Blooms from early summer, 4 months from planting
- SPECIAL NOTES: Needs to be planted where its tendency to reseed will not be a

problem. Fertilizing is unnecessary as Dahlbergs like poor soil

DAHLIA

DAHLIA HYBRIDA
Perennial

Dahlias are perennials grown from tubers, like Tuberous Begonias and from seed as tender annuals. At the end of the growing season, you can dig up the tubers, store them over the winter, and plant them again in the spring. In milder climates they will winter over in the ground. Dahlias are available in an extensive color range, in both tall and dwarf varieties, and in many flower forms and sizes. They make excellent cutting flowers, are very long-lasting and showy, and they bloom freely all season long. Some varieties have distinctive bronze foliage.

- DEGREE OF DIFFICULTY: Easy
- USES: Bedding, borders, cutting
- HEIGHT: 1'–5'
- COLORS: All except blue
- SIZE OF BLOOM: 1"–5"
- FROST TOLERANCE: Half-hardy. Some varieties are tender
- PREFER: Cooler weather, but tolerate warm
- WHEN TO SOW INDOORS: 4–6 weeks before last frost
- DAYS TO GERMINATION: 8–15
- WHEN TO SOW OUTDOORS OR SET TRANSPLANTS: After all danger of frost is past; should only be started indoors if earlier bloom is important

- SOIL CONDITIONS: Well-drained, rich, moist, high in organic material
- DISTANCE BETWEEN PLANTS: 6"–24"
- SUNLIGHT REQUIREMENTS: Full sun
- WATERING: Keep well-watered; will not flower well in hot climates unless kept moist
- DAYS TO BLOOM/BLOOMING PERIOD: Bloom freely from early summer until frost
- SPECIAL NOTES: Tall types may require staking. Dahlias should be fed heavily and regularly. Tubers can be dug up in the fall and stored for replanting the following spring

DELPHINIUM

DELPHINIUM ELATUM
Perennial grown as Annual

Delphinium is usually grown as an annual, but if mulched heavily it will winter-over quite successfully for future seasons. It is difficult to grow in hot climates, preferring long cool summers. In fact, it is hard to grow almost anywhere as it usually needs staking, frequent applications of fertilizer, and is prone to attack from several diseases and pests. But if you succeed with Delphinium, the results are quite breathtaking as both the height of the plant and the colors of the flowers are spectacular. See Larkspur, page 179.

- DEGREE OF DIFFICULTY: Moderately difficult
- USES: Borders, backgrounds, cutting

STAKING TALL FLOWERS

Some tall flowers, including Snapdragons, Hollyhocks, Delphiniums and Larkspur often require staking to keep the flowers from sprawling on the ground or the stems from breaking in the wind. Certain vines, like Morning Glory, also need support; trellises or netting are very effective for such plants.

Thin bamboo stakes, readily available at garden stores or through catalogues (or others which will not be visually obtrusive), are usually best for tall flowers. The stake should be placed in the ground at planting time to avoid root damage. Tie string or a twist-tie in a figure eight, putting the stem in one loop and the stake in the other. Tie the string securely to the stake, and loosely around the flower stem.

- HEIGHT: 4'–7'
- COLORS: Blues, pinks, purple, white
- SIZE OF BLOOM: 2½"–3"
- FROST TOLERANCE: Half-hardy
- PREFERS: Cool weather
- WHEN TO SOW INDOORS: Late winter. 8–10 weeks before setting out
- DAYS TO GERMINATION: 10–18
- WHEN TO SOW OUTDOORS OR SET TRANSPLANTS: Sow outdoors in spring or summer; set transplants in early spring
- SOIL CONDITIONS: Moist, well drained, loose, rich, slightly alkaline
- DISTANCE BETWEEN PLANTS: 2'–3'
- SUNLIGHT REQUIREMENTS: Full sun
- WATERING: Keep well watered
- DAYS TO BLOOM/BLOOMING PERIOD: Late spring into early summer; may bloom again in fall if cut back nearly to ground after first bloom
- SPECIAL NOTES: Deadhead spent blossoms. Delphinium requires a lot of fertilization. Staking is usually required. Aphids and slugs are drawn to Delphinium. Spray plants with soap spray to repel aphids, and handpick slugs. Diseases which sometimes attack include black spot, crown rot, yellows and powdery mildew. See pages 45–47 for control measures

DWARF MORNING GLORY

CONVOLVULUS TRICOLOR
Annual

Not related to Morning Glory vines but with a similar trumpet-shaped flower, the Dwarf Morning Glory does not climb. Instead its more compact growth is used well as an edging. Known originally for its bright blue color, and now also available in pinks and purple shades, Dwarf Morning Glory's funnel-shaped flower has a yellow center surrounded by white. The plant can be hard to find in seed catalogues, but if you prevail, it is easy to grow, likes poor and dry soil, and will give you pretty flowers for not much effort.

- DEGREE OF DIFFICULTY: Easy
- USES: Bedding, edging, rock gardens
- HEIGHT: 12″
- COLORS: Bright blue (easiest to find), also purple, lilac, pink, rose
- SIZE OF BLOOM: 1″–2″
- FROST TOLERANCE: Half-hardy
- PREFERS: Warm weather
- WHEN TO SOW INDOORS: Can be started 4–6 weeks before last frost, but it is better to start it outdoors as it does not transplant well. If you want to start it indoors, use individual peat pots
- DAYS TO GERMINATION: 5–7
- WHEN TO SOW OUTDOORS OR SET TRANSPLANTS: After all danger of frost
- SOIL CONDITIONS: Well-drained, sandy, not very rich soil
- DISTANCE BETWEEN PLANTS: 8″–12″

- SUNLIGHT REQUIREMENTS: Full sun
- WATERING: Moderate; do not overwater or allow soil to remain very wet
- DAYS TO BLOOM/BLOOMING PERIOD: Spring until frost
- SPECIAL NOTES: Nick the outer hard seed coat, or soak the seed in warm water overnight before planting. Sidedressing is not advisable, as these plants like poor soil

---

DUSTY MILLER

SENECIO CINERARIA
Perennial grown as Annual

Low-growing Dusty Miller is a perennial plant popularly grown as an annual in many gardens. (Another rare perennial, also called Dusty Miller, is in the Chrysanthemum family.) Senecio is cultivated for its uniquely-colored leaves, which are velvety, grey-green to silvery-white, and finely cut. They provide an excellent foil for other brilliantly-colored blooms in the border or behind them in beds. Dusty Miller is easy to grow, tolerant of heat, drought, and even accepts partial shade and sandy, dry soil.

- DEGREE OF DIFFICULTY: Easy
- USES: Edging, bedding, borders, planters
- HEIGHT: 1′–2½′
- COLORS: Yellow or cream blooms in terminal clusters

- SIZE OF BLOOM: 1½″, in terminal clusters
- FROST TOLERANCE: Half-hardy
- PREFERS: Warm weather
- WHEN TO SOW INDOORS: 8–10 weeks before last frost
- DAYS TO GERMINATION: 7–15; do not cover seeds
- WHEN TO SOW OUTDOORS OR SET TRANSPLANTS: Start early indoors, and set out just before last frost
- SOIL CONDITIONS: Well-drained, light and rich
- DISTANCE BETWEEN PLANTS: 8″–10″
- SUNLIGHT REQUIREMENTS: Full sun to partial shade
- WATERING: Keep lightly watered
- DAYS TO BLOOM/BLOOMING PERIOD: Blooms in late summer
- SPECIAL NOTES: Remove flowers as they appear, and shear to prevent legginess

---

ENGLISH DAISY

BELLIS PERENNIS
Biennial grown as Annual

The charming little English Daisy does not appear in every seed catalogue, but those that do carry it usually offer several varieties. It is easy to grow and likes some shade. Each plant is a clump with double or semi-double flowers in white and rich shades of red and pink, all with yellow centers. The English Daisy is technically a biennial, but is frequently grown as an annual, often to surround a patch of Pansies, which also like shade.

- DEGREE OF DIFFICULTY: Easy
- USES: Edgings, low beds, borders
- HEIGHT: 4″–6″
- COLORS: White, pinks, red, purple
- SIZE OF BLOOM: 1″–3″ single or double flowers
- FROST TOLERANCE: Treated as a tender annual in cold climates
- PREFERS: Cool weather
- WHEN TO SOW INDOORS: In midwinter for spring blooming
- DAYS TO GERMINATION: 10–15
- WHEN TO SOW OUTDOORS OR SET TRANSPLANTS: In mild climates, in late summer for early spring bloom; in other areas, in early spring for late spring bloom; set out transplants as soon as ground can be worked
- SOIL CONDITIONS: Light, moist and rich
- DISTANCE BETWEEN PLANTS: 6″
- SUNLIGHT REQUIREMENTS: Full sun or light shade
- WATERING: Likes moist soil; keep well-watered
- DAYS TO BLOOM/BLOOMING PERIOD: Early spring if planted previous fall in milder climates; late spring or early summer when planted early spring
- SPECIAL NOTES: English Daisies can be planted in the lawn, and benefits from monthly fertilizing

FIRECRACKER PLANT

CUPHEA IGNEA
Also called Mexican Cigar Flower
Annual

The Firecracker Plant is usually grown indoors, where it will flower through the winter. Interesting and easy to grow, it is equally effective for outdoor bedding or baskets,  producing an abundance of small tubular flowers with black tips. It is fairly tolerant of neglect, being both heat and drought resistant, and tolerant of excessive watering. It may reseed in warmer climates.

- DEGREE OF DIFFICULTY: Easy
- USES: Edgings, rock garden, bedding, hanging baskets, house plant
- HEIGHT: 12″
- COLORS: Bright orange-scarlet
- SIZE OF BLOOM: 1″
- FROST TOLERANCE: Half-hardy
- PREFERS: Warm weather
- WHEN TO SOW INDOORS: 6–8 weeks before last frost date
- DAYS TO GERMINATION: 8–10; do not cover—seeds require light to germinate
- WHEN TO SOW OUTDOORS OR SET TRANSPLANTS: After all danger of frost is past
- SOIL CONDITIONS: Well-drained, loose and fertile
- DISTANCE BETWEEN PLANTS: 9″–12″
- SUNLIGHT REQUIREMENTS: Full sun or partial shade
- WATERING: Keep moist

Notes

- DAYS TO BLOOM/BLOOMING PERIOD: 4 months after germination; then flowers continually until frost
- SPECIAL NOTES: Feed with liquid fertilizer lightly every month. Will bloom year-round indoors

FLOWERING KALE

BRASSICA OLERACEA ACEPHALA
Annual

Flowering Kale is a stunning ornamental grown for its brilliantly-colored leaves. Flowering or Ornamental Cabbage, a different plant with similar growing habits, is often presented in catalogues side by side with Flowering Kale. Since the leaves of Flowering Kale display their best color after a light frost, you can time its early fall maturity: Start it indoors in late spring or early summer and set out the transplants in midsummer for a wonderful show of fall color.

- DEGREE OF DIFFICULTY: Easy
- USES: Bedding, edging, containers
- HEIGHT: 8″–15″
- COLORS: Green, greenish-purple, or bluish-green outer leaves with rose-red, white or purple inner leaves
- SIZE OF BLOOM: The rosette of leaves is 12″ across

- FROST TOLERANCE: Hardy
- PREFERS: Definitely cool to cold weather
- WHEN TO SOW INDOORS: 6–8 weeks before setting out; sow in midwinter for spring maturity, in late spring or early summer for autumn display
- DAYS TO GERMINATION: 10–14
- WHEN TO SOW OUTDOORS OR SET TRANSPLANTS: For spring maturity, set out thoroughly hardened off transplants several weeks before the last expected frost date. For fall maturity, direct-seed or set out transplants in midsummer
- SOIL CONDITIONS: Moist, well-drained and rich
- DISTANCE BETWEEN PLANTS: 15″–18″
- SUNLIGHT REQUIREMENTS: Full sun
- WATERING: Keep evenly moist
- DAYS TO BLOOM/BLOOMING PERIOD: Color is best after first frost; continues until late fall or early winter depending on climate
- SPECIAL NOTES: Fertilize moderately. The plant makes a dramatic centerpiece for the table. It is, in fact, edible

FLOWERING TOBACCO

NICOTIANA ALATA
Also called Ornamental Tobacco
Annual

Listed under Nicotiana in most seed catalogues, Flowering Tobacco has trumpet-like, star-shaped flowers that are very sweetly scented. The older varieties opened only at night and on sunless days, but many cultivars now available stay open all day. Nicotiana is fragrant in the evening, is very easy to grow, and is available in many disease-resistant and earlier-blooming varieties that tolerate adverse weather conditions. *Nicotiana Tabacum* is the species grown commercially as smoking tobacco.

- DEGREE OF DIFFICULTY: Easy
- USES: Bedding, borders
- HEIGHT: 1'–4'
- COLORS: White, pink, red, mauve, even a green
- SIZE OF BLOOM: 2"–4" long by 2" wide
- FROST TOLERANCE: Tender
- PREFERS: Warm weather
- WHEN TO SOW INDOORS: 6–8 weeks before last frost date; do not cover seed—requires light for germination
- DAYS TO GERMINATION: 10–20
- WHEN TO SOW OUTDOORS OR SET TRANSPLANTS: After all danger of frost is past
- SOIL CONDITIONS: Rich, moist, well-drained
- DISTANCE BETWEEN PLANTS: 10"–12"
- SUNLIGHT REQUIREMENTS: Light shade to full sun
- WATERING: Prefers regular watering; needs generous watering in hot, dry weather
- DAYS TO BLOOM/BLOOMING PERIOD: 6 weeks from seed; until frost; some hybrids bloom from June until frost
- SPECIAL NOTES: All *Nicotiana alata* is fragrant. The leaves are said to have narcotic, or poisonous properties. A sidedressing of potash and lime is beneficial

FORGET-ME-NOT

MYOSOTIS SYLVATICA
Biennial grown as Annual

Forget-me-not is a low-growing, tiny-flowered biennial, but is generally treated as an annual. It grows well around water and is great for bog gardens. It also naturalizes well, but should have moist soil and partial shade to really perform best. Forget-me-not is easy to grow, early-blooming, produces masses of color, and is excellent for bouquets. It's also wonderful for interplanting with spring bulbs since they arrive in bloom at the same time. Its soft low growth conceals the growth of and sets off the brilliance of Daffodils, Tulips, Iris.

- DEGREE OF DIFFICULTY: Easy
- USES: Ground cover, edging, border, bedding, planters
- HEIGHT: 6"–12"
- COLORS: Mostly blue, but also pink and white
- SIZE OF BLOOM: ½"
- FROST TOLERANCE: Hardy
- PREFERS: Cool weather
- WHEN TO SOW INDOORS: 4–6 weeks before setting out
- DAYS TO GERMINATION: 7–15
- WHEN TO SOW OUTDOORS OR SET TRANSPLANTS: In late summer for bloom the following spring, or in spring for summer bloom; set transplants in early spring
- SOIL CONDITIONS: Rich, well-drained, moist
- DISTANCE BETWEEN PLANTS: 8"–12"

- SUNLIGHT REQUIREMENTS: Light shade
- WATERING: Keep very well watered
- DAYS TO BLOOM/BLOOMING PERIOD: 6 weeks from spring seeding
- SPECIAL NOTES: Reseeds freely. Fertilize bi-monthly

FOUR O'CLOCK

MIRABILIS JALAPA
Also called Marvel of Peru, Beauty of the Night
Perennial grown as Annual

Called Four O'Clock because the flowers open in the afternoon, this delightful plant is very easy to grow, extremely fragrant when the flowers open, and tall enough so its foliage can serve easily as a hedge. Flowers of many different colors often appear on a single plant. Four O'Clock is a perennial usually grown as an annual. It can be found in most catalogues, but usually only one variety is available.

- DEGREE OF DIFFICULTY: Very easy
- USES: Bedding, background, borders, annual hedges
- HEIGHT: 18"–36"
- COLORS: White, yellow, red, pink, some bicolored, often has several colors on same plant
- SIZE OF BLOOM: 1"–2"
- FROST TOLERANCE: Half-hardy
- PREFERS: Warm weather
- WHEN TO SOW INDOORS: 6–8 weeks before final frost
- DAYS TO GERMINATION: 7–10

- WHEN TO SOW OUTDOORS OR SET TRANSPLANTS: After final frost; direct-seeds easily
- SOIL CONDITIONS: Tolerates a wide range, even poor soil; prefers light, well-drained soil
- DISTANCE BETWEEN PLANTS: 12"–24"
- SUNLIGHT REQUIREMENTS: Full sun, tolerates partial shade
- WATERING: Keep well-watered
- DAYS TO BLOOM/BLOOMING SEASON: Summer through frost
- SPECIAL NOTES: Roots may be dug after the tops die from frost, stored in a cool, dry place, and replanted in the spring. A perennial in warm climates, it may self-sow freely. Fertilize monthly

FOXGLOVE

DIGITALIS
Perennial

Digitalis, with its tall stalks of bell-shaped blooms, is one of those plants that is very difficult to categorize. It is available in annual, biennial and perennial forms, although generally considered a biennial which can survive as a perennial under the right conditions. The advantage of the one annual form available is that it flowers the first year from seed. Foxglove is easy to grow and its exotic flowers bloom profusely in beautiful colors. Foxglove is the botanical source of the medication digitalis, and is considered to be poisonous

- DEGREE OF DIFFICULTY: Moderately easy
- USES: Background, borders
- HEIGHT: 1'–6'
- COLORS: White, yellow, pinks, purples
- SIZE OF BLOOM: 1"–3"
- FROST TOLERANCE: Hardy
- PREFERS: Cool weather
- WHEN TO SOW INDOORS: 6–10 weeks before last frost; seeds need light to germinate
- DAYS TO GERMINATION: 10–20
- WHEN TO SOW OUTDOORS OR SET TRANSPLANTS: In spring or early summer; harden off transplants and set out several weeks before last frost
- SOIL CONDITIONS: Moderately rich, well-drained but moist
- DISTANCE BETWEEN PLANTS: 12"–24"
- SUNLIGHT REQUIREMENTS: Partial shade or full sun
- WATERING: Keep well watered
- DAYS TO BLOOM/BLOOMING PERIOD: Late spring and early summer
- SPECIAL NOTES: Remove spent blooms for second flowering, but leave some for purposes of self-sowing. Can be used as a cutting flower, but it is considered to be poisonous

GARDEN BALSAM

IMPATIENS BALSAMINA
Also called Lady Slipper
Annual

Balsam is an old-fashioned favorite that is easy to grow for continuous summer bloom. The plants of the Garden Balsam are literally covered with flowers which are sometimes double, have a pleasant waxy texture and resemble either Camellias or small roses. The flowers come in a wide range of colors.

- DEGREE OF DIFFICULTY: Moderately easy
- USES: Bedding, borders, containers
- HEIGHT: 12"–36"
- COLORS: Cerise, mauve, scarlet, red, pink, purple, white
- SIZE OF BLOOM: 1"–2"
- FROST TOLERANCE: Tender
- PREFERS: Warm weather
- WHEN TO SOW INDOORS: 6–8 weeks before last frost
- DAYS TO GERMINATION: 8–15
- WHEN TO SOW OUTDOORS OR SET TRANSPLANTS: After all danger of frost
- SOIL CONDITIONS: Loose, rich, well-drained, sandy, high in organic matter
- DISTANCE BETWEEN PLANTS: 6"–12"
- SUNLIGHT REQUIREMENTS: Full sun where it is cooler, partial shade where summers are hot
- WATERING: Keep well watered
- DAYS TO BLOOM/BLOOMING PERIOD: 65 days from seed; early summer until frost
- SPECIAL NOTES: Balsam needs uniform moisture throughout the seedling stage,

but will not tolerate overwatering. Keep well fertilized and deadhead spent blossoms

GARDEN VERBENA

VERBENA HYBRIDA
Annual

Found in some seed catalogues under Verbena, this spreading plant can be a challenge to grow. It's a slow germinator and therefore shouldn't be direct-seeded—it takes too long and at a low rate of success. The seed is also sensitive to overwatering. Once up, the plant is susceptible to mildew and though it will withstand both heat and drought, it may cease to flower during hot periods. If you take it on, however, the results are worth the effort. Verbena spreads out nicely and produces an airy carpet of Forget-me-not-sized flowers in a range of very brilliant primary colors, blooming continuously from late spring until late fall. Verbena was once known for being delightfully fragrant, but the original scent has been bred out of many of the hybrids now available.

- DEGREE OF DIFFICULTY: Very temperamental
- USES: Beds, borders, edgings, ground cover, cutting
- HEIGHT: 6″–12″
- COLORS: Pink, red, purple, yellow, white, blue

- SIZE OF BLOOM: 2″–3″
- FROST TOLERANCE: Half-hardy
- PREFERS: Warm weather
- WHEN TO SOW INDOORS: 12–14 weeks before last frost
- DAYS TO GERMINATION: 10–20
- WHEN TO SOW OUTDOORS OR SET TRANSPLANTS: Set out transplants after all danger of frost is past
- SOIL CONDITIONS: Light, sandy, rich, well-drained
- DISTANCE BETWEEN PLANTS: 8″–12″
- SUNLIGHT REQUIREMENTS: Full sun
- WATERING: Do not overwater; likes well-drained or dry soil
- DAYS TO BLOOM/BLOOMING PERIOD: Late spring through late fall
- SPECIAL NOTES: When started indoors, Verbena seed needs darkness, but it is not good to cover it with soil because it does not do well when too wet. The best idea is to lay the seeds on moist soil and cover the flat with black plastic. Apply compost every two weeks for increased flower production

GERANIUM

PELARGONIUM × HORTORUM; × DOMESTICUM; × PELTATUM
Treat as Annual

Geraniums have long been a favorite garden and container annual. Originally propagated only by cuttings because they never grew dependably true from seed, many hybrids are

Notes

now available which do. "Many" is an understatement: there are trailing types, scented varieties, dwarfs, doubles, zonal foliage types, and many other variations. The scented types come in a startling selection of fragrances: apple, peppermint, coconut, lemon and oak. There's even a chocolate variety.

The general culture of all Geraniums is enough alike to consider them here together. They must be started indoors as they have a very long initial growth period. You can look for slightly earlier-flowering varieties, but even these will take longer than most annuals to get going and so must be started quite early as well. Depending on the climate, Geraniums will flower all year, then winter-over quite well; or, if brought inside, will bloom throughout the year. In warmer regions, look for newer varieties that may be more tolerant of heat and humidity. Geraniums are vigorous and trouble-free and produce abundant cheery color—especially the glowing red—in return for some moderate attention.

- DEGREE OF DIFFICULTY: Moderate
- USES: Bedding, borders, containers, house plants, hanging baskets, ground cover, greenhouse plant
- HEIGHT: 12″–36″
- COLORS: Pinks, rose, red, white, purple
- SIZE OF BLOOM: 1″–3″
- FROST TOLERANCE: Tender
- PREFERS: Warm, but not hot, weather
- WHEN TO SOW INDOORS: 12–16 weeks before last frost
- DAYS TO GERMINATION: 5–15
- WHEN TO SOW OUTDOORS OR SET TRANSPLANTS: Set transplants after all danger of frost is past; direct-seeding difficult, but possible in mild climates
- SOIL CONDITIONS: Moist, rich, well-drained, high in organic material, slightly acid
- DISTANCE BETWEEN PLANTS: 8″–15″
- SUNLIGHT REQUIREMENTS: Full sun
- WATERING: Keep very well watered
- DAYS TO BLOOM/BLOOMING PERIOD: 4–5 months from seed; spring until frost
- SPECIAL NOTES: Keep well fertilized. Deadhead flowers to encourage bloom. In pots, keep Geraniums slightly crowded, as they flower better with a little root constriction. Martha Washington and Ivy (trailing type) are popular varieties

GLOBE AMARANTH

GOMPHRENA GLOBOSA
Annual

The small but radiant thistle-like flowers of Gomphrena are, if not spectacular, quite colorful, and the plant is very easy to grow. It tolerates drought and heat very well, it likes poor soil and  keeps producing flowers under all kinds of adverse conditions. When dried, the blooms are excellent and long-lasting, holding color and form indefinitely. They also make fine cutting flowers for the same reasons.

- DEGREE OF DIFFICULTY: Easy
- USES: Bedding, edging, planters, cutting, dried
- HEIGHT: 12″–30″
- COLORS: Purple, white, orange, pink, lavender, yellow
- SIZE OF BLOOM: 1″
- FROST TOLERANCE: Tender
- PREFERS: Warm weather
- WHEN TO SOW INDOORS: 6–8 weeks before last frost date
- DAYS TO GERMINATION: 14–20
- WHEN TO SOW OUTDOORS OR SET TRANSPLANTS: After last frost
- SOIL CONDITIONS: Sandy, light, well-drained
- DISTANCE BETWEEN PLANTS: 10″–15″
- SUNLIGHT REQUIREMENTS: Full sun
- WATERING: Moderate; tolerates drought
- DAYS TO BLOOM/BLOOMING PERIOD: Midsummer to frost
- SPECIAL NOTES: For drying, cut flowers before they are fully opened or begin to elongate

GLORIOSA DAISY

RUDBECKIA HIRTA
Also called Brown-Eyed Susan
Perennial grown as Annual

Rudbeckia is a short-lived perennial commonly grown in colder climates as an annual. Bred from the original Black-eyed Susan, Gloriosa tolerates poor soil, drought and heat very well; in fact, the hotter the summer the better. Its brilliant yellow flowers with their dark centers bloom profusely and make long-lasting cutting flowers.

- DEGREE OF DIFFICULTY: Easy
- USES: Borders, bedding, rock garden, background, cutting
- HEIGHT: 2′–3′
- COLORS: Gold, yellow, bronze, orange, mahogany or brown
- SIZE OF BLOOM: 3″–7″
- FROST TOLERANCE: Half-hardy
- PREFERS: Warm, even hot, weather
- WHEN TO SOW INDOORS: 6–8 weeks before last frost
- DAYS TO GERMINATION: 5–10
- WHEN TO SOW OUTDOORS OR SET TRANSPLANTS: In spring; start indoors where summers are short
- SOIL CONDITIONS: Well-drained, moist, rich soil high in organic matter; but tolerates poor soil and drought
- DISTANCE BETWEEN PLANTS: 12″–24″
- SUNLIGHT REQUIREMENTS: Full sun
- WATERING: Keep well-watered
- DAYS TO BLOOM/BLOOMING PERIOD: Blooms easily first year if started early enough (either inside or outside); later summer into fall

- SPECIAL NOTES: Keep well-fertilized. Tall varieties may need staking

---

GODETIA

CLARKIA AMOENA
Also called Farewell-to-Spring, Satin Flower
Annual

Although Godetia is in the same family as Clarkia and considered a hybrid of the same genus, it is distinctly different and therefore listed separately here and in seed catalogues. As with Clarkia, it is available more often in British seed catalogues than in those from the United States. The bushy plants are smothered with dazzling flowers which have shimmering satiny petals. An excellent cutting flower, Godetia thrives in areas with cool summer nights and in soil with excellent drainage. It does not transplant well, so start it directly outdoors where you want it to grow. Successive plantings may extend the blooming season.

- DEGREE OF DIFFICULTY: Easy
- USES: Beds, borders, rock gardens, cutting
- HEIGHT: 12″–30″
- COLORS: White, pinks, purples, reds, lilac
- SIZE OF BLOOM: 1″–2″
- FROST TOLERANCE: Hardy
- PREFERS: Cool weather
- WHEN TO SOW INDOORS: Not an indoor starter

- DAYS TO GERMINATION: 7–10
- WHEN TO SOW OUTDOORS OR SET TRANSPLANTS: In spring or in climates with mild winters, sow in fall for bloom the following spring; barely cover seeds which need light to germinate
- SOIL CONDITIONS: Light and sandy, not rich with excellent drainage
- DISTANCE BETWEEN PLANTS: 8″–10″
- SUNLIGHT REQUIREMENTS: Partial shade to full sun; the hotter the summer, the more important shade becomes
- WATERING: Do not overwater
- DAYS TO BLOOM/BLOOMING PERIOD: 70 days from seeding; summer until frost in cooler climates, early summer only in hot climates

---

GOLDEN AGERATUM

LONAS INODORA OR LONAS ANNUA
Also Called Yellow Ageratum, African Daisy
Annual

As you can see, this is another plant with nomenclature problems. One of the many called African Daisy (though it looks nothing like a Daisy) it shares its other common names with the little Blue Ageratum which it only remotely resembles—certainly not in color. Beyond that, it also has two Latin designations in general use: both *Lonas inodora* and *L. annua*. In spite of its numerous names, it's

_____ *Notes* _____

usually only offered in one variety—a plant with very bright yellow flowers borne in dense low-growing clusters that bloom from early summer until frost. They are excellent and long-lasting as cut flowers.

- DEGREE OF DIFFICULTY: Easy
- USES: Edging, borders, rock gardens, cutting
- HEIGHT: 10″–12″
- COLORS: Yellow
- SIZE OF BLOOM: ¼″–⅓″ flowers in branched 2″ clusters
- FROST TOLERANCE: Half-hardy
- PREFERS: Cool weather, not heat-resistant
- WHEN TO SOW INDOORS: 6–8 weeks before last frost date
- DAYS TO GERMINATION: 5–7 days. Cover seeds completely—they require darkness to germinate
- WHEN TO SOW OUTDOORS OR SET TRANSPLANTS: After all danger of frost
- SOIL CONDITIONS: Average, well-drained soil
- DISTANCE BETWEEN PLANTS: 6″–12″
- SUNLIGHT REQUIREMENTS: Full sun
- WATERING: Keep moderately watered
- DAYS TO BLOOM/BLOOMING PERIOD: 8–10 weeks from seed; late spring until frost
- SPECIAL NOTES: Deadhead spent blossoms

HAWK'S BEARD

CREPIS RUBRA
Annual

Although very difficult to find in most seed catalogues, Hawk's Beard is an interesting and easy to grow Daisy-like annual. It thrives in any type of garden soil, tolerates dry conditions, and does beautifully planted in unthinned masses. It makes a good cutting flower; but cut as soon as flowers open, for they quickly dry and become as feathery as spent Dandelions.

- DEGREE OF DIFFICULTY: Easy
- USES: Borders, edging, cutting
- HEIGHT: 8″–14″
- COLORS: Pink, red, white
- SIZE OF BLOOM: 1″–1½″
- FROST TOLERANCE: Hardy
- PREFERS: Cool weather
- WHEN TO SOW INDOORS: 6–8 weeks before setting out
- DAYS TO GERMINATION: 5–7
- WHEN TO SOW OUTDOORS OR SET TRANSPLANTS: Sow seeds in spring, set transplants after danger of frost
- SOIL CONDITIONS: Poor but well-drained
- DISTANCE BETWEEN PLANTS: 4″–6″
- SUNLIGHT REQUIREMENTS: Full sun
- WATERING: Keep well-drained
- DAYS TO BLOOM/BLOOMING PERIOD: In summer and fall
- SPECIAL NOTES: Will do well when crowded

HELIOTROPE

HELIOTROPIUM ARBORESCENS
Also Called Cherry Pie
Perennial grown as Annual

Heliotrope is a perennial grown as a tender annual. Preferring rich soil, it produces clusters of small, richly colored fragrant blooms and makes an excellent cutting flower. Heliotrope is also wonderful as an indoor plant in winter, enlivening the environment with its fruity fragrance.

- DEGREE OF DIFFICULTY: Easy
- USES: Border, bedding, containers, indoor plant, cutting
- HEIGHT: 15″–30″
- COLORS: Purple, violet
- SIZE OF BLOOM: ¼″
- FROST TOLERANCE: Tender
- PREFERS: Warm weather
- WHEN TO SOW INDOORS: 10–12 weeks before last frost
- DAYS TO GERMINATION: 1–4 weeks
- WHEN TO SOW OUTDOORS OR SET TRANSPLANTS: Not a good outdoor starter: germination time is long and plant too sensitive to frost to sow outdoors; set transplants well after all danger of frost
- SOIL CONDITIONS: Well-drained and rich
- DISTANCE BETWEEN PLANTS: 12″
- SUNLIGHT REQUIREMENTS: Full sun
- WATERING: Moderate
- DAYS TO BLOOM/BLOOMING PERIOD: Summer until frost; brought inside before frost, will continue to bloom all winter
- SPECIAL NOTES: Keep regularly fertilized

HIBISCUS

HIBISCUS MOSCHEUTOS
Also Called Rose Mallow, Swamp Mallow
Perennial and Annual

Hibiscus is a spectacular and very showy plant with incredibly large and colorful flowers. The common species *moscheutos* is a perennial which may be treated as as an annual, but there are other species, both annual and perennial, also available. Started early enough, most will bloom the first year from seed. To over-winter in colder climates, you may need to mulch the plants to protect from frost burn. All varieties prefer moist, even wet, soil, but will tolerate drier conditions. Regrettably, Hibiscus will not work as a cutting flower as it wilts within an hour of picking.

- DEGREE OF DIFFICULTY: Moderately easy
- USES: Background, hedges, borders
- HEIGHT: 2′–6′; some varieties grow up to 8′
- COLORS: Pink, purples, red, white, yellow
- SIZE OF BLOOM: 8″–12″
- FROST TOLERANCE: Half-hardy; some varieties are hardy
- PREFERS: Warm weather
- WHEN TO SOW INDOORS: 8–10 weeks before last frost; if seed not yet scarified by seed company, nick the seedcoat or soak seed in water before planting to hasten germination
- DAYS TO GERMINATION: 10–20
- WHEN TO SOW OUTDOORS OR SET TRANSPLANTS: Sow outdoors in spring, or in summer up to 2 months before frost; set transplants after danger of frost is past
- SOIL CONDITIONS: Moist and high in organic matter
- DISTANCE BETWEEN PLANTS: 2′–3′
- SUNLIGHT REQUIREMENTS: Full sun to partial shade
- WATERING: Keep well-watered
- DAYS TO BLOOM/BLOOMING PERIOD: Midsummer until frost; most varieties will bloom first year from seed if started early enough
- SPECIAL NOTES: Keeping the soil rich will increase plant size and flower production

HOLLYHOCK

ALCEA ROSEA
Also Sold as Althaea Rosea
Annual

Hollyhocks are an old-fashioned favorite, producing flowers in a wide range of beautiful colors on very long spikes, available now in double, ruffled and fluted forms as well as the original single variety. They self-sow readily but produce inferior or weaker flowers the second or third year. So though Hollyhocks are technically perennials, they should be treated as half-hardy annuals and planted anew every year or two. Once Hollyhocks were available only as tall plants, but dwarf varieties have been developed which are also best grown as annuals. Look for disease-resistant varieties.

- DEGREE OF DIFFICULTY: Easy
- USES: Background, borders, screen
- HEIGHT: 4'–9'; dwarf form: 2'
- COLORS: Pinks, rose, red, white, yellow, apricot
- SIZE OF BLOOM: 3"–6"
- FROST TOLERANCE: Half-hardy
- PREFERS: Warm weather
- WHEN TO SOW INDOORS: For flowers the first year, in early spring 6–8 weeks before last frost date
- DAYS TO GERMINATION: 10–20; barely cover seeds, which need light to germinate
- WHEN TO SOW OUTDOORS OR SET TRANSPLANTS: For first-year bloom, must start indoors; set transplants after all danger of frost is past
- SOIL CONDITIONS: Well-drained and rich
- DISTANCE BETWEEN PLANTS: 12"–18"
- SUNLIGHT REQUIREMENTS: Full sun
- WATERING: Keep heavily watered
- DAYS TO BLOOM/BLOOMING PERIOD: Early summer until frost
- SPECIAL NOTES: Deadhead spent blossoms to prevent self-sowing. Hollyhocks suffer from rust disease, so choose resistant varieties. Tall varieties may require staking. Feed heavily during flowering period

HONESTY

LUNARIA ANNUA
Also called Money Plant, Moonwort, Silver Dollar
Biennial

Honesty is known primarily for its translucent silver seedpods, which, when dried, make great and lasting decorations. Honesty flowers are generally purple, but sometimes white; all are fragrant. It can be grown as an annual if started early enough, but will produce better plants and flowers if grown as a biennial and sown in midsummer for bloom the following spring. It is easy to grow, and both the flowers and seedpods are delightful.

- DEGREE OF DIFFICULTY: Easy
- USES: Beds, cutting, dried
- HEIGHT: 18"–36"
- COLORS: Purple, white
- SIZE OF BLOOM: 1"
- FROST TOLERANCE: Biennial, which can be grown as a hardy annual
- PREFERS: Cool weather
- WHEN TO SOW INDOORS: Very early, but easy to grow when started outdoors
- DAYS TO GERMINATION: 10–14
- WHEN TO SOW OUTDOORS OR SET TRANSPLANTS: Early spring, or sow in midsummer for blooms next season
- SOIL CONDITIONS: Average and well-drained
- DISTANCE BETWEEN PLANTS: 12"–15"
- SUNLIGHT REQUIREMENTS: Sun or partial shade
- WATERING: Moderate watering

- DAYS TO BLOOM/BLOOMING PERIOD: Usually second season, late spring and early summer
- SPECIAL NOTES: Plants die after they bloom, so let some set seeds for the following year. Recommended variety: annua

ICE PLANT

MESEMBRYANTHEMUM CHRYSTALLINUM
Also Called Sea Fig, Sea Marigold or Fig Marigold
Annual

The Ice Plant is a succulent related to the smaller Livingstone Daisy (see page 179). It has shining yellow blooms and leaves covered with glistening ice-like dots, whence comes the plant's name. Ice Plant makes an excellent ground cover, especially for areas with poor soil, and is best suited to dry, arid climates. However, it will flower in most regions if started early and not excessively fertilized. Ice Plant tolerates both salt spray and drought.

- DEGREE OF DIFFICULTY: Moderate
- USES: Edging, beds, rock gardens, planters
- HEIGHT: 8"
- COLORS: White, pink
- SIZE OF BLOOM: ¾"–1¼"
- FROST TOLERANCE: Half-hardy

- PREFERS: Cool weather
- WHEN TO SOW INDOORS: 10 weeks before last frost
- DAYS TO GERMINATION: 15–20—seeds need darkness to germinate
- WHEN TO SOW OUTDOORS OR SET TRANSPLANTS: After danger of frost is past
- SOIL CONDITIONS: Sandy, average, dry
- DISTANCE BETWEEN PLANTS: 6"–10"
- SUNLIGHT REQUIREMENTS: Full sun
- WATERING: Water sparingly
- DAYS TO BLOOM/BLOOMING PERIOD: Spring and early summer

IMPATIENS

IMPATIENS WALLERANA
Also Called Patient Plant, Busy Lizzie, Patient Lucy, Sultana
Annual

Impatiens is one of America's favorite flowers, primarily because it is so versatile. The plants can produce dazzling color in shady areas, and there are hybrid varieties such as Blitz and Gom which are  also tolerant of sun; they do as well in boxes and hanging planters as they do in beds; and they can make beautiful carpet-like covers at the base of shade trees. Impatiens is available in a huge range of colors including orange, red, pink, white, coral and purple. There are standard varieties and dwarfs, and single and double varieties. The leaves can be smooth and variegated.

Impatiens will live for many years in a frost-free environment, but will be killed in a hard frost. If you live in a colder climate, bring the plants indoors when the weather turns cold and they'll bloom all winter long.

- DEGREE OF DIFFICULTY: Moderately easy
- USES: Borders, bedding, hanging baskets, containers, house plants
- HEIGHT: 6"–24"
- COLORS: White, pink, red, mauve, scarlet, orange, lavender, purple
- SIZE OF BLOOM: 1"–2"
- FROST TOLERANCE: Tender
- PREFERS: Warm weather
- WHEN TO SOW INDOORS: 10–12 weeks before last frost—need light for germination
- DAYS TO GERMINATION: 14–21
- WHEN TO SOW OUTDOORS OR SET TRANSPLANTS: Not a good outdoor starter; set out transplants after danger of last frost is past
- SOIL CONDITIONS: Well-drained, sandy, moist, high in organic material
- DISTANCE BETWEEN PLANTS: 10"–15"
- SUNLIGHT REQUIREMENTS: Shade or partial shade, especially in areas with hot summers but will tolerate full sun if not too hot or if kept very well watered
- WATERING: Make certain soil is always moist, but never waterlogged
- DAYS TO BLOOM/BLOOMING PERIOD: Early summer until frost outside; several months longer if brought inside
- SPECIAL NOTES: Moderate fertilizing will produce many blooms, but do not overfertilize. Cut back to encourage new growth

_____ *Notes* _____

_____ *Notes* _____

JOHNNY-JUMP-UP

VIOLA TRICOLOR
Perennial

Look under Pansy if you are having trouble finding these in seed catalogues. If that fails, try "Viola." Like Pansy and Viola, Johnny-jump-up is a perennial sometimes grown as a hardy annual.
It is very early-blooming, with masses of small flowers. It thrives best in cool weather. Not many varieties are available, but this flower, found in most catalogues, is considered to be an old-fashioned favorite. Johnny-jump-up reseeds quite readily, accounting, in part, for its name.

- DEGREE OF DIFFICULTY: Easy
- USES: Bedding, edging, rock gardens
- HEIGHT: 7"–12"
- COLORS: Purple and yellow
- SIZE OF BLOOM: ¾"
- FROST TOLERANCE: Hardy
- PREFERS: Cool weather
- WHEN TO SOW INDOORS: 10–12 weeks before setting outside
- DAYS TO GERMINATION: 10–20—needs darkness to germinate; may benefit from refrigerating 4–5 days before germination
- WHEN TO SOW OUTDOORS OR SET TRANSPLANTS: After last expected heavy frost
- SOIL CONDITIONS: Rich, moist and well-drained
- DISTANCE BETWEEN PLANTS: 4"–6"
- SUNLIGHT REQUIREMENTS: Sun to partial shade
- WATERING: Keep well watered

- DAYS TO BLOOM/BLOOMING PERIOD: Very early spring
- SPECIAL NOTES: Keep moderately fertilized. Pick faded flowers

KINGFISHER DAISY

FELICIA BERGIERANA
Annual

The Kingfisher Daisy is closely related to and almost a miniature of the Blue Daisy, preferring nearly identical conditions. The main appeal of this Daisy is its small stature and its radiantly blue flowers, each on a single stem. Like the Blue Daisy, it grows best in cool climates and needs a well-drained soil. Neither Blue nor Kingfisher Daisies are as common as they deserve to be and can be difficult to find in catalogues.

- DEGREE OF DIFFICULTY: Moderate
- USES: Edging, borders
- HEIGHT: 4"–8"
- COLORS: Bright blue
- SIZE OF BLOOM: ¾"
- FROST TOLERANCE: Half-hardy
- PREFERS: Cool weather
- WHEN TO SOW INDOORS: Early spring
- DAYS TO GERMINATION: 20–30
- WHEN TO SOW OUTDOORS OR SET TRANSPLANTS: Sow outdoors in early spring; set transplants after danger of frost

- SOIL CONDITIONS: Well-drained, somewhat dry
- DISTANCE BETWEEN PLANTS: 8″–12″
- SUNLIGHT REQUIREMENTS: Full sun
- WATERING: Water moderately during dry periods, and always keep well-drained
- DAYS TO BLOOM/BLOOMING PERIOD: Midsummer until frost
- SPECIAL NOTES: This species will do best in northern climates

LARKSPUR

CONSOLIDA AMBIGUA
Also Called Annual Delphinium, Rocket Larkspur
Annual

Larkspur is an early-blooming, beautiful annual that resembles the perennial Delphinium but is somewhat smaller. It has tall showy spikes of flowers in white, blue, pinks and purples that bloom most of the summer. Some newer varieties are more base-branching, but all types thrive in sunny but cool conditions. Larkspur is especially nice as a cut flower.

- DEGREE OF DIFFICULTY: Moderate
- USES: Beds, borders (especially as background), cutting
- HEIGHT: 1′–4′
- COLORS: Pink, blue, white, purple
- SIZE OF BLOOM: 1″–3″
- FROST TOLERANCE: Hardy
- PREFERS: Cool weather

- WHEN TO SOW INDOORS: 6–8 weeks before setting out; does not transplant easily so use peat pots or pellets; cover seeds completely—need darkness to germinate
- DAYS TO GERMINATION: 8–15
- WHEN TO SOW OUTDOORS OR SET TRANSPLANTS: Sow in early spring or in fall if winters are mild—seedlings very frost-hardy; set transplants out in early spring
- SOIL CONDITIONS: Slightly alkaline, rich and loose soil
- DISTANCE BETWEEN PLANTS: 1′–3′
- SUNLIGHT REQUIREMENTS: Full sun
- WATERING: Keep well watered
- DAYS TO BLOOM/BLOOMING PERIOD: Late spring to end of summer
- SPECIAL NOTES: Keep well fed. Mulch when plants are 12″–18″ to keep the roots cool. Remove faded flowers for prolonged blooming season. Recommended variety: Imperial Blue Bell

LIVINGSTONE DAISY

DOROTHEANTHUS BELLIDIFORMIS
Perennial

The low-growing and very colorful Livingstone Daisy is sometimes listed with Ice Plant or under *Mesembryanthemum criniflorum*, an old botanical name, in seed catalogues. A succulent, it thrives in cool, sunny areas and, like Ice Plant, tolerates both salt spray and drought. It is most popular in the southwest but can be grown almost anywhere. It has intensely colored Daisy-like flowers and, along with its other uses, is especially easy to grow as a ground cover.

- DEGREE OF DIFFICULTY: Moderate
- USES: Ground cover, bedding, edging, planters
- HEIGHT: 3″
- COLORS: Pink, red, white, yellows, cream
- SIZE OF BLOOM: 3″
- FROST TOLERANCE: Half-hardy
- PREFERS: Warm weather
- WHEN TO SOW INDOORS: 10–12 weeks before last frost
- DAYS TO GERMINATION: 10–20. Darkness is needed for germination, but do not cover the very fine seeds with soil; better to put the whole flat in a dark place or place the flat in a black plastic bag
- WHEN TO SOW OUTDOORS OR SET TRANSPLANTS: After danger of frost is past
- SOIL CONDITIONS: Sandy, dry, average
- DISTANCE BETWEEN PLANTS: 6″–12″
- SUNLIGHT REQUIREMENTS: Full sun
- WATERING: Water sparingly
- DAYS TO BLOOM/BLOOMING PERIOD: Spring and early summer

LOBELIA

LOBELIA ERINUS
Annual

Many different cultivars of Lobelia are available in most catalogues. It is one of the best edging and ground-cover plants, spreading quickly and carpeting the ground with myriad small flowers  in jewel-like shades. These are only two of Lobelia's many uses. Its intense, vivid colors are without comparison, especially its superb deep blue. It likes cool weather, grows well in full sun to partial shade, and, if cut back, will bloom repeatedly until late fall. In very hot climates, plant in partial shade. Because its seedlings take a long time to grow, it is best to start Lobelia inside.

- DEGREE OF DIFFICULTY: Moderate
- USES: Ground cover, bedding, edging, borders, hanging baskets, rock gardens, containers
- HEIGHT: 4″–8″
- COLORS: Blues, white, violet, reds
- SIZE OF BLOOM: ½″–¾″
- FROST TOLERANCE: Hardy
- PREFERS: Cool weather, but tolerates heat if given shade
- WHEN TO SOW INDOORS: 10–12 weeks before last frost
- DAYS TO GERMINATION: 14–21
- WHEN TO SOW OUTDOORS OR SET TRANSPLANTS: Set transplants after all danger of frost is past
- SOIL CONDITIONS: Sandy, rich, high in organic material
- DISTANCE BETWEEN PLANTS: 4″–6″
- SUNLIGHT REQUIREMENTS: Full sun or partial shade
- WATERING: Keep well watered

- DAYS TO BLOOM/BLOOMING PERIOD: All summer
- SPECIAL NOTES: For repeated bloom, cut back after first flush of bloom is past

---

LOVE-IN-A-MIST

NIGELLA DAMASCENA
Also Called Devil-in-the-Bush
Annual

Love-in-a-mist produces an abundance of uniquely shaped flowers in beautiful hues that last well when cut and are especially good for dried arrangements. The  seedpods are also good for drying. Seeds can be sown outside in fall where winters are mild for late winter or early spring bloom. The neat and compact plants develop unusual thread-like foliage. The plant's flowering season is short, so it is a good idea to make successive sowings for continuous summer bloom.

- DEGREE OF DIFFICULTY: Moderately difficult
- USES: Borders, bedding, cutting, dried seed pods
- HEIGHT: 12″–24″; dwarf forms: 6″–8″
- COLORS: Blue, white, mauve, lavender, pinks
- SIZE OF BLOOM: 1½″
- FROST TOLERANCE: Hardy
- PREFERS: Cool weather

- WHEN TO SOW INDOORS: 4–6 weeks before setting out, but does not transplant well—best sown outdoors
- DAYS TO GERMINATION: 10–15
- WHEN TO SOW OUTDOORS OR SET TRANSPLANTS: Sow outdoors as soon as ground can be worked
- SOIL CONDITIONS: Average soil, with excellent drainage
- DISTANCE BETWEEN PLANTS: 8″–12″
- SUNLIGHT REQUIREMENTS: Full sun
- WATERING: Water only when soil gets dry
- DAYS TO BLOOM/BLOOMING PERIOD: Mid- to late summer
- SPECIAL NOTES: The flowers are followed by seedpods which are also used for drying, so don't deadhead, but note that the plant reseeds readily if seedpods are not quickly harvested. Fertilize monthly

---

LUPINE

LUPINUS POLYPHYLLUS
Perennial

Lupine is a perennial which is frequently grown from seed. It thrives best in areas with cool summers and high humidity, but is viable in the northeast if mulched to keep the roots cool in the summer and safe from deep frost in the winter. It is available in a wide range of flower colors on huge showy spikes.

- DEGREE OF DIFFICULTY: Moderately difficult

- USES: Background, bedding, borders, cutting
- HEIGHT: 2'–4'
- COLORS: Red, yellow, white, pink, blue, purple, orange
- SIZE OF BLOOM: ½"–1"
- FROST TOLERANCE: Hardy
- PREFERS: Cool weather
- WHEN TO SOW INDOORS: 8–10 weeks before setting out; nick seeds or soak 24 hours before sowing in individual peat pots or pellets—Lupine resents transplanting; seeds need darkness to germinate
- DAYS TO GERMINATION: 12–20
- WHEN TO SOW OUTDOORS OR SET TRANSPLANTS: Early spring
- SOIL CONDITIONS: Average, well drained
- DISTANCE BETWEEN PLANTS: 18"–24"
- SUNLIGHT REQUIREMENTS: Full sun to partial shade
- WATERING: Water when dry
- DAYS TO BLOOM/BLOOMING PERIOD: Blooms in late spring and early summer
- SPECIAL NOTES: Deadhead spent spikes. Will self-sow. Mulch the roots to keep them cool, especially in areas with warm summers

MARIGOLDS

TAGETES
Annual

Marigolds are considered America's most popular annual, and for good reason. They are the flower workhorses of the American garden. For one thing, they are quite beautiful to look at—their yellows, oranges, reds are rich and alluring—and for another, they repel pests. Their strong scent deters the dreaded Mexican bean beetle, and their roots produce an exudate which naturally repels nematodes, which makes Marigolds valuable in the vegetable garden too. In fact, they are perfect in almost every garden application and there seems to be one for all of them: Marigolds come in every height from 8" to 3', in growing patterns from compact to bushy, and in all those colors—there's even a white hybrid now.

Most of the literally dozens of Marigold varieties either bloom early or can be induced to bloom early by starting them inside, and all continue to bloom until frost. They require little care—nothing is easier to grow than a Marigold—and they provide masses of color. Native to Mexico, the name comes from Mary's Gold, as the flowers were called by Spaniards who placed them on the altars of the Virgin Mary when they found them in the New World.

MARIGOLD
TAGETES ERECTA
Called African Marigold or American Marigold

Erecta is the tallest Marigold variety; its common name of "American Marigold" is further confused since dwarf varieties of American Marigolds have become available, so stick with the Latin when you look for it. Erecta have the largest blooms, and, after years of painstaking plant breeding, are finally available in white as well as the traditional yellow-orange range. They take longer to bloom than other Marigolds, so it is advisable to start them early inside.

_____ *Notes* _____

_____ *Notes* _____

- DEGREE OF DIFFICULTY: Very easy
- USES: Bedding, edging, borders, cutting
- HEIGHT: 18″–36″
- COLORS: Yellow, orange, white
- SIZE OF BLOOM: 2″–6″
- FROST TOLERANCE: Half-hardy
- PREFERS: Warm weather
- WHEN TO SOW INDOORS: 6–8 weeks before last frost
- DAYS TO GERMINATION: 5–7
- WHEN TO SOW OUTDOORS OR SET TRANSPLANTS: 2–3 weeks before last frost, when ground is warm
- SOIL CONDITIONS: Average to enriched, with good drainage
- DISTANCE BETWEEN PLANTS: 6″–18″
- SUNLIGHT REQUIREMENTS: Full sun
- WATERING: Moderate, don't leave standing in water
- DAYS TO BLOOM/BLOOMING PERIOD: 60–70 days from seed; spring to frost
- SPECIAL NOTES: Too much fertilization can create lush foliage at the expense of flowers. Pick faded flowers to induce bushiness and longer flowering. Recommended variety: Inca Hybrids. Except for the rare (and unpopular) odorless hybrids, Marigolds will repel insect pests

MARIGOLD
TAGETES PATULA
Called French Marigold

French Marigolds were the original dwarf variety. They are very easy to grow and have the tidy habit of keeping uniform and compact. The flowers are often crested and sometimes bicolor, and they bloom abundantly and constantly.

- DEGREE OF DIFFICULTY: Very easy
- USES: Beds, low borders, edgings, cutting
- HEIGHT: 6″–18″
- COLORS: Yellow, orange, both often marked with red; cultivars exist from purer yellows to nearly red
- SIZE OF BLOOM: 2″–3″ single or double
- FROST TOLERANCE: Half-hardy
- PREFERS: Warm weather
- WHEN TO SOW INDOORS: 6–8 weeks before last frost
- DAYS TO GERMINATION: 5–7
- WHEN TO SOW OUTDOORS OR SET TRANSPLANTS: 2–3 weeks before last frost, when ground has warmed
- SOIL CONDITIONS: Average, with good drainage
- DISTANCE BETWEEN PLANTS: 6″–10″
- SUNLIGHT REQUIREMENTS: Full sun
- WATERING: Moderate; keep well-drained
- DAYS TO BLOOM/BLOOMING PERIOD: 6 weeks from seed; spring until frost
- SPECIAL NOTES: Pick faded flowers. Try the dwarf double-crested varieties

MARIGOLD
TAGETES HYBRIDS
Also Called Triploid Hybrids, Mule Marigolds

The Triploid Hybrids are said to be the brightest of all the Marigolds. They have the tidiness of the French, and the vigor and flower-size of the American. They are sterile and set no seed,  and so they give all their energy to flower production and bloom profusely. They have a lower-than-average germination rate, so plant them generously.

- DEGREE OF DIFFICULTY: Very easy
- USES: Bedding, edging, borders, cutting
- HEIGHT: 10″–14″
- COLORS: Orange, yellow, red
- SIZE OF BLOOM: 2″–2½″, single and double
- FROST TOLERANCE: Half-hardy
- PREFERS: Warm weather; these are especially heat-tolerant
- WHEN TO SOW INDOORS: 6–8 weeks before last frost
- DAYS TO GERMINATION: 7–10
- WHEN TO SOW OUTDOORS OR SET TRANSPLANTS: Just before last frost, when ground is warm
- SOIL CONDITIONS: Average
- DISTANCE BETWEEN PLANTS: 12″
- SUNLIGHT REQUIREMENTS: Full sun
- WATERING: Water moderately
- DAYS TO BLOOM/BLOOMING PERIOD: 50–60 days from seed; spring to frost
- SPECIAL NOTES: Like other Marigolds, these repel insect pests. Try Red and Gold varieties. Deadhead spent blossoms

MEXICAN SUNFLOWER
TITHONIA ROTUNDIFOLIA
Annual

One of the most heat-resistant and largest of annuals, this tall plant is easy to grow and provides a splash of new color later in the summer. It produces flowers that are a brilliant, rich yellow or red-orange color, and large, velvety grey-green leaves. Mexican Sunflower is an excellent choice for the back of a border.

SEARING CUT FLOWERS FOR DRIED ARRANGEMENTS

Flowers with hollow stems, like Dahlias and Mexican Sunflowers, and those that exude sap or milky juice when cut, like Poppies, require special treatment if they are to be dried. First, as usual, cut stems at an angle with a sharp knife or scissors. Then, to seal them off, the open stem-bottoms should either be held under boiling water for several seconds, or seared with a flame, after which they should be plunged immediately into a cold water bath. This process stops the flowers from "bleeding," and improves both their quality and shelf-life in dried arrangements.

- DEGREE OF DIFFICULTY: Easy
- USES: Borders, backgrounds, cutting
- HEIGHT: 4′–6′
- COLORS: Yellow, gold, red-orange
- SIZE OF BLOOM: 3″–4″
- FROST TOLERANCE: Half-hardy
- PREFERS: Warm weather
- WHEN TO SOW INDOORS: 6–8 before last frost, but easy to start outdoors
- DAYS TO GERMINATION: 7–15
- WHEN TO SOW OUTDOORS OR SET TRANSPLANTS: After all danger of frost is past
- SOIL CONDITIONS: Average, good drainage
- DISTANCE BETWEEN PLANTS: 2′
- SUNLIGHT REQUIREMENTS: Full sun
- WATERING: Only if soil very dry; tolerates heat and drought
- DAYS TO BLOOM/BLOOMING PERIOD: Summer and early fall
- SPECIAL NOTES: Staking may be necessary. Sear the hollow stems to prolong the life of flowers used for cutting—see page 183

MIGNONETTE
RESEDA ODORATA
Annual

As the second part of its Latin name would indicate, the essential reason to grow Mignonette is for its fragrance. The yellowish flowers are nothing special to look at, but their fragrance is divine, enlivening indoor arrangements and long-lasting bouquets.

Mignonette really likes cool weather, so give it a partially shaded spot in your garden. And because it resents transplanting, it is best to start seeds directly outdoors.

- DEGREE OF DIFFICULTY: Easy
- USES: Bedding, borders, containers, cutting
- HEIGHT: 12″–18″
- COLORS: Greenish-yellow, yellowish-white
- SIZE OF BLOOM: ⅓″
- FROST TOLERANCE: Hardy
- PREFERS: Cool weather
- WHEN TO SOW INDOORS: 6 weeks before setting out, but best sown outside
- DAYS TO GERMINATION: 4–10; do not cover seeds; need light to germinate
- WHEN TO SOW OUTDOORS OR SET TRANSPLANTS: As soon as the ground can be worked
- SOIL CONDITIONS: Moist, well-drained, enriched with organic matter
- DISTANCE BETWEEN PLANTS: 6″–12″
- SUNLIGHT REQUIREMENTS: Full sun to partial shade
- WATERING: Keep moist
- DAYS TO BLOOM/BLOOMING PERIOD: All summer
- SPECIAL NOTES: Look for an heirloom variety—it is bound to have better fragrance than newer types. Fertilize lightly every month

MONKEY FLOWER

MIMULUS × HYBRIDUS GRANDIFLORUS
Annual

The freckle-faced Monkey Flower is truly a shade-loving annual. It can tolerate sun only in cooler climates, but in warmer areas, where the usual problem is to find flowers that will tolerate heat but don't require sun, the Monkey Flower is a natural to plant along with Impatiens and Begonias and the few other shade-tolerant annuals. It needs moist ground, and thrives when planted near water. It is frost-tolerant, free-blooming and the newer types are more vigorous and produce blooms even earlier. Some varieties have flowers that are mixed yellow and red, and some are one color with tinges of another.

- DEGREE OF DIFFICULTY: Moderately difficult
- USES: Bedding, borders, rock gardens, containers
- HEIGHT: 6″–8″
- COLORS: Red, or red and yellow, pinks and white
- SIZE OF BLOOM: 2″
- FROST TOLERANCE: Half-hardy
- PREFERS: Cool weather
- WHEN TO SOW INDOORS: 10–12 weeks before last frost
- DAYS TO GERMINATION: 7–14; do not cover seeds
- WHEN TO SOW OUTDOORS OR SET TRANSPLANTS: After danger of frost is past; in milder climates, may sow seed in fall for late winter and early spring bloom

- SOIL CONDITIONS: Moist, rich, well-drained
- DISTANCE BETWEEN PLANTS: 6″
- SUNLIGHT REQUIREMENTS: Shade
- WATERING: Keep very well-watered
- DAYS TO BLOOM/BLOOMING PERIOD: 7–9 weeks from sowing; all summer
- SPECIAL NOTES: In the United States it is best grown in Northern California, but many newer varieties can be grown in parts of the country with hotter summers and brought inside for winter bloom. Monkey Flower likes to stay moist, grows well near streams or ponds, and even tolerates flooding. Mulch to help keep soil moist. Fertilize regularly. Deadhead spent blossoms

MORNING GLORY

IPOMOEA
Annual

This large group of climbing flowers contains seven or eight different species, including Morning Glory Vine, Moonflower Vine, Cypress Vine and Cardinal Climber, but they are all similar enough to consider together here. Morning Glory is usually found in catalogues under one of its common names, occasionally under *Ipomoea*. Some varieties produce very fragrant blooms that open at dusk. Plants grow up or down, or trail, but most need support. They tolerate dry conditions, and even prefer poor soil. Although Morning Glories flower abundantly until frost, the individual blooms last only a day. The plants are quick-growing, and flowering increases after the initial burst and as cooler weather approaches. Some varieties have flowers that open in the evening.

- DEGREE OF DIFFICULTY: Moderately easy
- USES: Trailing over fences, porches, trellises, dead trees, screens
- HEIGHT: 8'–30'
- COLORS: Blue, white, purple, pink, red
- SIZE OF BLOOM: 1½"–4"
- FROST TOLERANCE: Half-hardy
- PREFERS: Warm weather
- WHEN TO SOW INDOORS: 4–6 weeks before last frost
- DAYS TO GERMINATION: 5–15
- WHEN TO SOW OUTDOORS OR SET TRANSPLANTS: After all danger of frost is past. Some varieties dislike transplanting, so if you start them inside, use individual peat pots or pellets, and set them in their permanent location carefully
- SOIL CONDITIONS: Sandy, light, well-drained, preferably low in fertility
- DISTANCE BETWEEN PLANTS: 12"–24"
- SUNLIGHT REQUIREMENTS: Full sun
- WATERING: Do not overwater; tolerates drought
- DAYS TO BLOOM/BLOOMING PERIOD: July until frost
- SPECIAL NOTES: The outer coats of the seeds need to be nicked, or soaked in warm water for 24 hours before planting to hasten the end of dormancy. All the taller varieties need some support. Sidedressing is unnecessary as all forms of *Ipomoea* prefer poor soil

NASTURTIUM

TROPAEOLUM MAJUS
Annual

Nasturtium is very easy to grow, and offers wonderful color when interplanted in the vegetable garden. It tolerates drought and thrives in poor soil, and yet still manages to bloom profusely all summer long. If you live in an area of hot, humid summers, look for varieties that specify greater tolerance of those conditions, since Nasturtium generally prefers a cooler, drier environment. Some varieties are fragrant. Look for specialized types for bedding, baskets and climbing.

The leaves, flowers and seeds of Nasturtium are all edible. Leaves are generally tossed in fresh salads, while blossoms are dipped in batter for tempura.

- DEGREE OF DIFFICULTY: Very easy
- USES: Bedding, edging, trellising, screens, hanging baskets, planters
- HEIGHT: 12"; can have runners up to 12'
- COLORS: Yellow, red, orange, white, pinks, mahogany, bicolored
- SIZE OF BLOOM: 2½"
- FROST TOLERANCE: Hardy
- PREFERS: Cool weather
- WHEN TO SOW INDOORS: Able to start indoors, does just as well started outdoors
- DAYS TO GERMINATION: 7–14
- WHEN TO SOW OUTDOORS OR SET TRANSPLANTS: After danger of frost is past
- SOIL CONDITIONS: Dry, light, sandy, poor, well-drained
- DISTANCE BETWEEN PLANTS: 12"
- SUNLIGHT REQUIREMENTS: Full sun

_____ *Notes* _____

Notes

- WATERING: Keep moist, but do not waterlog
- DAYS TO BLOOM/BLOOMING PERIOD: Early summer until frost
- SPECIAL NOTES: Sidedressing is not desirable; rich soil produces foliage at the expense of flowers

NEMESIA

NEMESIA STRUMOSA
Also Called Pouch Nemesia
Annual

Nemesia is a bushy plant fairly smothered in flowers, giving the effect of a carpet of glowing color. The flowers are an interesting shape, with a pouch at the base, and come in a very wide range of colors. They are borne on square stems with lance-shaped leaves. Nemesia is similar to Snapdragon, and they can be planted effectively together. It is hard to grow in areas with very hot summers.

- DEGREE OF DIFFICULTY: Moderately difficult
- USES: Edging, pots, bedding, borders, rock gardens, cutting
- HEIGHT: 12″–18″
- COLORS: White, yellow, bronze, cream, pink, purple, orange, red
- SIZE OF BLOOM: 1″
- FROST TOLERANCE: Half-hardy
- PREFERS: Cool weather
- WHEN TO SOW INDOORS: 4–6 weeks before final frost date
- DAYS TO GERMINATION: 7–14

- WHEN TO SOW OUTDOORS OR SET TRANSPLANTS: After all danger of frost is past
- SOIL CONDITIONS: Well-drained, rich, moist
- DISTANCE BETWEEN PLANTS: 6″
- SUNLIGHT REQUIREMENTS: Full sun to partial shade
- WATERING: Keep well-watered
- DAYS TO BLOOM/BLOOMING PERIOD: Summer until frost
- SPECIAL NOTES: Nemesia does not tolerate high humidity and heat, and does best in areas with long, cool summers. In other areas, start them early inside and set them out in the spring for several weeks of flowering. Keep well fertilized, and pinch plants back to encourage bushiness and increase flowering

PAINTED TONGUE

SALPIGLOSSIS SINUATA
Also Called Velvet Flower
Annual

This lovely plant of radiant color is available in most catalogues, but usually in only one or two varieties. Heat-resistant strains are the most desirable, so look for them. Painted Tongue is a very interesting and gorgeous flower, but not commonly grown. The blooms are trumpet-shaped, velvety and showy, some with contrasting veining. Try a few plants if you have the space; you'll be delighted you

did. It's also a good plant for a cool greenhouse.

Painted Tongue is best started indoors. The seeds need darkness to germinate but are very fine, so it is best just to press them into the soil—do not cover—and keep them away from light.

- DEGREE OF DIFFICULTY: Moderate
- USES: Beds, borders, backgrounds, cutting
- HEIGHT: 2'–3'
- COLORS: Red, blue, yellow, pink
- SIZE OF BLOOM: 2"–3"
- FROST TOLERANCE: Tender
- PREFERS: Cool summers
- WHEN TO SOW INDOORS: 8 weeks before last frost
- DAYS TO GERMINATION: 15–20
- WHEN TO SOW OUTDOORS OR SET TRANSPLANTS: After all danger of frost is past
- SOIL CONDITIONS: Loose, rich, well drained
- DISTANCE BETWEEN PLANTS: 8"–12"
- SUNLIGHT REQUIREMENTS: Full sun
- WATERING: Keep evenly moist
- DAYS TO BLOOM/BLOOMING PERIOD: Through summer in cool climates; heat and high humidity "burn" it (turn foliage and blooms whitish)
- SPECIAL NOTES: Salpiglossis is sensitive to nitrogen burn; use only compost or aged manure as sidedressing

PANSY

VIOLA × WITTROCKIANA
Also Called Heartsease, and sometimes called Viola
Perennial grown as Annual

The common names of this very popular garden flower are confusing as there is a close relationship to other flowers among them. For instance, Pansies, Violets, Violas and Johnny-jump-ups are grouped together as one flower in some catalogues, and listed separately in others. The species *Wittrockiana* is the one I usually consider to be Pansies. A perennial grown as an annual, Pansies do not thrive in heat but will bloom for long periods under cool conditions. Some varieties now available tolerate heat better, but the best-looking varieties are cool-weather flowers. In milder climates Pansies over-winter well, their foliage remaining evergreen. If started early indoors, Pansies will flower very early and continue to bloom through the coolest parts of the spring and summer.

- DEGREE OF DIFFICULTY: Easy
- USES: Borders, bedding, rock gardens, edging, planters, cutting
- HEIGHT: 4"–9"
- COLORS: Purple, red, blue, yellow, white, pink, orange, scarlet, carmine, many in combinations, with both plain and marked faces
- SIZE OF BLOOM: 2"–5"
- FROST TOLERANCE: Very hardy
- PREFERS: Cool weather
- WHEN TO SOW INDOORS: 10–12 weeks before setting out
- DAYS TO GERMINATION: 10–20

- WHEN TO SOW OUTDOORS OR SET TRANSPLANTS: Set after heavy frost; in mild climates, direct-seed in late summer for early spring blooming
- SOIL CONDITIONS: Moist, rich, well-drained
- DISTANCE BETWEEN PLANTS: 4"–6"
- SUNLIGHT REQUIREMENTS: Moderate sun to partial shade
- WATERING: Keep well watered
- DAYS TO BLOOM/BLOOMING PERIOD: If started indoors or wintered over: from very early spring through mild summer until frost; in hot climates, up to mid-summer
- SPECIAL NOTES: Keep well fertilized. Pansy seeds need darkness to germinate. Putting seed containers in the refrigerator 4–5 days after sowing may help germination. Keep plants pinched back and pick faded flowers

PETUNIA

PETUNIA × HYBRIDA
Annual

The variety of Petunias available is legion. You can get singles and doubles, picotees, large blooms, bicolors, dwarf, and fringed and ruffled versions of this wonderfully colorful and free-blooming plant. Choose varieties resistant to disease caused by cool damp weather. Otherwise, pick the colors, shapes and sizes that will best fit your gardening needs, and enjoy them all summer long.

- DEGREE OF DIFFICULTY: Easy
- USES: Borders, bedding, window boxes, hanging planters
- HEIGHT: 8″–18″
- COLORS: White, red, pink, violet, blue, yellow, striped, bicolored
- SIZE OF BLOOM: 2″–4″
- FROST TOLERANCE: Half-hardy
- PREFERS: Warm weather
- WHEN TO SOW INDOORS: 10 weeks before last frost; do not cover seeds
- DAYS TO GERMINATION: 10
- WHEN TO SOW OUTDOORS OR SET TRANSPLANTS: After danger of frost
- SOIL CONDITIONS: Light, sandy loam, but will perform well in poor, even excessively alkaline soil
- DISTANCE BETWEEN PLANTS: 12″
- SUNLIGHT REQUIREMENTS: Full sun
- WATERING: Keep well-watered
- DAYS TO BLOOM/BLOOMING PERIOD: Spring until frost
- SPECIAL NOTES: Apply compost monthly, and water thoroughly. Petunias can get leggy in the hot sun, so shear or pinch back after first wave of blooming

PHLOX

PHLOX DRUMMONDII
Also Called Annual Phlox
Annual

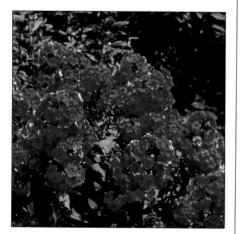

Annual Phlox is easy to grow, blooms from early summer until fall, and is available in a wide range of brilliant colors. It is quick-blooming, and can be sown directly outdoors in early spring or even

later for summer flowers—thanks to the availability of heat-resistant varieties. Phlox resents transplanting, so start it outdoors in well-drained soil. It's a good cutting flower, and since continuous cutting promotes flowering, keep your scissors handy. However, though plants tolerate some heat, they may stop blooming during the hottest part of the summer. For some reason, the weakest seedlings often produce the best color. Improved dwarf varieties that produce bushy plants blanketed by masses of flowers are increasingly available.

- DEGREE OF DIFFICULTY: Easy
- USES: Bedding, borders, rock gardens, edging, containers, cutting
- HEIGHT: 6″–20″
- COLORS: White, blue, crimson, pinks, red, some bicolors
- SIZE OF BLOOM: 1″–1½″
- FROST TOLERANCE: Half-hardy
- PREFERS: Cool weather
- WHEN TO SOW INDOORS: Not a good indoor starter
- DAYS TO GERMINATION: 6–15; needs darkness to germinate, so cover seeds completely
- WHEN TO SOW OUTDOORS OR SET TRANSPLANTS: As soon as ground can be worked
- SOIL CONDITIONS: Loose, sandy, light, rich loam, with excellent drainage
- DISTANCE BETWEEN PLANTS: 6″–12″; does well when crowded
- SUNLIGHT REQUIREMENTS: Full sun
- WATERING: Keep moist; water early in the day
- DAYS TO BLOOM/BLOOMING PERIOD: Summer until frost
- SPECIAL NOTES: When you are thinning the seedlings, remember that the smallest or weakest ones often produce the best color; you might choose to keep a few of the runts to see what happens. Keep Phlox heavily fertilized, and remove flowers as they fade

PINCUSHION FLOWER

SCABIOSA ATROPURPUREA
Also Called Sweet Scabious and Mourning Bride
Annual

Found generally under Scabiosa in seed catalogues, the Pincushion Flower is long-stemmed, fragrant and often fully double. It is an unusual and infrequently grown plant, but is finally available in more and more catalogues. Pincushion Flowers come in a range of colors and are good for bouquets and as cut flowers.

- DEGREE OF DIFFICULTY: Easy
- USES: Bedding, borders, cutting
- HEIGHT: 12″–36″
- COLORS: Purple, pink, white, blue, red
- SIZE OF BLOOM: 2″–4″
- FROST TOLERANCE: Half-hardy
- PREFERS: Warm weather
- WHEN TO SOW INDOORS: 4–5 weeks before last frost
- DAYS TO GERMINATION: 10–15
- WHEN TO SOW OUTDOORS OR SET TRANSPLANTS: After all danger of frost is past
- SOIL CONDITIONS: Well-drained, rich, preferably alkaline
- DISTANCE BETWEEN PLANTS: 8″–15″
- SUNLIGHT REQUIREMENTS: Full sun
- WATERING: Water moderately, preferably early in the day
- DAYS TO BLOOM/BLOOMING PERIOD: Early spring to fall
- SPECIAL NOTES: Fertilize moderately. May require staking

PLUMED THISTLE

CIRSIUM JAPONICUM
Biennial

Hard to find in seed catalogues, and then in only one variety—Thistle—Cirsium produces rose-red flowers which are especially nice for arrangements in fresh or dried bouquets. It does not transplant well, so start it outdoors. Once up, it is easy to grow and tolerates poor soil, but be careful: it has a tendency to spread quickly. Keep the flowers cut to prevent excessive self-sowing.

- DEGREE OF DIFFICULTY: Easy
- USES: Borders, cutting, dried
- HEIGHT: 2′–2½′
- COLORS: Rose-red
- SIZE OF BLOOM: 1″–2″
- FROST TOLERANCE: Hardy. Biennial grown as a hardy annual
- PREFERS: Cool weather
- WHEN TO SOW INDOORS: Best to sow in place outdoors
- DAYS TO GERMINATION: 15–18
- WHEN TO SOW OUTDOORS OR SET TRANSPLANTS: Early spring
- SOIL CONDITIONS: Any garden soil
- DISTANCE BETWEEN PLANTS: 12″
- SUNLIGHT REQUIREMENTS: Sun or partial shade
- WATERING: Tolerates occasional drought
- DAYS TO BLOOM/BLOOMING PERIOD: Late summer and early fall
- SPECIAL NOTES: Cirsium can become weedy, so beware its uncontrolled spreading

POPPY

PAPAVER RHOEAS, P. NUDICAULE, P. ORIENTALE
Annual and Perennial

Several Poppy varieties are considered here: Rhoeas, called Field Poppy or Shirley Poppy, which is an annual; Nudicaule, called Iceland Poppy, which is a perennial grown as an annual; and Orientale, called Oriental Poppy, which is a perennial. All will bloom the first year from seed if started early enough. Poppies are spectacular plants, with long-stemmed, silky flowers of paper-like petals in brilliant colors that are wonderful for fresh arrangements. Gardeners frequently complain that the perennial Oriental Poppy does not flower for a long enough time, is easily damaged by wind, and dies down in summer, leaving bare spots. Although these criticisms are founded in truth, to experience the beauty of the flowers in bloom, however evanescent, is just compensation.

- DEGREE OF DIFFICULTY: Moderate
- USES: Borders, rock gardens, beds, cutting
- HEIGHT: Rhoeas: 1′–3′; Nudicaule: 1′–2′; Orientale: 2′–4′
- COLORS: Pinks, red, orange, purple, white
- SIZE OF BLOOM: 1″–4″
- FROST TOLERANCE: Hardy
- PREFERS: Cool weather
- WHEN TO SOW INDOORS: 6–8 weeks before last frost; Poppies resent transplanting, so if you start them inside, use individual peat pots
- DAYS TO GERMINATION: 6–15

Notes

_____ *Notes* _____

- WHEN TO SOW OUTDOORS OR SET TRANSPLANTS: Sow outdoors in place in early spring; the Shirley Poppy, which is the annual, can be sown a little later in spring. Iceland Poppy can be sown outside in fall in milder climates. Set transplants in spring
- SOIL CONDITIONS: Very well drained, slightly rich
- DISTANCE BETWEEN PLANTS: 10″–12″ except Orientale: 15″–18″
- SUNLIGHT REQUIREMENTS: Full sun to light shade
- WATERING: Water moderately
- DAYS TO BLOOM/BLOOMING PERIOD: Orientale: mid-spring to early summer; Nudicaule: spring until frost; Rhoeas: summer
- SPECIAL NOTES: Successive plantings of the annual Poppy will produce a longer blooming season. Poppies may require staking. For cut flowers: pick them before the buds open and seal the stems by searing with a flame

PORTULACA

PORTULACA GRANDIFLORA
Also Called Rose Moss
Annual

Portulaca is a very easy annual to grow because it likes dry and sunny conditions, and poor, hot soil. It has soft spiky leaves, is covered with lavish Rose-like flowers— some double—of brilliant

hue, and carpets the ground with splashes of color throughout the summer. Newer varieties produce flowers that stay open all day long.

- DEGREE OF DIFFICULTY: Easy
- USES: Bedding, edging, ground cover, rock garden, borders, containers
- HEIGHT: 4″–8″
- COLORS: White, yellow, cream, gold, purple, red, pinks
- SIZE OF BLOOM: 1″–2½″
- FROST TOLERANCE: Tender
- PREFERS: Warm weather; tolerates drought and heat
- WHEN TO SOW INDOORS: 4–6 weeks before setting out; easy to direct-seed
- DAYS TO GERMINATION: 7–15
- WHEN TO SOW OUTDOORS OR SET TRANSPLANTS: After all danger of frost is past
- SOIL CONDITIONS: Average, dry, sandy, well-drained
- DISTANCE BETWEEN PLANTS: 12″–24″
- SUNLIGHT REQUIREMENTS: Full sun
- WATERING: Water only when soil has dried out; never overwater
- DAYS TO BLOOM/BLOOMING PERIOD: 30–70 days from seed; all summer
- SPECIAL NOTES: Look for varieties which produce blooms that do not close at all during the daytime, even in cloudy weather. Self-sows easily

POT MARIGOLD

CALENDULA OFFICINALIS
Annual

Generally found under Calendula in seed catalogues which offer several varieties, the Pot Marigold is an easy-to-grow annual that performs best in cool weather. You might want to try a second planting in late summer for fall bloom. Pot Marigold produces sunny blooms early in the spring, but look for varieties that are more heat-resistant and you will have blooms into the heat of midsummer as well. Calendula is long-lasting as a cut flower.

- DEGREE OF DIFFICULTY: Easy
- USES: Bedding, cutting
- HEIGHT: 12″–24″
- COLORS: White, cream, gold, orange and yellow
- SIZE OF BLOOM: 2″–4″
- FROST TOLERANCE: Hardy
- PREFERS: Cool weather; does poorly in hot climates
- WHEN TO SOW INDOORS: Early spring for summer blooming; in summer for fall or winter
- DAYS TO GERMINATION: 10–14; darkness needed for germination
- WHEN TO SOW OUTDOORS OR SET TRANSPLANTS: As soon as ground can be worked
- SOIL CONDITIONS: Rich soil
- DISTANCE BETWEEN PLANTS: 12″–15″
- SUNLIGHT REQUIREMENTS: Full sun
- WATERING: Keep well watered
- DAYS TO BLOOM/BLOOMING PERIOD: Spring until frost
- SPECIAL NOTES: Feed every 2–3 weeks. Remove spent blooms. Pot Marigolds will bloom constantly in a cool greenhouse

---

PRIMROSE

PRIMULA
Perennial

Primroses are perennials—some varieties of which are grown as annuals—but will flower the first year from seed if started early enough. They must be kept moist at all times during germination, and should be well-watered thereafter. Shade protection is essential during germination and initial growth, and mature plants prefer a little shade as well. Primroses thrive in soil rich in organic material. They are relatively easy to grow, are a delight to behold outside, and thrive beautifully when brought indoors for winter bloom.

Primroses are available in most seed catalogues and are grown all over the United States, but to understand how much of an English favorite they are you have to look at the pages upon pages of tremendously different varieties in seed catalogues from Great Britain.

- DEGREE OF DIFFICULTY: Moderately easy
- USES: Bedding, borders, edging, containers
- HEIGHT: 4″–18″
- COLORS: All colors, but not every color appears in every variety
- SIZE OF BLOOM: ½″–2″
- FROST TOLERANCE: Some hardy, some half-hardy
- PREFERS: Cool weather
- WHEN TO SOW INDOORS: Late fall, winter or early spring; before sowing rinse seeds with cold water or refrigerate for several weeks; seeds need light and humidity to germinate, so place flats in clear plastic bags or under glass
- DAYS TO GERMINATION: 10–20
- WHEN TO SOW OUTDOORS OR SET TRANSPLANTS: Hardier varieties: fall or early spring; all varieties in fall in milder climates; set transplants after spring frost
- SOIL CONDITIONS: Well-drained but very moist, loose, slightly acid, high in organic matter
- DISTANCE BETWEEN PLANTS: 6″–12″
- SUNLIGHT REQUIREMENTS: Partial shade; a cool location best
- WATERING: Must be well-watered, especially during dry spells; should never allow to dry out
- DAYS TO BLOOM/BLOOMING PERIOD: Several months but will bloom first year if started early enough; early spring
- SPECIAL NOTES: Keep the soil rich in organic material

SAPPHIRE FLOWER

BROWALLIA SPECIOSA
Annual

Like Begonias, Browallia are annuals that thrive in shade and make excellent ever-blooming house plants. But, though Browallia are easier to grow than Begonias, they are much less common.  They make wonderful hanging baskets, with velvety, star-shaped, cool-colored flowers over emerald green foliage.

- DEGREE OF DIFFICULTY: Moderately easy
- USES: Bedding, borders, containers, house plant
- HEIGHT: 10″–18″
- COLORS: White, shades of blue-purple, violet
- SIZE OF BLOOM: 1″–2″
- FROST TOLERANCE: Tender
- PREFERS: Warm weather
- WHEN TO SOW INDOORS: 6–8 weeks before last frost
- DAYS TO GERMINATION: 14–21; need light to germinate
- WHEN TO SOW OUTDOORS OR SET TRANSPLANTS: Should not be sown directly outdoors; set transplants after all danger of frost is past
- SOIL CONDITIONS: Well-drained, rich
- DISTANCE BETWEEN PLANTS: 6″–10″
- SUNLIGHT REQUIREMENTS: Prefer partial shade, also grows well in full sun
- WATERING: Keep soil evenly moist, but do not overwater
- DAYS TO BLOOM/BLOOMING PERIOD: Mid-spring until frost; if brought inside will bloom all winter

- SPECIAL NOTES: Fertilize lightly; overfertilizing produces foliage at the expense of flowers. Look for varieties that are low-growing and bushy, unless you prefer cultivars that trail or sprawl

SCARLET SAGE

SALVIA SPLENDENS
Perennial grown as Annual

Found under Salvia in most catalogues, Scarlet Sage—the best-known of *S. splendens*—has densely packed fiery red spikes over glossy dark green foliage. The plant is also available in several other colors, but hummingbirds especially love the red Salvia, which gardeners have always used to provide a blaze of red in massed borders and beds. Scarlet Sage can be planted in full sun or partial shade, generally the former in the north and the latter in the south; the pastel colors do better in partial shade in any region as they tend to fade in full sun. The plant dislikes high humidity but tolerates heat well. Dwarf varieties are available.

- DEGREE OF DIFFICULTY: Easy
- USES: Bedding, borders, edging, planters, cutting
- HEIGHT: 6″–36″
- COLORS: Red, white, violet, salmon, rose
- SIZE OF BLOOM: 1½″
- FROST TOLERANCE: Tender
- PREFERS: Warm weather
- WHEN TO SOW INDOORS: 8–10 weeks before last frost

- DAYS TO GERMINATION: 12–15; needs light to germinate—do not cover seeds
- WHEN TO SOW OUTDOORS OR SET TRANSPLANTS: After soil warms; set transplants after all danger of frost is past
- SOIL CONDITIONS: Rich, moist, well-drained
- DISTANCE BETWEEN PLANTS: 6″–18″
- SUNLIGHT REQUIREMENTS: Full sun to partial shade (full sun in north, partial shade in south)
- WATERING: Keep well watered, especially during dry spells
- DAYS TO BLOOM/BLOOMING PERIOD: Early summer until frost
- SPECIAL NOTES: Fertilize monthly. Seeds do not live long and should not be stored; always use fresh seeds

SHASTA DAISY

CHRYSANTHEMUM × SUPERBUM
Perennial

The Shasta Daisy is a perennial Chrysanthemum that will bloom the first year from seed if started early enough. It blooms all summer long, and its foliage will last well into fall. Easy to grow from  seed, its abundant, showy flowers on long, strong stems are great for cutting as they are extremely long-lasting in fresh arrangements.

- DEGREE OF DIFFICULTY: Easy
- USES: Beds, borders, edging, cutting
- HEIGHT: 1″–3″

- COLORS: White
- SIZE OF BLOOM: 3"–6"
- FROST TOLERANCE: Hardy
- PREFERS: Cool weather
- WHEN TO SOW INDOORS: 8–10 weeks before setting out
- DAYS TO GERMINATION: 8–14
- WHEN TO SOW OUTDOORS OR SET TRANSPLANTS: Can sow from early spring to 2 months before frost; set transplants in spring
- SOIL CONDITIONS: Well drained, moist, rich
- DISTANCE BETWEEN PLANTS: 12"–24"
- SUNLIGHT REQUIREMENTS: Sun to partial shade
- WATERING: Keep well watered
- DAYS TO BLOOM/BLOOMING PERIOD: Spring through summer
- SPECIAL NOTES: Occasional addition of organic material to the soil is helpful. Remove faded flowers to encourage more blooming

SHOO-FLY PLANT

NICANDRA PHYSALODES
Also called Apple-of-Peru
Perennial

Nicandra is a perennial grown as a half-hardy annual. It is an old-fashioned favorite said to repel flies and other insects. Not very difficult to grow, you might try the plant among the

vegetables for these qualities. In summer, the Shoo-fly presents delicate blue flowers, followed by papery, lantern-like seed cases which are used in dried arrangements. Surprisingly, it is hard to find in catalogues.

- DEGREE OF DIFFICULTY: Moderately difficult
- USES: Borders, mixed beds, dried
- HEIGHT: 2'–4'
- COLORS: Pale blue
- SIZE OF BLOOM: 1"–2"
- FROST TOLERANCE: Half-hardy
- PREFERS: Warm weather
- WHEN TO SOW INDOORS: 8–10 weeks before setting out
- DAYS TO GERMINATION: 15–20
- WHEN TO SOW OUTDOORS OR SET TRANSPLANTS: After all danger of frost
- SOIL CONDITIONS: Average soil with good drainage
- DISTANCE BETWEEN PLANTS: 2'
- SUNLIGHT REQUIREMENTS: Full sun
- WATERING: Moderate
- DAYS TO BLOOM/BLOOMING PERIOD: Summer
- SPECIAL NOTES: Fertilize monthly

SNAPDRAGON

ANTIRRHINUM MAJUS
Perennial

Snapdragons are garden favorites all over the country. The spikes of blooms (sometimes as many as 15 per plant) come in a large range of lavish colors, bloom for a long period, have a

_____ *Notes* _____

cinnamon scent, and are among the best cut flowers. Snapdragons are an excellent choice in all varieties: the dwarf versions make excellent edgings; the half-dwarf types are wonderful for massing in beds; and the tallest are good for background and cutting. To promote the growth of flowering side-shoots, the central bud should be removed when transplanting, and the plant kept generally pinched back whenever flower spikes get a little long.

- DEGREE OF DIFFICULTY: Easy
- USES: Beds, borders, cutting
- HEIGHT: 6″–3′
- COLORS: Red, white, yellow, pink
- SIZE OF BLOOM: 1½″
- FROST TOLERANCE: Half-hardy
- PREFER: Cool weather
- WHEN TO SOW INDOORS: 6–8 weeks before last frost
- DAYS TO GERMINATION: 10–14
- WHEN TO SOW OUTDOORS OR SET TRANSPLANTS: When soil has warmed; set transplants early, as soon as ground can be worked
- SOIL CONDITIONS: Sandy, light, well drained
- DISTANCE BETWEEN PLANTS: 6″–8″
- SUNLIGHT REQUIREMENTS: Full sun
- WATERING: Water moderately
- DAYS TO BLOOM/BLOOMING PERIOD: Late spring to frost
- SPECIAL NOTES: Pinch young plants to encourage branching. Fertilize monthly. Flower production and bushier plants will be encouraged by cutting freely

SNOW-ON-THE-MOUNTAIN

EUPHORBIA MARGINATA
Annual

Like Dusty Miller, Snow-on-the-mountain is grown for its foliage: cool, green, white-edged and long-lasting. It is extremely easy to grow and thrives in absolutely any kind of soil—moist, dry, hot—and does well in sun or shade. There is only one thing wrong with this plant: the milky juice exuded from its stems can seriously irritate both skin and eyes, so wear gloves and glasses when handling it.

- DEGREE OF DIFFICULTY: Very easy
- USES: Bedding, borders, background
- HEIGHT: 18″–24″
- COLORS: Green leaves with white margins
- SIZE OF BLOOM: Tiny and insignificant
- FROST TOLERANCE: Half-hardy
- PREFERS: Warm weather
- WHEN TO SOW INDOORS: Not an indoor starter
- DAYS TO GERMINATION: 10–20
- WHEN TO SOW OUTDOORS OR SET TRANSPLANTS: Sow in place after last frost date
- SOIL CONDITIONS: Any soil is fine
- DISTANCE BETWEEN PLANTS: 8″–12″
- SUNLIGHT REQUIREMENTS: Full sun or partial shade
- WATERING: Moderate

SPIDER FLOWER

CLEOME HASSLERANA
Annual

Producing showy, unusual, fragrant clouds of flowers atop clean foliage, the Spider Flower is easy to grow and an excellent conversation piece among gardening friends. It is heat and drought resistant, and not particular about the kind of soil in which it is grown. It is hard to find in seed catalogues, and there are few varieties offered when you do. But with its Orchid-like flowers and distinctive demeanor, Spider Flower is worth looking for.

- DEGREE OF DIFFICULTY: Easy
- USES: Background, beds, borders, cutting
- HEIGHT: 3'–6'
- COLORS: Lavender, white, pinks
- SIZE OF BLOOM: 2"–3"
- FROST TOLERANCE: Half-hardy
- PREFERS: Warm weather
- WHEN TO SOW INDOORS: 4–6 weeks before last frost
- DAYS TO GERMINATION: 10–14
- WHEN TO SOW OUTDOORS OR SET TRANSPLANTS: After all danger of frost is past
- SOIL CONDITIONS: Any soil is okay, but does best in sandy soil
- DISTANCE BETWEEN PLANTS: 1'–3'
- SUNLIGHT REQUIREMENTS: Full sun
- WATERING: Do not overwater
- DAYS TO BLOOM/BLOOMING PERIOD: Late spring until frost

DRYING EVERLASTING FLOWERS

Everlastings are plants (Strawflowers, Scabiosa Stellata, Globe Amaranth and Bells of Ireland, to name a few) whose flowers can be easily and effectively dried for arrangements, as they retain their color and form for a long time. Other flowers can also be used for dried arrangements, but they require a more complicated preparation, including the use of drying agents.

The flowers of everlastings should be picked at just the right moment to ensure their lasting qualities. For example, some should be cut before the flowers have fully opened (Yarrow and Strawflower); some as they begin to open (Thistles), and still others when they are fully opened (Bells of Ireland, Globe Amaranth and Scabiosa). Check the individual seed packets for specific information about the everlastings you have planted.

All everlastings should be picked when they are as dry as possible—never immediately after a rainfall or when they are still covered with dew. After cutting, strip off all the leaves, tie the flowers in bunches, and hang them upside-down in a cool, dark, dry and well ventilated place for several weeks. When they are fully dried, they are ready for whatever types of arrangements please you.

STARFLOWER

SCABIOSA STELLATA
Annual

The Starflower is an everlasting grown primarily for its seed heads, which make interesting dried flowers. It produces little florets with star-like centers, and is a very effective counterpoint when used with other everlastings in dried arrangements. It is found under both Starflower and Scabiosa in catalogues.

- DEGREE OF DIFFICULTY: Moderately easy
- USES: Dried
- HEIGHT: 6"–24"
- COLORS: Blue, rose, white
- SIZE OF BLOOM: 1½"
- FROST TOLERANCE: Half-hardy
- PREFERS: Warm weather
- WHEN TO SOW INDOORS: 4–5 weeks before last frost
- DAYS TO GERMINATION: 10–15
- WHEN TO SOW OUTDOORS OR SET TRANSPLANTS: After all danger of frost is past
- SOIL CONDITIONS: Rich, loose, well-drained, preferably alkaline
- DISTANCE BETWEEN PLANTS: 8"–15"
- SUNLIGHT REQUIREMENTS: Full sun
- WATERING: Water moderately
- DAYS TO BLOOM/BLOOMING PERIOD: Flowers develop quickly into seed heads

STATICE

LIMONIUM SINUATUM
Also called Sea Lavender or Notchleaf
Sea Lavender
Biennial

Statice is a half-hardy
biennial commonly grown
as an annual. It is
especially good for
seashore growing as it
tolerates salt spray very
well. Its erratic blooming
habits make it hard to
predict exactly when it will be in bloom,
but it is available in a good range of bright
colors and dries very well for everlasting
arrangements.

- DEGREE OF DIFFICULTY: Moderately
  difficult
- USES: Borders, rock gardens, cutting,
  dried
- HEIGHT: 12″–30″
- COLORS: White, yellow, red, blue, pinks
- SIZE OF BLOOM: ⅜″ borne in clusters
  atop stalks
- FROST TOLERANCE: Half-hardy
- PREFERS: Warm weather
- WHEN TO SOW INDOORS: 8–10 weeks
  before last frost; resents transplanting so
  use individual peat pots
- DAYS TO GERMINATION: 15–20
- WHEN TO SOW OUTDOORS OR SET
  TRANSPLANTS: After danger of frost
- SOIL CONDITIONS: Sandy, light, well-
  drained, not very rich
- DISTANCE BETWEEN PLANTS: 12″–24″
- SUNLIGHT REQUIREMENTS: Full sun;
  tolerates heat, drought, salt spray
- WATERING: Water only when dry; do not
  overwater
- DAYS TO BLOOM/BLOOMING PERIOD: All
  summer

- SPECIAL NOTES: Look for seeds that are
  advertised "clean," which means they have
  had the fluff around them removed for
  easier planting. To dry, cut fully opened
  flowers and hang them upside down in a
  dark, cool place

STOCK

MATTHIOLA INCANA,
LONGIPETALA
Perennial grown as Annual

These are the best known
of these fragrant, quick-
blooming cool-weather
lovers. *Matthiola incana,*
called Stock, or Brompton
Stock, or Gillyflower, has
richly packed blooms on
stems ranging from 15″

(for dwarf types) to 30″ high. *Matthiola
longipetala,* known as Evening Stock, is not
much to look at by comparison but opens
gloriously in the evening to release a lovely
fragrance. Some Stocks are biennials and
some annuals, and all are excellent cultivars,
easy to grow, and fast blooming. They are
excellent cutting flowers too, so you can
enjoy their rich fragrance inside as well.

- DEGREE OF DIFFICULTY: Moderate
- USES: Borders, bedding, edging, planters,
  cutting
- HEIGHT: 12″–30″
- COLORS: White, cream, pink, red, purple,
  lavender, rose, blue, yellow
- SIZE OF BLOOM: 1″

- FROST TOLERANCE: Some hardy, some
  half-hardy
- PREFERS: Cool weather
- WHEN TO SOW INDOORS: 6–8 weeks
  before last frost
- DAYS TO GERMINATION: 7–10: do not
  cover seeds—need light for germination
- WHEN TO SOW OUTDOORS OR SET
  TRANSPLANTS: Sow in spring; set
  transplants after danger of frost is past
- SOIL CONDITIONS: Moist, rich, sandy
- DISTANCE BETWEEN PLANTS: 10″–15″
- SUNLIGHT REQUIREMENTS: Full sun or
  light shade; use cool location, does not
  tolerate heat well
- WATERING: Keep soil evenly moist but
  do not overwater
- DAYS TO BLOOM/BLOOMING PERIOD:
  Most bloom early, some 7 weeks from
  seed; will bloom in the winter indoors; in
  milder areas can be sown in fall for late
  winter and early spring blooming
- SPECIAL NOTES: Fertilize frequently

STRAWFLOWER

HELICHRYSUM BRACTEATUM
Also called Everlasting
Annual

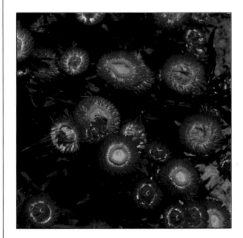

The Strawflower is
considered the finest, and
is probably the most
popular, of the
everlastings grown in the
home garden. Its ability
to hold shape and color is
almost everlasting indeed.
It is very easy to grow, likes long, hot
summers, and will even tolerate poor soil. It

is reliable and trouble-free and provides beautiful concentrated color all summer long. Some seed companies will supply drying instructions on request. See Special Notes, below.

- DEGREE OF DIFFICULTY: Easy
- USES: Borders, rock gardens, cutting, dried
- HEIGHT: 1'–3'
- COLORS: Yellow, red, white, pink, salmon, purple
- SIZE OF BLOOM: 1"–3"; Monstrosum variety has larger head
- FROST TOLERANCE: Half-hardy
- PREFERS: Long, hot summers
- WHEN TO SOW INDOORS: 4–6 weeks before last frost—needs light to germinate
- DAYS TO GERMINATION: 7–10
- WHEN TO SOW OUTDOORS OR SET TRANSPLANTS: After last frost
- SOIL CONDITIONS: Porous, sandy, light, well-drained, alkaline
- DISTANCE BETWEEN PLANTS: 9"–15"
- SUNLIGHT REQUIREMENTS: Full sun
- WATERING: Moderate watering, during very dry spells only
- DAYS TO BLOOM/BLOOMING PERIOD: From early summer until frost
- SPECIAL NOTES: Deadhead spent blooms regularly. Tall plants may need staking. For drying, flowers should be cut when they are partially open, and hung upside down in a dark place. The stems are too fragile to last, so when flower heads dry, they should be cut from the stems and attached to wires

SUMMER FORGET-ME-NOT

ANCHUSA CAPENSIS
Also called Cape Forget-Me-Not
Annual

Called Summer Forget-me-not because of its similarity to the well-known spring bloomer—to which it is related—this is a showy bloomer with masses of tiny brilliant ultramarine blue flowers on compact plants. Although it is known mainly for the vividness of its blue color, a rare pink is also available, but hard to find. The plant is relatively easy to grow, likes poor soil, and can bloom from early summer until frost.

- DEGREE OF DIFFICULTY: Moderately easy
- USES: Rock gardens, background, borders, cutting
- HEIGHT: 8"–18"
- COLORS: Intense ultramarine blue
- SIZE OF BLOOM: ¼"
- FROST TOLERANCE: Hardy
- PREFERS: Cool weather
- WHEN TO SOW INDOORS: 6–8 weeks before last frost
- DAYS TO GERMINATION: 14–21
- WHEN TO SOW OUTDOORS OR SET TRANSPLANTS: After danger of frost is past
- SOIL CONDITIONS: Average to poor, with good drainage
- DISTANCE BETWEEN PLANTS: 10"–12"
- SUNLIGHT REQUIREMENTS: Full sun
- WATERING: Water moderately
- DAYS TO BLOOM/BLOOMING PERIOD: Early summer until frost

Notes

- SPECIAL NOTES: Shear to 6″ after each wave of blooming to encourage flowering until frost. The plant really likes cool weather and may cease to bloom in the hottest part of the summer, but if cut back will flower again in the cooler days of late summer. Feed little, if any, as it prefers poor soil

SUNFLOWER

HELIANTHUS
Annual

I used to think of Sunflowers as the huge stalks you planted at the back of the garden to attract lovely birds and whose seeds you could eat (if the birds left any).  Now, thanks to the hybrids that have appeared in recent years, the Sunflower is a far more stylish and versatile plant. There are dwarf varieties that produce one double mum-like flower per plant, and other types which bear many blossoms. All are very easy to grow and do well in any garden soil.

The three best-known species are: *Helianthus annuus,* called the Common Sunflower, grows 4′–6′ with yellow single or double flowers blooming in late summer; *Helianthus debilis,* which grows 4′–5′ with yellow or white flowers 3″ across, and blooms midsummer until frost; and *Helianthus giganteus,* the Giant Sunflower, growing 9′–12′ tall with light yellow flowers up to 1′ across, and blooming in late summer and early fall.

- DEGREE OF DIFFICULTY: Very easy to grow
- USES: Background, borders
- HEIGHT: 4′–10′; dwarf varieties: 15″–30″
- COLORS: Mostly yellow, some bronzes and reds
- SIZE OF BLOOM: 3″ to 1′
- FROST TOLERANCE: Hardy
- PREFERS: Warm weather
- WHEN TO SOW INDOORS: 4–6 weeks before last frost—but so easy to start outside, better to give indoor space to more difficult flowers
- DAYS TO GERMINATION: 10–14
- WHEN TO SOW OUTDOORS OR SET TRANSPLANTS: After all danger of frost is past
- SOIL CONDITIONS: Light, average-to-dry; tolerates poor soil
- DISTANCE BETWEEN PLANTS: 2′–4′
- SUNLIGHT REQUIREMENTS: Full sun
- WATERING: Regularly, but tolerates both heat and drought
- DAYS TO BLOOM/BLOOMING PERIOD: Will bloom over a long season

SWAN RIVER DAISY

BRACHYCOME IBERIDIFOLIA
Annual

This plant from Australia has profuse, almost wall-to-wall masses of fragrant Daisies amid interesting feathery foliage. It is not long-blooming and requires successive plantings for continuous show, nor does it bloom well when the weather gets hot. Nevertheless, it is easy to grow and deserves a try in your garden. The display is impressive when you keep it going.

- DEGREE OF DIFFICULTY: Easy
- USES: Edgings, borders, rock gardens
- HEIGHT: 8"–16"
- COLORS: Blue, white, rose, violet
- SIZE OF BLOOM: 1"–1½"
- FROST TOLERANCE: Half-hardy
- PREFERS: Cool weather
- WHEN TO SOW INDOORS: 4–6 weeks before last frost
- DAYS TO GERMINATION: 10–18
- WHEN TO SOW OUTDOORS OR SET TRANSPLANTS: After last frost
- SOIL CONDITIONS: Moist, rich, well-drained
- DISTANCE BETWEEN PLANTS: 6"
- SUNLIGHT REQUIREMENTS: Full sun
- WATERING: Keep moderately watered
- DAYS TO BLOOM/BLOOMING PERIOD: Blooms in the summer
- SPECIAL NOTES: Make successive plantings for continuous bloom

SWEET PEA

LATHYRUS ODORATUS
Annual

The Sweet Pea is normally a spring bloomer, but some newer varieties will actually bloom all summer long. The plant is easy to grow, and is available in climbing vine types which may require staking, and bush types, which do not. It is an old-fashioned favorite with fragrant flowers in beautiful colors which last well when cut and brought indoors. Because it does not do well in the heat, start Sweet Pea early inside, or very early in an outdoor bed prepared the preceding fall. Sweet Pea is very common in England, and you might want to look in seed catalogues from Great Britain for older, more fragrant (but shorter-blooming) varieties.

- DEGREE OF DIFFICULTY: Easy
- USES: Beds, borders, containers, fences, screens, trellises, cutting
- HEIGHT: Vines: 6'; bush types: 30"
- COLORS: Purple, rose, pink, red, white, lavender, blue
- SIZE OF BLOOM: 2" each, borne 1–5 blooms per stem
- FROST TOLERANCE: Hardy
- PREFERS: Cool weather
- WHEN TO SOW INDOORS: 4–6 weeks before setting out; nick seed coat or soak seeds 24 hours before planting
- DAYS TO GERMINATION: 10–14
- WHEN TO SOW OUTDOORS OR SET TRANSPLANTS: Early spring; ground should be prepared in the fall for spring planting. May be planted in the fall in mild climates

- SOIL CONDITIONS: Deeply worked, rich, well-drained, high in organic matter, slightly alkaline
- DISTANCE BETWEEN PLANTS: 6"–12"
- SUNLIGHT REQUIREMENTS: Full sun
- WATERING: Keep very well watered
- DAYS TO BLOOM/BLOOMING PERIOD: Spring and early summer; newer varieties may bloom even in hotter weather
- SPECIAL NOTES: Fertilize regularly and frequently. Taller types may require staking. Mulch roots to keep them cool. Cut back to encourage branching and to stimulate flowering. Careful and constant deadheading of spent blooms will greatly encourage longer flowering. To prevent root-rot disease, do not plant in the same spot two years in a row

SWEET WILLIAM

DIANTHUS BARBATUS
Biennial grown as Annual

This Dianthus is usually found in seed catalogues under Sweet William, but sometimes under Dianthus as well. It is normally a biennial grown as an annual, but some newer annual varieties are now available. In either case, *Dianthus barbatus* is quite fragrant, long-blooming and showy. If sown early in spring, Sweet William will flower from spring on, and in mild areas may winter-over to flower again the following spring. Some newer annual varieties have larger, often double, flowers.

- DEGREE OF DIFFICULTY: Moderately easy
- USES: Edging, bedding, borders, cutting
- HEIGHT: 4″–12″
- COLORS: Red, purple, white, bicolored
- SIZE OF BLOOM: ⅓″–½″
- FROST TOLERANCE: Hardy
- PREFERS: Cool weather
- WHEN TO SOW INDOORS: 6–8 weeks before last frost
- DAYS TO GERMINATION: 8–15
- WHEN TO SOW OUTDOORS OR SET TRANSPLANTS: After danger of frost
- SOIL CONDITIONS: Well-drained, alkaline
- DISTANCE BETWEEN PLANTS: 6″–12″
- SUNLIGHT REQUIREMENTS: Full sun to partial shade
- WATERING: Water moderately
- DAYS TO BLOOM/BLOOMING PERIOD: If started indoors early, in early spring of first year
- SPECIAL NOTES: Deadhead spent blossoms

TAHOKA DAISY

MACHAERANTHERA TANACETIFOLIA
Annual

Seeds for the Tahoka Daisy are extremely difficult to find in catalogues. The flowers are blue or lavender-blue with gold centers, and the foliage is lacy. Although it thrives best in cool climates, it will produce flowers in warmer areas, but for a shorter period of time. It tolerates poor soil.

- DEGREE OF DIFFICULTY: Easy
- USES: Border, cutting
- HEIGHT: 12″–24″
- COLORS: Blue, lavender, with gold centers
- SIZE OF BLOOM: 2″–2½″
- FROST TOLERANCE: Half-hardy
- PREFERS: Cool climates
- WHEN TO SOW INDOORS: 6–8 weeks before last frost date
- DAYS TO GERMINATION: 25–30
- WHEN TO SOW OUTDOORS OR SET TRANSPLANTS: Sow in early spring; set transplants after danger of hard frost
- SOIL CONDITIONS: Average, well-drained
- DISTANCE BETWEEN PLANTS: 9″
- SUNLIGHT REQUIREMENTS: Full sun
- WATERING: Water moderately
- DAYS TO BLOOM/BLOOMING PERIOD: Late spring until frost
- SPECIAL NOTES: Deadhead spent blooms. The dormancy of the seeds should be broken by mixing them with moist peat moss or placing them in some other moistened planting medium and then refrigerating for 2–3 weeks

TOADFLAX

LINARIA MAROCCANA
Annual

Toadflax is rarely planted but definitely deserves greater popularity. It is easy, showy, and very long-flowering, with blooms that first appear in spring and last clear until frost. It can be both

one of the first and one of the last annuals to bloom in the garden. The flowers resemble miniature Snapdragons and come in a range of rich colors over gray-green foliage.

- DEGREE OF DIFFICULTY: Easy
- USES: Borders, bedding, rock gardens, edging, cutting
- HEIGHT: 8″–12″
- COLORS: Yellow, blue, pink, red, bronze, orange, white, multicolored
- SIZE OF BLOOM: ½″
- FROST TOLERANCE: Hardy
- PREFERS: Cool weather
- WHEN TO SOW INDOORS: 4–6 weeks before setting out, but unnecessary—very easy to direct-seed
- DAYS TO GERMINATION: 7–15
- WHEN TO SOW OUTDOORS OR SET TRANSPLANTS: As soon as the ground can be worked
- SOIL CONDITIONS: Light, loose, sandy, well-drained
- DISTANCE BETWEEN PLANTS: 4″–8″
- SUNLIGHT REQUIREMENTS: Full sun
- WATERING: Water moderately
- DAYS TO BLOOM/BLOOMING PERIOD: Early spring until frost
- SPECIAL NOTES: Frequently self-sows. Can be planted in the fall in milder climates. Fertilize monthly

TRANSVAAL DAISY

GERBERA JAMESONII
Also called Barberton Daisy
Annual

Found under Gerbera in seed catalogues, and best grown where the summers are long and humid. Transvaal Daisy is becoming increasingly popular in cooler regions as a garden plant which  can be brought inside when summer ends and grown as a houseplant. It must be sown indoors early to gain a jump on its long growing season (3½ months from seed for some varieties), but the beauty of the flowers, especially as very long-lasting cutting flowers, makes it worth the effort. Transvaal Daisy is available in a range of brilliant colors and sizes.

- DEGREE OF DIFFICULTY: It is tricky to grow, requiring specific care during its rather long growing period
- USES: Borders, low beds, cutting; dwarf varieties as indoor plants
- HEIGHT: 12″–24″; dwarf varieties: 6″–10″
- COLORS: Orange, yellow, red, pink, scarlet, white, rose, crimson, violet
- SIZE OF BLOOM: 4″–5″
- FROST TOLERANCE: Half-hardy (can tolerate some light frost); technically a tender perennial grown as an annual in colder climates
- PREFERS: Warm weather but likes cool evenings
- WHEN TO SOW INDOORS: Late winter or early spring, as early as 10–14 weeks before last frost date; faster-growing strains are appearing—check catalogues to determine dates for varieties
- DAYS TO GERMINATION: 15–25; seeds need light to germinate
- WHEN TO SOW OUTDOORS OR SET TRANSPLANTS: Too slow-growing to sow outdoors; set transplants after all danger of frost is past
- SOIL CONDITIONS: Well-drained, moist, slightly acid
- DISTANCE BETWEEN PLANTS: 12″–15″
- SUNLIGHT REQUIREMENTS: Full sun, tolerates some shade; likes afternoon shade where summers very hot
- WATERING: Keep moist; water during dry spells, but do not overwater
- DAYS TO BLOOM/BLOOMING PERIOD: 3½ months from sowing in the newer varieties
- SPECIAL NOTES: Seed does not store from one season to the next, so use only fresh seed. Fertilize lightly twice a month

TREASURE FLOWER

GAZANIA RIGENS
Perennial

Usually found under Gazania in seed catalogues, Treasure Flower has thick leaves of a beautiful silvery-green color and brightly-colored Daisy-like flowers which close at night and on

_____ *Notes* _____

cloudy days. It thrives best in dry, hot, desert-like climates, but can be grown with success almost anywhere if given soil that is extremely well-drained.

- DEGREE OF DIFFICULTY: Easy
- USES: Bedding, edging, rock gardens, ground cover
- HEIGHT: 6"–15"
- COLORS: Yellow, gold, orange, pink, red, cream
- SIZE OF BLOOM: 3"–6"
- FROST TOLERANCE: Tender
- PREFERS: Warm weather
- WHEN TO SOW INDOORS: 6–8 weeks before last frost; cover seeds—need darkness to germinate—and keep them moist but not wet
- DAYS TO GERMINATION: 8–14
- WHEN TO SOW OUTDOORS OR SET TRANSPLANTS: After all danger of frost
- SOIL CONDITIONS: Light, sandy soil
- DISTANCE BETWEEN PLANTS: 8"–12"
- SUNLIGHT REQUIREMENTS: Full sun
- WATERING: Avoid overwatering; tolerates both heat and drought
- DAYS TO BLOOM/BLOOMING PERIOD: July until frost
- SPECIAL NOTES: Look for varieties that offer "clean seed," which means that they have had the fluff around them removed for easier planting

TREE MALLOW

LAVATERA ARBOREA, LAVATERA TRIMESTRIS
Annual

Tree Mallow is related to Hollyhocks. It is not commonly grown, but should be because it is easy and quick to grow and provides continuous, beautiful color. The plants have dense, bushy mounds which are excellent for backgrounds because of their considerable height, and the foliage remains beautiful long after frost has destroyed other annuals.

- DEGREE OF DIFFICULTY: Moderately easy
- USES: Border, hedge or screen, background, cutting
- HEIGHT: 2½'–4'
- COLORS: Dark red, pinks, rose, white
- SIZE OF BLOOM: 2"–4"
- FROST TOLERANCE: Hardy
- PREFERS: Cool weather
- WHEN TO SOW INDOORS: Not a great indoor starter, but seeds can be sown (use individual peat pots or pellets) 6–8 weeks before setting out
- DAYS TO GERMINATION: 15–21
- WHEN TO SOW OUTDOORS OR SET TRANSPLANTS: Early spring
- SOIL CONDITIONS: Well-drained, average soil
- DISTANCE BETWEEN PLANTS: 18"–24"
- SUNLIGHT REQUIREMENTS: Full sun
- WATERING: Keep well-watered
- DAYS TO BLOOM/BLOOMING PERIOD: Midsummer until frost; foliage turns bronze and stays attractive after frost
- SPECIAL NOTES: Fertilize monthly. Remove faded flowers to prolong bloom

VINCA

CATHARANTHUS ROSEUS
Also Called Periwinkle
Annual

Depending on which catalogue you are looking at, this plant can be found under any of the names above; it's also known as Madagascar Periwinkle. Whatever you call it, it is a wonderful

annual, thriving almost anywhere under conditions that might discourage other plants. Unaffected by disease or insects, it is extremely easy to grow, spreads out nicely, survives both heat and drought well, and blooms luxuriantly and constantly from early spring to frost over glossy, lush foliage. The bright flowers are long-lasting and do not fade. Because it is a slow-grower, it must be started indoors. It prefers warm soil, self-sows easily, and is a natural for climates that are too hot for many plants. All in all, this flower puts on quite a show for only a minimum of gardener-effort.

- DEGREE OF DIFFICULTY: Easy
- USES: Low beds, borders, ground cover, hanging baskets, planters
- HEIGHT: 3″–18″
- COLORS: Pinks, white, mauves, lavenders, some with red centers
- SIZE OF BLOOM: 1″–2″
- FROST TOLERANCE: Tender
- PREFERS: Warm, or even hot, weather
- WHEN TO SOW INDOORS: 12 weeks before last frost; do not overwater seedlings
- DAYS TO GERMINATION: 15–20; germinate in total darkness
- WHEN TO SOW OUTDOORS OR SET TRANSPLANTS: Outdoor sowings will not mature early enough to flower; set transplants after all danger of frost is past
- SOIL CONDITIONS: Any well-drained garden soil
- DISTANCE BETWEEN PLANTS: 12″
- SUNLIGHT REQUIREMENTS: Full sun or partial shade
- WATERING: Keep evenly moist, but tolerates drought and heat; definitely do not overwater
- DAYS TO BLOOM/BLOOMING PERIOD: Early spring to frost

VIOLA

VIOLA CORNUTA
Also Called Bedding Pansy, Tufted Pansy, Horned Violet
Annual

The Viola, like Johnny-jump-ups and Violets, is a cousin of the Pansy and can appear in seed catalogues under its own name or with the Pansies. Also like the Pansy, it is a perennial usually grown

as an annual. It will bloom the first year if sown early, and produces long-lasting flowers on small neat plants. Shear the tops after plants bloom to encourage renewed flowering once the hottest part of the summer has past. The Viola is usually more tolerant of hot weather than either Violets or Pansies and is especially good for woodland plantings. Because they are less arresting than Pansies, they are also very popular to interplant with and set off spring-flowering bulbs such as Tulips and Daffodils.

- DEGREE OF DIFFICULTY: Easy
- USES: Borders, edging, rock gardens, planters
- HEIGHT: 6″–10″
- COLORS: Yellow, white, red, blue, orange, pinks, purples, apricot
- SIZE OF BLOOM: 1″–2″
- FROST TOLERANCE: Very hardy
- PREFERS: Cool weather
- WHEN TO SOW INDOORS: 8–10 weeks before setting out
- DAYS TO GERMINATION: 10–12; after sowing, cover seeds—they require darkness to germinate—and chill in refrigerator several days
- WHEN TO SOW OUTDOORS OR SET TRANSPLANTS: Set transplants a few weeks before last frost
- SOIL CONDITIONS: Rich, loose, high in organic material, moist
- DISTANCE BETWEEN PLANTS: 6″
- SUNLIGHT REQUIREMENTS: Sun to partial shade
- WATERING: Keep well watered
- DAYS TO BLOOM/BLOOMING PERIOD: Early spring through fall if not too hot
- SPECIAL NOTES: Keep well fertilized. Pick faded blossoms regularly

VIOLET

VIOLA ODORATA
Also Called Sweet Violet, English Violet
Perennial grown as Annual

The Violet, yet another member of the Pansy family, may be found in seed catalogues under Pansy, Violet, or occasionally Viola, although it is a rare offering to begin with.

Also a perennial grown as an annual, it is longer-lived than the Pansy, and flowers profusely in early spring and again in the fall. Violets thrive best in cool and moist conditions. The charming flowers on this old-fashioned plant have clear crisp colors and are pleasantly fragrant.

- DEGREE OF DIFFICULTY: Easy
- USES: Edging, rock gardens, ground cover
- HEIGHT: 4″–5″
- COLORS: Lavender blue, violet, purple, white
- SIZE OF BLOOM: 1″
- FROST TOLERANCE: Hardy
- PREFERS: Cool weather
- WHEN TO SOW INDOORS: In midwinter
- DAYS TO GERMINATION: 10–20; needs darkness to germinate; chilling seeds may aid germination
- WHEN TO SOW OUTDOORS OR SET TRANSPLANTS: Sow outdoors in early spring or late summer
- SOIL CONDITIONS: Moist, rich, cool
- DISTANCE BETWEEN PLANTS: 6″–8″
- SUNLIGHT REQUIREMENTS: Partial shade is best
- WATERING: Keep moist

- DAYS TO BLOOM/BLOOMING PERIOD: Flowers early if planted early, then flowers again in fall
- SPECIAL NOTES: Keep well fertilized. Mulch to keep cool and moist in the summer

---

WALLFLOWER

CHEIRANTHUS CHEIRI
Perennial grown as Annual

The Wallflower is found in seed catalogues under its common name when it is found at all. It is a perennial grown as an annual that thrives best in cool coastal or mountainous places, and

in other areas with long cool summers. It blooms easily the first year from seed, and, in milder climates, may keep blooming for many years; indoors it is winter-blooming. The four-petaled clustered flowers are fragrant and brilliantly colored on bushy plants. Wallflower will tolerate poor soil.

- DEGREE OF DIFFICULTY: Moderately easy
- USES: Bedding, borders, rock gardens, cutting
- HEIGHT: 12″–30″
- COLORS: Mainly orange, yellow and apricot; some bronze, purple, red
- SIZE OF BLOOM: 1″
- FROST TOLERANCE: Half-hardy
- PREFERS: Cool weather
- WHEN TO SOW INDOORS: In midwinter, 6–8 weeks before setting out; grows easily when direct-sown

- DAYS TO GERMINATION: 5–7
- WHEN TO SOW OUTDOORS OR SET TRANSPLANTS: Early spring
- SOIL CONDITIONS: Average and well-drained
- DISTANCE BETWEEN PLANTS: 12″–15″
- SUNLIGHT REQUIREMENTS: Full sun to light shade
- WATERING: Water regularly to keep soil moist
- DAYS TO BLOOM/BLOOMING PERIOD: Some varieties start blooming in spring, others from early summer until late fall
- SPECIAL NOTES: Good for bouquets

WAX BEGONIA

BEGONIA SEMPERFLORENS-CULTORUM
Annual

The Wax Begonia is one of the most versatile annuals in the garden. It has attractive, distinctive foliage and blooms abundantly and almost continuously from early spring through frost. Botanically a perennial, it is treated as an annual in all but the warmest regions. There are countless hybrids available in various shapes and forms. Some have clusters of small flowers, others sport larger double or single blossoms. Begonias will bloom under almost any light conditions but prefer light shade. They are usually grown from stem cuttings and are somewhat daunting to grow from seed: the seed is tiny and requires bright light and constant, evenly moist soil to germinate, and initial growth is quite slow. However it's not impossible with a little luck and the right conditions. Sow the seeds lightly in flats on a mixture of sand, soil and peat moss. Wrap the flats in plastic to maintain high humidity and moisture, and give them a weekly feeding of soluble fertilizer. Once set out in the garden, they like to grow in a soil rich in organic matter.

- DEGREE OF DIFFICULTY: Difficult but not impossible and definitely worth the effort
- USES: Borders, edging, bedding, house plant, containers
- HEIGHT: 6″–12″
- COLORS: Pinks, white, reds
- SIZE OF BLOOM: 1″–2″
- FROST TOLERANCE: Half-hardy
- PREFERS: Warm weather
- WHEN TO SOW INDOORS: 3–5 months before last frost
- DAYS TO GERMINATION: 2–4 weeks
- WHEN TO SOW OUTDOORS OR SET TRANSPLANTS: Cannot effectively be sown outdoors; set transplants after last frost
- SOIL CONDITIONS: Well-drained and rich
- DISTANCE BETWEEN PLANTS: 8″–10″
- SUNLIGHT REQUIREMENTS: Light shade is best but hybrids tolerate medium shade and full sun if temperature stays below 90°F
- WATERING: Allow soil to dry out between waterings
- DAYS TO BLOOM/BLOOMING PERIOD: Mid-spring until frost, sometimes beyond
- SPECIAL NOTES: Frequent and heavy sidedressing using lots of organic matter is appropriate

WISHBONE FLOWER

TORENIA FOURNIERI
Annual

The Wishbone Flower is so named because of the unusual wishbone shape of two stamens in its yellowish center. Readily available in catalogues, it grows well in shade, and is a fine indoor plant,  flowering the year round. Wishbone Flower prefers cool conditions, indoors and out. Its dwarf, bushy plants are covered with a profusion of brilliantly-colored blooms from early summer until frost.

- DEGREE OF DIFFICULTY: Easy
- USES: Bedding, borders, edging, containers, hanging baskets
- HEIGHT: 8″–12″
- COLORS: Purple or violet with a yellow or white throat
- SIZE OF BLOOM: 1″
- FROST TOLERANCE: Tender
- PREFERS: Warm weather
- WHEN TO SOW INDOORS: 10–12 weeks before last frost
- DAYS TO GERMINATION: 15–20; needs light to germinate
- WHEN TO SOW OUTDOORS OR SET TRANSPLANTS: After danger of frost is past
- SOIL CONDITIONS: Rich, moist, well-drained, high in organic matter
- DISTANCE BETWEEN PLANTS: 6″–8″
- SUNLIGHT REQUIREMENTS: Partial shade; tolerates full sun only in cool climates
- WATERING: Keep well-watered

Notes

- DAYS TO BLOOM/BLOOMING PERIOD: Summer until frost
- SPECIAL NOTES: Can be potted and brought inside as houseplant for indoor color during the winter

YARROW

ACHILLEA
Also Called Milfoil
Perennial

There are several types of Yarrow: *Achillea filipendulina*; which is Fernleaf Yarrow: *A. millefolium*, or Common Yarrow; and *A. ptarmica*, usually called Sneezewort. There are also several commonly occuring hybrids. Height, color and bloom size vary among the many varieties, so check catalogues for those best suited to your area and taste. Yarrow has a ferny foliage which is quite beautiful itself. The plant is long-lived, tolerates drought and heat, and does well in poor soil. The flowers are lovely for both cutting and drying. Keep an eye on *Ptarmica* as it can be invasive. You will get flowers the first year from seed started in early spring.

- DEGREE OF DIFFICULTY: Very easy
- USES: Rock gardens, borders, cutting, dried
- HEIGHT: 6″–4′
- COLORS: Yellow, white, rose-red

- SIZE OF BLOOM: Flowers are ¼″–¾″ in clusters 1″–6″ across
- FROST TOLERANCE: Hardy
- PREFERS: Warm weather
- WHEN TO SOW INDOORS: 8–10 weeks before setting out
- DAYS TO GERMINATION: 5–15; needs light to germinate
- WHEN TO SOW OUTDOORS OR SET TRANSPLANTS: Sow in early spring or summer; set transplants in spring
- SOIL CONDITIONS: Well-drained, dry, average to poor fertility
- DISTANCE BETWEEN PLANTS: 1′–2′
- SUNLIGHT REQUIREMENTS: Full sun
- WATERING: Moderate watering is best, preferably not late in the day
- DAYS TO BLOOM/BLOOMING PERIOD: Most in June and July, again in September; some varieties continuously June through September
- SPECIAL NOTES: Taller varieties may need staking. Soil that is too rich is bad for Yarrow. Deadheading spent blossoms will prolong the flowering season, and cutting back after summer blooming will encourage another bloom time in September

ZINNIA

ZINNIA ELEGANS, HAAGEANA, ANGUSTIFOLIA
Also Called Common Zinnia, Youth-and-Old-Age, Mexican Zinnia
Annual

Zinnias are among the most popular annuals grown; they are easy and quick to grow from seed and produce vibrantly colorful flowers. Many, many varieties, types and colors are available to

choose from, in a wide range of bloom sizes and plant heights. Zinnias are difficult to transplant, so either direct-seed outdoors or if you start them indoors, use individual peat pots. They are intolerant of dampness and high humidity and have a tendency to mildew, so be sure of good air circulation. Water them early in the day and try to keep water off the foliage. Beyond that, just enjoy their variety of color, bloom size and beauty both in the garden and in the home, where they make a fabulous cut flower.

- DEGREE OF DIFFICULTY: Easy
- USES: Borders, bedding, planters, edging, background, cutting
- HEIGHT: 6"–40"
- COLORS: Almost every color but blue
- SIZE OF BLOOM: 1"–7"
- FROST TOLERANCE: Half-hardy; some varieties billed as tender
- PREFERS: Warm weather
- WHEN TO SOW INDOORS: Far better started outside; but to start inside, sow in individual pots 4 weeks before setting out
- DAYS TO GERMINATION: 5–10
- WHEN TO SOW OUTDOORS OR SET TRANSPLANTS: After the ground has warmed up; cover seeds lightly and keep moist during germination
- SOIL CONDITIONS: Rich, well-drained, high in organic matter
- DISTANCE BETWEEN PLANTS: 6"–12"
- SUNLIGHT REQUIREMENTS: Full sun
- WATERING: Water regularly, early in day, at ground level—avoid getting the foliage wet (Zinnias prone to mildew)
- DAYS TO BLOOM/BLOOMING PERIOD: Early summer until frost
- SPECIAL NOTES: Keep well fertilized. Pinch young plants. Once in bloom, keep plants well cut. Many varieties will produce more flowers and bushier plants the more flowers you cut. Deadhead all spent blossoms

MONTH-BY-MONTH
CALENDAR

❦

*These calendar pages are for your
personal gardening notes. Use them to
jot down month-by-month plans and records
of garden activities from planting to
transplanting to harvesting.*

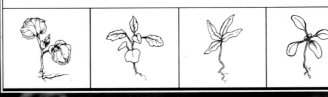

❧ *JANUARY NOTES* ❧

SEEDS PLANTED LAST YEAR ❧ SEEDS TO GROW

THIS YEAR ❧ THIS YEAR'S PLANTING SCHEDULE

❧ FROST DATES

❦ FEBRUARY NOTES ❦

HARDY SEEDS TO START INDOORS

❦ ORDERING SEEDS ❦ NOTES ON HYBRIDS

❦ TEMPERATURE RECORDS

_____

_____

_____

_____

_____

_____

_____

_____

_____

_____

_____

_____

_____

_____

_____

_____

_____

_____

_____

_____

❦ MARCH NOTES ❦

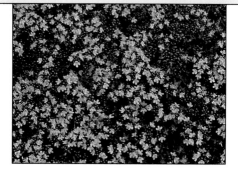

REMOVING WINTER MULCHES ❦ SOIL TESTING

❦ TILLING ❦ FERTILIZING

❦ SOWING HARDY SEEDS OUTDOORS

_____

_____

_____

_____

_____

_____

_____

_____

_____

_____

_____

_____

_____

_____

_____

_____

_____

_____

_____

❧ APRIL NOTES ❧

PLANTING ❧ NEW TOOLS ❧ WATERING

❧ RAINFALL

❦ MAY NOTES ❦

WEEDING ❦ WATERING ❦ CULTIVATING
❦ THINNING ❦ FERTILIZING

❦ JUNE NOTES ❦

CULTIVATING ❦ THINNING ❦ WEEDING
❦ WATERING ❦ DIRECT SOWING

❦ JULY NOTES ❦

PEST CONTROL ❦ SUCCESSION PLANTINGS
❦ WEEDING ❦ WATERING

🍂 *AUGUST NOTES* 🍂

WATERING 🍂 WEEDING 🍂 SIDE DRESSING

🍂 HARVESTING

🍒 *SEPTEMBER NOTES* 🍒

PRUNING 🍒 SIDE DRESSING 🍒 TOP DRESSING

🍒 FERTILIZING

OCTOBER NOTES

TRANSPLANTING TO COLD FRAME

❧ PRESERVING SURPLUS ❧ GARDEN CLEANUP

❧ FROST PROTECTION ❧ FROST DATES

❧ NOVEMBER NOTES ❧

FINAL HARVESTS ❧ RECONDITIONING AND
TESTING SOIL ❧ SITE CLEARING

❦ DECEMBER NOTES ❦

REPAIR OF TOOLS ❦ ORDERING SEED CATALOGUES
❦ YEAR-END GARDEN REVIEW

Butchart Gardens (Victoria, British Columbia) is one of the world's most stunning formal gardens.

Glossary of Useful Terms

ANNUAL: A plant which completes its life cycle—from seed to flower to fruit to seed—in one year. See biennial and perennial.

ANTHER: The tip of the stamen containing pollen.

AXIL: The angle made by a leaf or branch with the stem or with another branch.

BICOLOR: A flower of two principal colors.

BIENNIAL: A plant which starts from seed and completes its growth cycle in two years.

BLANCHING: The process of eliminating light from a plant or plant part for purpose of lightening its color.

BLOCK PLANTING: Wide row planting in diamond-shaped or staggered pattern.

BOLTING: When a plant shoots up a seed stalk (where flowers appear on it almost immediately) prematurely; going to seed. This can happen almost overnight with some species, such as lettuce. The plant loses its edibility upon bolting: leaves become bitter and tough, so preventing bolting is important crop care.

BRACT: A modified leaf that is usually small and surrounds a flower cluster.

BROADCAST: To scatter seed uniformly over an entire area, not in rows or other patterns.

BULB: A scaley bud, generally grown underground.

CLOCHE: A cover of glass or plastic that is put over plants to protect them from cold temperatures.

CLOVE: A segment of a bulb (notably of garlic or shallot) used as seed stock.

COLD FRAME: A bottomless box with a glass lid set outdoors in which plants are started from seed or protected from the weather; warmed by solar energy only (see hotbed).

COMPANION PLANTING: The practice of adjacent planting of two or more crops for best space utilization, pest-control, or other benefits.

COMPOST: Decomposed organic matter which, like humus, fertilizes and improves soil.

COTYLEDON: An embryonic leaf, differing in form from and preceding "true" leaves.

CROP ROTATION: The practice of alternating crops on a piece of land to avoid depleting the soil of nutrients and to discourage insects and diseases.

CROSS-POLLINATION: The transfer of pollen from the anthers of one species to the stigma of another, as in the case of sweet corn and popcorn.

CULTIVAR: Cultivated variety grown by breeders, not found in nature.

CUT BACK: To prune or reduce.

CUTTING: A segment of a plant (e.g. a leaf or piece of stem or root) that is cut off and used as stock to grow a new plant.

DEADHEAD: Removal of spent flower blossoms.

DETERMINATE: Plants with a terminal bud (at the ends of branches) which stops growth of that branch at a certain point. See terminal bud.

DICOTYLEDON: A plant whose seed has two leaves; grows out from its base. See monocotyledon.

DIVISION: To separate roots of a plant for propagation.

DORMANT: Alive, but resting, not growing. Seeds in seed packets are dormant.

EMBRYO: The rudimentary plant contained within the seed.

ENDOSPERM: The layer storing plant nourishment in certain seeds.

EVERBLOOMING: A plant that flowers throughout its entire growing season.

EVERLASTINGS: Flowers that hold their color and form indefinitely when dried.

FRUIT: The ripened ovary of a flower which contains the seed.

GREEN MANURING: To plant a crop for the express purpose of plowing it under to improve the quality of the soil.

HALF-HARDY: Plants that can tolerate light frosts and some limited cold weather.

HARDENING OFF: The process of gradually introducing seedlings grown indoors to outside weather conditions.

HARDINESS: The ability of a plant to tolerate cold.

HARDY: Able to withstand frost.

HEIRLOOM: Old-fashioned seed variety.

HOTBED: Identical in structure and purpose to a cold frame, but has added heating supply, either electrical element or decomposing manure.

HOTCAP: A heat-gathering device for tender seedlings.

HUMUS: Decomposed organic material.

HYBRID: A plant grown from a seed that was produced by crossing two different plant varieties.

INDETERMINATE: Plants whose growth pattern is continuous, unchecked by a terminal bud. See terminal bud.

INTERPLANTING: Planting different crops together in the same patch.

LAYERING: Propagating a plant by burying a portion of its stem and allowing it to take root.

LEACHING: The loss of nutrients that results from water passing through the soil.

LOAM: Soil that is a mixture of silt and sand with some clay.

MONOCOTYLEDON: A plant that has one seed leaf, and grows up from its base, such as corn and onions. See dicotyledon.

MULCH: A layer of materials spread thickly or thinly over the ground to inhibit weeds, protect from cold temperatures, conserve moisture, or enrich the soil.

MULE: A hybrid plant that is infertile and does not set seed on its own.

NPK: The three major plant nutrients; nitrogen (N), phosphorus (P_2O_5) and potassium (K_2O).

NODE: Where a leaf is produced on a plant stem.

OVARY: The hollow portion at the lower end of the pistil that contains ovules, or future seeds.

OVULE: The egg, or female cell, which when fertilized becomes a seed.

PERENNIAL: Plants whose life cycles last more than two years.

pH: The scale that measures acidity and alkalinity of soil, running from 0 (lowest acidity) to 14 (highest alkalinity), with 7 being neutral.

PERIANTH: The external envelope of a flower.

PICOTEE: A flower of one principle color with a margin of another color.

PHOTOSYNTHESIS: The process by which green leaves use sunlight to make carbohydrates.

PINCH, PINCH BACK: Removal of plant's growing tip to generate growth.

PISTIL: The female organ of the flower, comprising style with stigma at its top and ovary containing ovules at its lower end.

POLLEN: The tiny grains produced by anthers which fertilize the pistil.

POLLINATION: The transfer of pollen from anther to stigma. Self-pollination when it is within the same flower containing male and female organs, or a plant with both male and female flowers.

PRUNE: See pinch.

SCARIFICATION: Nicking or scratching the seed coat to aid germination.

ROOT DIVISION: See Division.

SEED: A fertilized, ripened ovule.

SEEDLING: A newly emerged plant.

SIDEDRESSING: A midseason application of organic fertilizer to the soil alongside the plant. And see topdressing.

STEMCUTTING: A section of plant stem used for propagating new plants.

STERILE: Infertile.

STIGMA: The portion of the pistil that receives pollen.

STRATIFICATION: Promoting germination by chilling a seed.

SUCCESSION PLANTING: Two or more sowings of one crop at different times to extend the growing season.

STYLE: The stalk between the ovary and the stigma.

TAPROOT: An extended central root.

TENDER: Plants that cannot withstand frost or survive over cold winters.

TERMINAL BUD: A flower cluster at the end of a stem or branch.

THINNING: Removing plants to leave necessary growing space between the remaining ones.

THRESH : To separate seed from chaff.

TILTH : The cultivation of garden soil; the state of being tilled.

TOPDRESSING : A midseason application of organic fertilizer to the soil around the stem of the plant. And see sidedressing.

TRACE ELEMENTS : Elements which plants need in very small quantities for survival.

TRANSPLANT : Moving a plant from one location to another.

TRELLIS : A support for climbing plants and flowers.

TUBER : The enlarged portion of an underground stem which contains buds or "eyes" from which new plants are grown.

VARIEGATED : Having color markings that differ from the main color.

VARIETY : A sub-group in a species. And see cultivar.

VIABILITY : The potential for a seed to germinate.

WIDE-ROW PLANTING : The planting of flowers and vegetables in bands anywhere from twelve inches to several feet wide and of any length.

WINTER-OVER : The ability of an insect or other organism to survive the winter.

WOODINESS, WOODY : When stems of herb plants become tough and unproductive.

LISTS OF
SEED SUPPLIERS

❦

VEGETABLE SEEDS

Allen, Sterling and Lothrop
191 U.S. Rt. 1
Falmouth, ME 04105

Brudy (John) Exotics
Rt. 1 Box 190
Dover, FL 33527

Butterbrooke Farm
78 Barry Rd.
Oxford, CT 06483

Comstock, Ferre & Co.
263 Main Street
Wethersfield, CT 06109

The Cook's Garden
Box 65
Londonderry, VT 05148

Dr. Yoo Farm
PO Box 290
College Park, MD 20740

Evans Plant Co.
PO Box 1649
Tifton, GA 31794

Far North Gardens
15621 Auburndale Ave.
Livonia, MI 48154

Ernest Hardison Seed Co.
PO Box 23072
Nashville, TN 37201

Kerncraft
434 W. Main St.
Kutztown, PA 19530

McConnell Nurseries Inc.
R.R.1
Port Burwell, Ontario
Canada NOJ ITO

McLaughlin's Seeds
PO Box 550
Mead, WA 99021

Steven E. Meredith Seeds
211 Oregon Pioneer Bldg.
Portland, OR 97204

Mountain Valley Seeds & Nurs.
2015 North Main
North Logan, UT 84321

Nichols Garden Nursery
1190 North Pacific Hwy.
Albany, OR 97321

Pony Creek Nursery
Tilleda, WI 54978

Otto Richter & Sons Ltd.
Box 26
Goodwood, Ontario
Canada LOC 1AO

Royce Seeds, Ltd.
Box 118-017
Cass City, MI 48726

Sanctuary Seeds
2388 W. 4th
Vancouver, B.C.
Canada V6K 1P1

Shepherd's Garden Seeds
7389 W. Zayante Road
Felton, CA 95018

Tsang and Ma
1306 Old Country Road
Belmont, CA 94002

Vermont Bean Seed Co.
Garden Lane
Bomoseen, VT 05732

Vita-Green Farms, Inc.
217 Escondido Ave.
Vista, CA 92083

Weeks Seed Co.
921 Dickinson Ave.
Greenville, NC 27834

GENERAL (FLOWERS AND VEGETABLES)

Abundant Life Seed Foundation
PO Box 772
Port Townsend, WA 98368

Agway Inc.
Box 4933
Syracuse, NY 13221

Alberta Nurseries & Seeds Ltd.
Box 20
Bowden, Alberta
Canada TOM OKO

Archias'
PO Box 109
Sedalia, MO 65301

Bonavista
Box 618
Frederick, MD 21701

Bishop Farm Seeds
Box 338
Belleville, Ontario
Canada K8N 5A5

Bountiful Gardens
5798 Ridgewood Rd.
Willits, CA 95490

Broom Seed Co.
PO Box 237
Rion, SC 29132

Buckerfields
PO Box 7000
Vancouver, B.C.
Canada V6B 4E1

Bunch's
321 Texas
Texarkana, TX 75501

Burgess Seed and Plant Co.
905 Four Seasons Rd.
Bloomington, IL 61701

W. Atlee Burpee Co.
300 Park Avenue
Warminster, PA 18974

California Gardeners Seed Co.
904 Silver Spur Rd.
Suite 414
Rolling Hills Est., CA 90274

Charles Seeds
Box 28, Sta. B.
Ottawa, Ontario
Canada KIP 6C3

William Dam Seeds Ltd.
Box 8400
Dundas, Ontario
Canada L9H 6M1

De Giorgi Co., Inc.
PO Box 413
Council Bluffs, IA 51502

Dominion Seed House
Georgetown, Ontario
Canada L7G 4A2

Early's Farm & Garden Centre
PO Box 3024
Saskatoon, Saskatchewan
Canada S7K 3S9

Epicure Seed Ltd.
PO Box 450
Brewster, NY 10509

Farmer Seed & Nursery Co.
818 N.W. 4th St.
Faribault, MN 55021

Henry Field Seed & Nursery
Shenandoah, IA 51601

Fisher's Garden Store
PO Box 236
Belgrade, MT 59714

Garden City Seeds
PO Box 297
Victor, MT 59875

Garden Delight Seed Co.
Box 55316
Madison, WI 53705

Garden Magic Seed Co.
310 Main St.
East Haven, CT 06512

Gateway Seed Co.
PO Box 906
Clinton, IA 52732

Gaze Seed Company Ltd.
PO Box 640
St. John's, Newfoundland
Canada A1C 5K8

Gleckler's Seedsmen
Metamora, OH 43540

Good Seed Co.
PO Box 702
Tonasket, WA 98855

Grace's Gardens
10 Bay Street
Westport, CT 06880

Jonathan Green & Sons Inc.
Box 9
Farmingdale, NJ 07727

Greenleaf Seeds
PO Box 89
Conway, MA 01341

Gurney's Seed & Nursery Co.
Yankton, SD 57078

Halifax Seed Company Ltd.
Box 8026
Halifax, Nova Scotia
Canada B3K 5L8

Joseph Harris Co.
3670 Buffalo Rd.
Rochester, NY 14624

Chas C. Hart Seed Co.
PO Box 9169
Wethersfield, CT 06109

H. G. Hastings Co.
1036 White Street, S.W.
PO Box 115535
Atlanta, GA 30310

Heirloom Gardens
PO Box 138
Guerneville, CA 95446

Herb Gathering, Inc.
5742 Kenwood
Kansas City, MO 64110

Ed Hume Seeds
PO Box 1450
Kent, WA 98032

Island Seed Co. Ltd.
PO Box 4278, Sta. A
Victoria, B.C.
Canada V8X 3XB

Japonica Seeds Inc.
PO Box 919
Jackson Heights, NY 11372

Jenkins Seed House
359 Ridout St. N.
London, Ontario
Canada N6A 4G3

Johnny's Selected Seeds
Albion, ME 04910

Johnson Seed Co.
227 Ludwig Ave.
Dousman, WI 53118

J. W. Jung Seed Co.
335 S. High St.
Randolph, WI 53957

Lagomarsino Seeds, Inc.
5675-A Power Inn Road
Sacramento, CA 95824

Lakeland Nurseries Sales
340 Poplar St.
Hanover, PA 17331

Landreth Seed Co.
180-188 W. Ostend
Baltimore, MD 21230

Lands-End Seeds
Crawford, CO 81415

Le Marché Seeds International
PO Box 566
Dixon, CA 95620

Oral Ledden & Sons
PO Box 7
Sewell, NJ 08080

Letherman's Inc.
1221 Tuscarawas St. E
Canton, OH 44707

Liberty Seed Co.
PO Box 806
New Philadelphia, OH 44663

Lindenberg Seeds Ltd.
803 Princess Ave.
Brandon, Manitoba
Canada R7A OP5

Lockhart Seeds, Inc.
PO Box 1361
Stockton, CA 95205

Long Island Seed and Plant
PO Box 1285
Riverhead, NY 11901

Lowden's Better Plants & Seeds
Box 7010
Lancaster, Ontario
Canada L9G 3L3

M. Q. Enterprises
4626 Glebe Farm Rd.
Sarasota, FL 33580

Earl May Seed & Nursery Co.
Shenandoah, IA 51603

McFayden Seeds
PO Box 1800
Brandon, Manitoba
Canada R7A 6N4

Mellinger's Inc.
2310 W. South Range
North Lima, OH 44452

Meyer Seed Co.
600 S. Caroline St.
Baltimore, MD 21231

Mountain Seed & Nursery
PO Box 9107
Moscow, ID 83843

Nationwide Seed & Supply
4801 Fegenbush Lane
Louisville, KY 40228

Native Seeds/Search
3950 W. New York Dr.
Tucson, AZ 85745

Robert Nicholson Seed Co.
PO Box 7790
Madison, WI 53707

Ontario Seed Company, Ltd.
PO Box 144
Waterloo, Ontario
Canada N2J 3Z9

Geo. W. Park Seed Co.
PO Box 31
Greenwood, SC 29646

Peace Seeds
1130 Tetherow Road
Williams, OR 95744

Porter & Son, Seedsmen
PO Box 104
Stephenville, TX 76401

Rawlinson Garden Seed
269 College Road
Truro, Nova Scotia
Canada B2N 2P6

Redwood City Seed Co.
PO Box 361
Redwood City, CA 94064

Reuter Seed Co.
320 N. Carrollton Ave.
New Orleans, LA 70119

Martin Rispens & Sons
3332 Ridge Rd. (Rear, Box 5)
Lansing, IL 60438

Rocky Mountain Seed Co.
1325 15th Street (PO Box 5204)
Denver, CO 80217

P. L. Rohrer & Bro. Inc.
PO Box 25
Smoketown, PA 17576

Roswell Seed Co.
115-117 S. Main St.
Roswell, NM 88201

Saunders Seed Co., Inc.
101 W. Broadway
Tipp City, OH 45371

Seeds For All
Keating Stage
Baker, OR 97814

Seedway, Inc.
Hall, NY 14463

Self-Sufficient Seeds
Barr Hollow Road
Woodward, PA 16882

R. H. Shumway Seedsman
PO Box 777
Rockford, IL 61105

Siegers Seed Co.
7245 Imlay City Road
Imlay City, MI 48444

Southern Exposure Seed Exchange
PO Box 158
North Garden, VA 22959

Southern Garden Co.
Box 888748
Dunwoody, GA 30338

Specialty Garden Supply
418 Sumner Street
Santa Cruz, CA 95062

Stokes Seeds Inc.
737 Main St., Box 548
Buffalo, NY 14240

Stokes Seeds Ltd.
Box 10
St. Catharines, Ontario
Canada L2R 6R6

Sunrise Enterprises
PO Box 10058
Elmwood, CT 06110

T & T Seeds, Inc.
830 S. 48th St., Box 338
Grand Forks, ND 58201

Geo. Tait & Sons, Inc.
990 Tidewater Drive
Norfolk, VA 23504

Territorial Seed Co.
PO Box 27
Lorane, OR 97451

Thompson & Morgan
PO Box 1308
Jackson, NJ 08527

Tillinghast Seed Co.
PO Box 738
La Conner, WA 98257

Tregunno Seeds Ltd.
126 Catharine St. N.
Hamilton, Ontario
Canada L8R IJ4

The Urban Farmer
PO Box 444
Convent Station, NJ 07961

Vermont Bean Seed Co.
Garden Lane
Bomoseen, VT 05732

Vesey's Seeds Ltd.
York, Prince Edward Island
Canada C0A 1P0

H. K. Webster Co.
PO Box 470
Concord, NH 03301

Wyatt-Quarles Seed Co.
PO Box 2131
Raleigh, NC 27602

HERBS

Abracadabra
PO Box 1040
Guerneville, CA 95446

Bonavista
Box 618
Frederick, MD 21701

High Altitude Gardens
PO Box 4238
Ketchum, ID 83340

Otto Richter & Sons Ltd.
Box 26
Goodwood, Ontario
Canada L0C 1A0

Royce Seeds, Ltd.
Box 118-017
Cass City, MI 48726

Sanctuary Seeds
2388 W. 4th
Vancouver, B.C.
Canada V6K 1P1

Seeds For All
Keating Stage
Baker, OR 97814

T & T Seeds, Inc.
830 S. 48th St., Box 338
Grand Forks, ND 58201

Vita-Green Farms, Inc.
217 Escondido Ave.
Vista, CA 92083

HEIRLOOM VARIETIES

Abracadabra
PO Box 1040
Guerneville, CA 95446

Alston Seed Growers
PO Box 266
Littleton, NC 27850

Bountiful Gardens
5798 Ridgewood Rd.
Willits, CA 95490

Bunch's
321 Texas
Texarkana, TX 75501

Burrell Seed Growers Co.
Box 150
Rocky Ford, CO 81067

De Giorgi Co., Inc.
PO Box 413
Council Bluffs, IA 51502

Fred's Plant Farm
Rt. 1, PO Box 707
Dresden, TN 38225

Gilfeather Turnip
Bill Schmidt
Rt. 1, Box 200
Brattleboro, VT 05301

Greenleaf Seeds
PO Box 89
Conway, MA 01341

Heirloom Gardens
PO Box 138
Guerneville, CA 95446

J. L. Hudson Seedsman
PO Box 1058
Redwood City, CA 94064

Johnson Seed Co.
227 Ludwig Ave.
Dousman, WI 53118

Lands-End Seeds
Crawford, CO 81415

Le Marché Seeds International
PO Box 566
Dixon, CA 95620

Long Island Seed and Plant
PO Box 1361
Stockton, CA 95205

Seeds Blum
Idaho City Stage
Boise, ID 83707

Southern Exposure Seed Exchange
PO Box 158
North Garden, VA 22959

Tregunno Seeds Ltd.
126 Catharine St. N.
Hamilton, Ontario
Canada L8R 1J4

SPECIALTY SEEDS

Alston Seed Growers
PO Box 266
Littleton, NC 27850

Becker's Seed Potatoes
R.R.1
Trout Creek, Ontario
Canada P0H 2L0

John Brudy Exotics
Rt. 1 Box 190
Dover, FL 33527

Burrell Seed Growers Co.
Box 150
Rocky Ford, CO 81067

The Cook's Garden
Box 65
Londonderry, VT 05148

The Cotton Boll
PO Box 156
Hayneville, AL 36040

Crockett Seeds
PO Box 237
Metamora, OH 43540

Early's Farm & Garden Center
PO Box 3024
Saskatoon, Saskatchewan
Canada S7K 3S9

Exotica Seed Co.
8033 Sunset Bl., Suite 125
West Hollywood, CA 90046

Far North Gardens
15621 Audurndale Ave.
Livonia, MI 48154

Fern Hill Farm
PO Box 185
Clarksboro, NJ 08020

Dean Foster Nurseries
Hartford, MI 49057

Fred's Plant Farm
Rt. 1, PO Box 707
Dresden, TN 38225

Fungi Perfecti
PO Box 7634
Olympia, WA 98507

Giant Watermelons
PO Box 141
Hope, AR 71801

Gilfeather Turnip
Bill Schmidt
Rt. 1, Box 200
Brattleboro, VT 05301

Gleckler's Seedsmen
Metamora, OH 43540

Glendale Enterprises
Rt. 3, Box 73-C
De Funiak Springs, FL 32433

Grace's Gardens
10 Bay St.
Westport, CT 06880

Chas. C. Hart Seed Co.
PO Box 9169
Wethersfield, CT 06109

Heirloom Gardens
PO Box 138
Guerneville, CA 95446

Horticultural Enterprises
PO Box 810082
Dallas, TX 75381

J. L. Hudson Seedsman
PO Box 1058
Redwood City, CA 94064

Island Seed Co. Ltd.
PO Box 4278, Sta. A
Victoria, B.C.
Canada V8X 3XB

Jackson & Perkins Co.
1 Rose Lane
Medford, OR 95701

Kalmia
PO Box 3881
Charlottesville, VA 22903

Kester's Wild Game Food Nurs.
PO Box V
Omro, WI 54963

Kurtzman's Mushroom Specialties
815 S. Harbor Way, #12
Richmond, CA 94804

Lagomarsino Seeds, Inc.
5675-A Power Inn Road
Sacramento, CA 95824

Lakeland Nurseries Sales
340 Poplar St.
Hanover, PA 17331

Le Jardin du Gourmet
West Danville, VT 05873

Le Marché Seeds International
PO Box 566
Dixon, CA 95620

Libby Creek Farm
PO Box 177
Carlton, WA 98814

Living Tree Centre
PO Box 797
Bolinas, CA 94924

Long Island Seed and Plant
PO Box 1285
Riverhead, NY 11901

M.Q. Enterprises
4626 Glebe Farm Rd.
Sarasota, FL 33580

Margrave Plant Co.
Gleason, TN 38229

McLaughlin's Seeds
PO Box 550
Mead, WA 99021

Steven E. Meredith Seeds
211 Oregon Pioneer Bldg.
Portland, OR 97204

Mushroompeople
PO Box 158
Inverness, CA 94937

Neal's Open Pollinated
417 N. 8th St. W.
Mt. Vernon, IA 52314

Necessary Trading Co.
Box 305
New Castle, VA 24127

Nichols Garden Nursery
1190 North Pacific Hwy.
Albany, OR 97301

The Pepper Gal
10536 119th Ave. N.
Largo, FL 33543

Peter Pepper Seeds
H. W. Alfrey
PO Box 415
Knoxville, TN 37901

Pinetree Garden Seeds
New Gloucester, ME 04260

Plants of the Southwest
1570 Pacheco St.
Santa Fe, NM 87501

Prairie State Commodities
PO Box 6
Trilla, IL 62469

Redwood City Seed Co.
PO Box 361
Redwood City, CA 94064

Reynas' Taos Pueblo Seed Co.
PO Box 189
Taos, NM 87571

Otto Richter & Sons Ltd.
Box 26
Goodwood, Ontario
Canada L0C 1A0

S & H Organic Acres
PO Box 27
Montgomery Creek, CA 96065

Siberia Seeds
Box 3000
Olds, Alberta
Canada T0M 1P0

Sunrise Enterprises
PO Box 10058
Elmwood, CT 06110

Tater-Mater Seeds
Thomas P. Wagner
Rt. 2
Wathena, KS 66090

Turtle Enterprises
Rt. 1
Box 242
Dalton, WI 53926

Otis Twilley Seed Co.
PO Box 65
Trevose, PA 19047

Vermont Bean Seed Co.
Garden Lane
Bomoseen, VT 05732

Weeks Seed Co.
921 Dickenson Ave.
Greenville, NC 27834

Wildlife Nurseries
PO Box 2724
Oshkosh, WI 54903

Willhite Seed Co.
PO Box 23
Poolville, TX 76076

Wilton's Organic Potatoes
PO Box 28
Aspen, CO 81611

CANADIAN SEEDS

Alberta Nurseries & Seeds Ltd.
Box 20
Bowden, Alberta
Canada T0M 0K0

Becker's Seed Potatoes
R.R.1
Trout Creek, Ontario
Canada P0H 2L0

Bishop Farm Seeds
Box 338
Belleville, Ontario
Canada K8N 5A5

Buckerfields
PO Box 7000
Vancouver, B.C.
Canada V6B 4E1

Charles Seeds
Box 28, Sta. B
Ottowa, Ontario
Canada K1P 6C3

William Dam Seeds Ltd.
Box 8400
Dundas, Ontario
Canada L9H 6M1

Dominion Seed House
Georgetown, Ontario
Canada L7G 4A2

Gaze Seed Company Ltd.
PO Box 640
St. John's, Newfoundland
Canada A1C 5K8

Halifax Seed Company Ltd.
Box 8026
Halifax, Nova Scotia
Canada B3K 5L8

Jenkins Seed House
359 Ridout St. N.
London, Ontario
Canada N6A 4G3

Lindenberg Seeds Ltd.
803 Princess Ave.
Brandon, Manitoba
Canada R7A 0P5

McConnell Nurseries Inc.
R.R.1
Port Burwell, Ontario
Canada N0J 1T0

McFayden Seeds
PO Box 1800
Brandon, Manitoba
Canada R7A 6N4

W. H. Perron Co. Ltd.
515 Labelle Blvd., Chomedey
Laval, Quebec
Canada H7V 2T3

Sanctuary Seeds
2388 W. 4th
Vancouver, B.C.
Canada V6K 1P1

Seed Centre Ltd.
Box 3867, Sta. D.
Edmonton, Alberta
Canada T5L 4K1

Stokes Seeds Ltd.
Box 10
St. Catharines, Ontario
Canada L2R 6R6

Tregunno Seeds Ltd.
126 Catharine St. N.
Hamilton, Ontario
Canada L8R 1J4

Vesey's Seeds Ltd.
York, Prince Edward Island
Canada C0A 1P0

SEEDS FOR SHORT SEASONS

High Altitude Gardens
PO Box 4238
Ketchum, ID 83340

Ed Hume Seeds
PO Box 1450
Kent, WA 98032

Lindenberg Seeds Ltd.
803 Princess Ave.
Brandon, Manitoba
Canada R7A 0P5

Mountain Seed & Nursery
PO Box 9107
Moscow, ID 83843

Vesey's Seeds Ltd.
York, Prince Edward Island
Canada C0A 1P0

SEEDS FOR SOUTHERN GARDENS

California Gardeners Seed Co.
904 Silver Spur Rd., Suite 414
Rolling Hills Est., CA 90274

Hastings
PO Box 4274
Atlanta, GA 30302

Southern Garden Co.
Box 888748
Dunwoody, GA 30338

Westwind Seeds
2509 N. Campbell Ave. #139
Tucson, AZ 85719

Wyatt-Quarles Seed Co.
PO Box 2131
Raleigh, NC 27602

SEEDS FOR NORTHERN GARDENS

Abundant Life Seed Foundation
PO Box 772
Port Townsend, WA 98368

Allen, Sterling and Lothrop
191 U.S. Rt. 1
Falmouth, ME 04105

Charles Seeds
Box 28, Sta. B.
Ottowa, Ontario
Canada K1P 6C3

Fisher's Garden Store
PO Box 236
Belgrade, MT 59714

Garden City Seeds
PO Box 297
Victor, MT 59875

Good Seed Co.
PO Box 702
Tonasket, WA 98855

Grace's Gardens
10 Bay St.
Westport, CT 06880

Johnny's Selected Seeds
Albion, ME 04910

W. H. Perron Co. Ltd.
515 Labelle Blvd., Chomedey
Laval, Quebec
Canada H7V 2T3

Seed Centre Ltd.
Box 3867, Sta. D.
Edmonton, Alberta
Canada T5L 4K1

T & T Seeds, Inc.
830 S. 48th St., Box 338
Grand Forks, ND 58201

FOREIGN SEEDS

Bountiful Gardens
5798 Ridgewood Rd.
Willits, CA 95490

William Dam Seeds Ltd.
Box 8400
Dundas, Ontario
Canada L9H 6M1

Dr. Yoo Farm
PO Box 290
College Park, MD 20740

Epicure Seed Ltd.
PO Box 450
Brewster, NY 10509

Japonica Seeds Inc.
PO Box 919
Jackson Heights, NY 11372

Kerncraft
434 W. Main Street
Kutztown, PA 19530

Le Marché Seeds International
PO Box 566
Dixon, CA 95620

Shepherd's Garden Seeds
7389 W. Zayante Road
Felton, CA 95018

Siberia Seeds
Box 3000
Olds, Alberta
Canada T0M 1P0

Sunrise Enterprises
PO Box 10058
Elmwood, CT 06110

Thompson & Morgan
PO Box 100
Farmingdale, NJ 07727

Tsang and Ma
1306 Old County Road
Belmont, CA 94002

The Urban Farmer
PO Box 444
Convent Station, NJ 07961

UNTREATED SEEDS

Abundant Seed Life Foundation
PO Box 772
Port Townsend, WA 98368

Butterbrooke Farm
78 Barry Rd.
Oxford, CT 06483

Sanctuary Seeds
2388 W. 4th
Vancouver, B.C.
Canada V6K 1P1

Tregunno Seeds Ltd.
126 Catharine St. N.
Hamilton, Ontario
Canada L8R 1J4

Westwind Seeds
2509 N. Campbell Ave. #139
Tucson, AZ 85719

INDEX

❧

PHOTOGRAPHY CREDITS